THe AWe-Manac
A Daily Dose of Wonder

by Jill Badonsky

The possibilities of creative effort
connected with the subconscious mind
are stupendous and imponderable.
They inspire one with awe.
—Napoleon Hill

RUNNING PRESS
PHILADELPHIA. LONDON

9   8   7   6   5   4   3   2   1
Digit on the right indicates the number of this printing

Library of Congress Control Number: 2008933240

ISBN 978-0-7624-3125-0

Cover and Interior design by Jill Badonsky
Edited by Jennifer Kasius
Typography: Tempus, Gilligan's Island, and a little Pot

Running Press Book Publishers
2300 Chestnut Street
Philadelphia, PA 19103-4371

Visit us on the web!
www.runningpress.com

TABLE OF CONTENTS TABLE OF CONTENTS TABLE OF CONTENTS

AcKNoWLedgMents

This work was made possible because of the belief my editor
Jennifer Kasius had in it. Jennifer, does that sentence even sound right?
Thanks to Bill Jones and all the folks at Running Press,
and to my agent Stephanie Kip Rostan.
thanks to my beloved spitual teacher, Jacob Glass

This is my thank you list and it's important to me because without my
friends I spend too much time alone and my thoughts inbreed and become
deformed and scary. Friends are precious.

Thanks to my non-biological family Donna Gray, Rena Tucker, Reba Spencer,
Marney Madridikus, Lisa Jaffee, Holly Wheeler, Rae Warde, Kim Cromwell,
Caitlin Kelley, Jim Billingsley, Anne Mery, Pattie Mosa, Meredith Deal, Steve
Ostrow, Kris Powell, Shirley Anderson, Eber Lambert, Jenn Simpson, Deb
Thompson, Caitlin Kelley, Lynda Treger, Dale Brown, Ellie Sanders, Randy
Herman, Rick Christensen, Bert and Amy Lawrence, Ron Kofron, all the
students who have taught me so much, the readers of my monthly
newsletter, my cats—Mambo and Sappho, and to that crazy, unpredicable,
ride called the creative process.
This would not have been made possible also without having an eccentric
mother and a funny father.

I dedicate The Awe-manac to the memory
of that funny dad.

Love,
Jill

Wonder can only be found in the present moment. The gentle breeze drawing together your fractured attention, the scent of cloves stealing you from worry, the sound of the waves reminding you that to be alive is something to believe in—those are gifts of the present.

We can live with wonder if we have or are open to, the ability to recognize the deep pleasure possible in a simple moment. But this ability is a skill like any other—it may take time and practice. We are impatient, we want to apply life-changing concepts to banish our challenges immediately. When the change is not sustained after the enthusiasm dies down, we often just give up instead of rinse and repeat. This book will teach you to forge on in trust, to practice the concepts over and over, a little at a time, imperfectly, until your mind effortlessly chooses the thought that exalts your existence rather than one that darkens it.

Give yourself permission to play, to stay true to yourself, to make compassion a hobby. The non-linear practice of moving forward two tiny steps and sideways one stumble is okay. In the long run, this will get you further than the other schemes that 85 percent of us give up on because we didn't do it perfectly or because it was too much too soon.

WELCOME
to the
AWe-MaNac

Prelude to Book in Awe Major

Everything starts as somebody's daydream. —Larry Niven

Dear Readers, Writers and Arithmetic:

Life is funny poetry. It comes with enjoyably odd tangents, good friends, and obligatory rendezvous with inconvenient shadows followed by sun salutations, wonder, and comfortable recliners from a year-end sale at Target. While writing this book I experienced one of THE darkest shadows of my life in terms of loss, hardship, confusion, estrangement, renegade biochemistry, mental gridlock, and failure to use my emergency brake. Overwhelm, self-sabotage, perfectionistic paralysis, fickle focus, dubious distractions, torrential self-torment, ludicrous preoccupation with email, napping, stare contests with lamp shades - I know all these well.

As I test-drove *The Awe-manac* I noticed that imbibing in Aha-phrodisiacs, Toasts-of-the-Day, and daily quote exposure became medicine. Being creative is the ultimate high of being alive and is able to lift us out of dark places and fogged-up outlooks.

I have sometimes been wildly, despairingly, acutely miserable, racked with sorrow, but through it all I still know quite certainly that just to be alive is a grand thing. —Agatha Christie

Creativity and inspiration are underused remedies and portals to a more incredible existence. How can we dispute that we were meant to exercise our creative muscles? For when we do, we achieve timelessness, bliss, kindness, energy, better health and the divine validation of creation.

AND the world is discovering that creativity is not assigned to a talented few - we are all creative. Our brains are designed to be creative, it is our divinity to create. Coping with life and with growing older are creative. Thinking is a creative act and most of us think, so creativity is the province of many. Creative passion lifts us from a mundane existence to one filled with wonder, with . . . awe.

Creative growth seems to thrive on permission to act with emphasis on passion, not perfection. James Joyce said, "A man's errors are his portals of discovery." Let's step through our errors and dance with discovery. Creativity thrives on lightness and play, so quit being so serious.

If we can open your mind to laughter, we can slip in a little information.
~Virginia Tooper

There is little success where there is little laughter.
~ Andrew Carnegie

The covers of this book are too far apart.
~ Ambrose Bierce

The staff of *The Awe-manac* (that would be me) invites you at your next available moment to look for the afternoon glow.

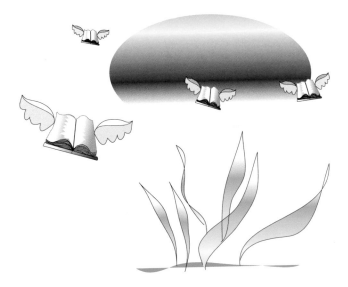

The afternoon glow is brightening the bamboos, the fountains are bubbling with delight, Let us dream of evanescence, and linger in the beautiful foolishness of things. —Okakura Kakuzo

Ahhh, "the beautiful foolishness of things." Foolishness can indeed be beautiful in moderation and with safety gear. It's all how you look at it.

You have entered *The Awe-manac*, sort of like an "almanac" but with that sublime state of "awe" instead of the overwhelming state of "al." Awe, in this particular awe-rena, means the wonder and cultivation of the mind's possibilities. A rock pile can become a cathedral if your mind has the right combination of perspective and possibility. It's all how you look at it.

The Old Farmer's Almanac was invented in 1766 by Robert Bailey Thomas. As you may know, *The Old Farmer's Almanac* is still published annually and provides information about the weather, sunrises, moon cycles, tides, crops, gardening, astrology, and things like that. Almanacs have also been known to advertise potions, magic elixirs, and special products that claim everything from making you younger and smarter and curing your ailments to ridding your house of dust bunnies.

Our Genuine Claim:

The Awe-manac will make you younger by providing a regular diet of creative thought. It will enhance your sex appeal because creative people are known to be more sexy, uninhibited, and resourceful. And no dust bunnies were harmed in the writing of this book—but I really should sweep now. But wait, there's more: next page, please hurry.

The AWe-MaNac WiLL aLSo HeLp yoU to:

◇ retrain your thinking to focus on thoughts that make you more confident, creative, and joy-filled

◇ see your day in a more desirable light

◇ be inspired by the many muses and amusing events there are in the world

◇ be reminded of the wonder of who you are

◇ develop habits that help you to activate the wonder of who you are, and have an abundance of creative prompts to use for yourself, classes, workshops, with coaching clients, or for writing, collage, art, doodling and just thinking

◇ turn a dread-locked attitude (that's an attitude that begins the day with "I have to...") into one of eager anticipation (and that would be an attitude of "I get to...")

◇ discover how life's daily events can entertain you, unearth your hidden cleverness, and accelerate what genius might already be flowing

◇ wake up your still life and send it dancing into morning glories

◇ celebrate moments of delight, wonder and amusement alone or with others

◇ feed your mind

◇ press purple periwinkles flat

let go of your limited thinking

NAVIGATING THE AWE-MANAC

This section gives you all you need to know in order to sail through your life with daily awe.

People often say that motivation doesn't last.
Well, neither does bathing, that's why we recommend it daily.
~Zig Ziglar

Read *The Awe-manac* as daily as possible so that the awe will last. If you miss a few days, get over it. In fact, you can miss a lot of days, just pick it up and continue—no need to go back to the days you skipped. No need to quit just because you're not perfect.

Perennial Applications

The Awe-manac can be used any time of the year, year after year. It can be your record, your reminder, and your spiritual rendezvous. Its spell will continue to upgrade your existence, keep you young, and remind you of your magnificence. Each time you return, it will gift you with new discoveries—so don't lose it under your bed or leave it in an airport.

If you are as anal as I am, read the detailed instructions starting on page 8. If not, just read this short table description and trust you will figure out the rest. You might want to stick a pink Post-it note, a silver paperclip, or a golden retriever on these pages so you can easily find them when you forget stuff.

MONTHLY ENTRY WAY AND DAILY HEADINGS	BRIEF DESCRIPTION
Astrological Spells	Ideas to charm you according to your star sign.
Tides	Setting intentions to what to let go of—ebbing—and what to do more of—flowing.
Vessel of Strength	A quote, a saying, a word, that you can call on when life throws you some turbulence.
Crops and Planting Tips	To cultivate lightness and laughter
Name Today	Give the day a title to make it more special or meaningful.
Daily Soul Vitamin	Read a quote to fortify your spirits and boost your outlook.
Toast of the Day	Calling undivided attention and honor to a small delight, a secret to a fulfilling existence.
Subliminal Messages, Potion Ads, Notes to Myself	Recurring messages and ads to persuade the mind to think more fulfilling thoughts and sell you some free inspiration.
Awe-servances	Events of the day, week or month chosen for the purpose of creative play and inspiration.
Dose of Mirth	Don't leave home without wit.
Today I get to	Frame your day with the spirit of childlike eagerness.
Journal Juju	Prompts for musing, reflection, discovery, esteem, processing, and doodling.
Aha-phrodisiacs	Guidelines, prompts, and spells for partaking in creative play.

MONTHLY ENTRY WAYS:
Things you will see at
the beginning of each month

ASTROLOGICAL SPELLS
Possible Effects: insight, direction, bafflement, amusement.
  Just read the description under your sign. Consider its potential for creative expression: if it inspires you to write or do art, make a list of ideas and then choose one and take a small step.

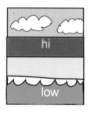

TIDES
Possible Effect: Awareness of intentions, which helps trigger their manifestation. Each month you will see a space to fill in your Ebbing and Flowing tides. Ask yourself the questions: What might I want to ebb or let go of this month, even if it's just 5 percent? Or where might I want to flourish or flow more, even if it's just 5 percent. Identifying it, writing it down, is one step to following the laws of subtraction and attraction. Examples: This month I'd like to ebb checking email so much and flow in the area of loving the fall weather.

VESSEL OF STRENGTH
Possible Effects: Reprogramming your mind, spirit, and reality according to the thoughts you choose to think, a better life directly related to the messages you tell yourself and the perspectives you choose, replacing tormenting thoughts with constructive thoughts.
  To further wax upon the ocean metaphor, a space is provided for you to choose a "vessel of strength." A powerful way to change your thinking is to replace thoughts that do not serve you with ones that will. At first this might seemed contrived, but with repetition you will soon believe and operate from your advanced higher messages. Writing them in *The Awe-manac* as well as posting them with sticky notes inside cabinets, clothes, and coffee cups can increase their effect. Tape to the inside of your glasses.*

MONTHLY CROPS and PLANTING TIPS
Possible Effect: Budding amusement.
  Just follow the instructions according to each monthly crop. Repeat annually.

* do not operate heavy equipment or cross busy freeways

Name Today

Possible Effects: Tapping into the healing power of amusement; adding enhanced meaning, novelty, and importance to the day, exercising your imagination muscles.

Without much thought or analysis, quickly give the day a name, a title, or a caption - randomly or methodically, imperfectly or precisely. Concern as to whether it makes sense is optional. Naming a day exercises your imagination a bit and makes the day a little more special. Skip it if it annoys you. But if you decide to do it, have fun with it. I have named days things like Mac, Abigail, Yoga in the Grocery Line Day, The Day That Ate My Brain, "Bleh!", Pay Attention to Blue Things Day, Dayo, Da-a-ay-o, Daylight Come and Me Wanna Buy Shoes... names like that. You will have fun reviewing previously named days when you go back through your *Awe-manac*. Some of them might even catch on annually with friends and family, leading to picnics and themed possibilities. You can name days first thing in the morning to carry a theme throughout the day or a name may surface in the evening according to what actually happened that day. Your names do not have to all be perky. "Bleh!" was just one of those blah days—when I called it Bleh, it was magically a little less Blah-ful.

The Awe-manac has not noted your personal special occasions. The staff did not have time to find out who would be reading the book and what stuff you celebrated, so here is your chance to fill in the Name Today with birthdays, anniversaries, made-up holidays and the date that your car rolled down the driveway.

DAILY SOUL VITAMINS

Possible Effects: Changing the voices in your head to more positive ones. Feeling fortified daily with inspiration, motivation, and a higher perspective.

The Awe-manac refers to quotes as Soul Vitamins because we believe that they: 1) are good for you, 2) should be taken regularly like vitamins to fortify your thoughts with essential inspiration.

When you find quotes that work especially well for you, they'll click with your intuition and ignite your heart energy. There is space provided in the back of the book called *The Soul Vitamin Cabinet*. Copying quotes here will keep your fortifiers in a place where you can easily reference them when you need attitude nourishment.

TOAST OF THE DAY

Possible Effects: Awakening to the sweetness of life that is there every day, fulfillment,

contentment, and a better complexion. This is a biggie in the awe-development department.

The Toast of the Day is designed to celebrate those little delights you might normally take for granted. You will notice that when you start paying attention to small sweet treasured moments, you will start to see more. With practice and patience, delight will begin to ricochet in the walls of your mind and the ensuing percussion will gently awaken you from the doldrums to spirited appreciation.

SUBLIMINAL MESSAGES and POTION ADS

Possible effects- gradual shift toward believing in messages that serve your higher self.

    The Awe-manac uses the power of repeat advertisement for mental and spiritual retraining. The advertising world has long known that we are highly susceptible to repeated suggestions. We can remember advertising ditties such as "I wish I were an Oscar Meyer wiener" for a lifetime but forget that we can be delightful when we are completely ourselves. If repeat advertising works for hot dogs and antacids, why not use it for thoughts that exalt our existence? We are bombarded daily with new information, so in order for the messages that we need to get through all the static, they definitely need some repetition. So when you see notes, ads, quotes, messages, and the like more than once - it is not a mistake. It's a public service announcement to reprogram your mind in a way you will really, really like. Be kind to yourself. A little dab will do ya.

"I Get To" Spell

Possible Effects: Energetically shifting to looking forward to your day rather than dreading it. You will often have space to make a daily "Today I get to ..." list. Although it sounds simple and somewhat fluffy, this easy exercise is one of the most powerful of all the potions in *The Awe-manac*.

    When filled in, this sentence changes the burdened overtone of an "I have to... " attitude to the light energy, motivation, and built-in gratitude of "I get to ..." Mind, body and spirit are often shifted with this simple reframe.

Examples:

◇ I get to work on my book.

◇ I get to watch my cat sunbathe with his head under the bed and his body in the sun.

    You can also dip into this potion throughout the day and just think things like "I get to write a report, I get to drive my car home." You will notice a change of temperament that follows the simple redesign of these words. Consider writing an "I got to..." list in the evening, .

AWE–SERVANCES

During my research for *The Awe-manac's* daily pages, I was truly in awe of all the celebrations that organizations and individuals have invented to honor various entities; everything from Hairball Day to comet commemorations, Chocolate Covered Cherry Day to Bald Eagles Day. And of course every day of the year has birthdays, anniversaries, and historical events that certainly deserve note and at least a cupcake.

There are whole books dedicated to the acknowledgment all of these events—the trivial to the profound. This book is not one of them, and because of that, many important and many more trivial events are not mentioned here. It's not that we mean to ignore, boycott, or be passive-aggressive; we just have a different mission and not enough space. If we tried to observe all of these designated occasions it would be a full-time job for a staff of thirty-two and at least seventeen of those people would be eating a lot of cake. All real observances noted in *The Awe-manac* are real except the ones the staff made up: they are delineated as *Awe-manac Generated Events* - which spells AGE in the hopes that they will be remembered through the ages. During my research I got to meet Ruth and Tom Roy, two eccentrically wonderful individuals who invented and formalized some of the fun holidays you will see in *The Awe-manac*. They gave me permission to use their holidays as long as I mentioned their website at www.wellcat.com.

JOURNAL JUJU

Possible Effects: Self realization, reinventing yourself, discovery, saving money on therapy, reflection, capturing moments, wisdom, insight, organized thinking, feeling grounded the rest of the day, idea generation, a good doodle.

Journal Juju are refreshingly original journal ideas that defy the mundane, unearth the archeology of your soul, and deliver profound solutions to esoteric ponderings. Feel free to tweak them to best meet your intuitive impulses.

Journal Juju's Credit Report

Possible effects: Increased self esteem, appreciation, awareness, motivation and a night's sleep filled with a feeling of accomplishment.

When prompted to do a credit report, take at least two minutes and write a list of things you are glad you did: little successes, both unexpected and expected things accomplished. Doing this just before sleep fills your spirit with a sense of esteem and reward and the next day you may find yourself motivated to do more. Repeat often, even without a prompt, when you just feel you need the fuel of some self-acknowledgement.

DOSE OF MIRTH

Possible effects: Positive effects of humor: perspective, lightening up, tension relief.

You will be provided with funny or sort of funny material almost every day to help you in-jest the spirit of medicinal mirth.

AHA-PHRODISIACS

Possible Effects: Increased creativity, enhanced amusement, running away without leaving home, reinventing yourself, timelessness, agelessness, fulfillment, increased sex appeal, contentment, becoming a better conversationalist.

Aha-phrodisiacs are your creative prompts. Partaking in them on or around the actual day of the celebration that triggered its existence can summon even more inspiration by virtue of the celebrated energy floating in the air. I think.

Simply read the Aha-phrodisiacs for thought-provoking, educational or even entertainment purposes or sip some to blossom with creative practice. They can trigger lively discussion with your favorite email mate, between sets of tennis, or during a shared fajita at dinner.

1. Title Wave

Titles that people have chosen for songs, paintings, and books are rich in poetic possibility and can be spot-on inspirational triggers for your own writing, art, and other creative outlets. So when you see "Title Wave," pick one of the titles for your inspiration, combine titles or take the words out of the titles and recombine titles, adding more words like a word pool for poetry, prose, or art inspiration. You can even just use one word of one of the titles. Play. Revisit each wave annually for a different twist each time.

2. Word Pool

When you see "Word Pool" it is your cue to jump in *sans* bathing suit, critic, or inhibitions. Take the provided words and play with them. Starting with a group of words and short phrases inspires combinations that lead to places you may not have considered going, and it can make starting easier. Explore poetry, prose, nonsense, a journal entry, a run-on sentence, a state of the union speech, a dialog between refrigerator mold and the yogurt, an observation about the sky, how-to instructions, how-come explanations. Add words. Make the words into a collage or drawing. You do not have to use all of the words. In fact, if one of the words triggers an idea for an off-the-wall subject, go with it, float down that stream of thinking.

3. Repeated Completions

The brain likes a repetitve rhythm and often volunteers surprising responses when we get into a repetitious roll. Completing and repeating an unfinished sentence differently each time over and over taps into spontaneous creative potential and often by-passes that ever-so annoying inner critic. It is an adventure to be sure and one of the most common exercises I have seen that results in amazing responses in writing workshops. To maximize results - go fast, and have little concern whether or not it makes sense.

4. Starter Fluid

When you see "Starter Fluid" just keep going with as little thought and as much speed and freedom as you can summon. Experiment with different points of view: first person, third person, first antelope, third owl, etc. Five minutes is a good amount of time to play with an unfinished sentence, or it may spur a whole weekend where you cannot stop.

5. Viewfinders

When you see Viewfinders, it means you get to try on various personas, attitudes, genres, and perspectives in order to think something different. You may look at the same topic through anger, then giddiness, then as an expert, then as an absentminded person. All these different "viewfinders" can give you a a new angle to explore and new angles are known to lead to fresh ideas.

6. Listing

When asked to do so (or whenever the heck you want) just list away - fast, imaginatively, furiously, having fun with it. Listing actually stretches your mind's flexibility and forges new neural pathways of resourcefulness, especially when you keep going past the point where you would normally stop.

7. Haiku

There's two ways *The Awe-manac* staff encourages you to write a haiku:
1) 5-7-5 syllables: First line with five syllables, second line seven syllables and third line with five syllables. Example: Let's write a haiku/ a short but powerful poem/ that ends quite quickly.
Or 2) One word, two words, a full sentence, two words, one word. (the words can have any number of syllables. Example: Haiku/, a journey/ Unrhyming poem short in length, long in effect/ Try one/ Begin.

Creativity Crash Course

There is a way through every creative block. The following tips are keys to many of them.

1. **SMALL STEPS:** Start projects and prompts using just two minutes at a time. Use those two minutes to think, daydream, set up a space or write and make art as a beginning. For creative thinking: practice new thoughts over and over, believing them, embodying them just 5 percent more each time.

2. **Lower your expectations at the beginning:** high expectations may immobilize you and inspire avoidance. Give yourself permission to be imperfect and ask yourself: How can I make this fun?

3. **ASK SMALL QUESTIONS:** The mind loves questions. Ask questions without expecting an immediate answer and your subconscious will happily percolate answers.

4. **Remind yourself what works:** What worked in the past? What's working now?

5. **Replace your inner discouraging voices with voices that encourage and empower you.** Even if those new voices feel contrived at the beginning, keep practicing them (believe them just 5 percent more each time). Remember: belief has carried many people farther than talent. The adjustment will be gradual, but eventually it will shift your confidence dramatically.

6. **Comparison is toxic in the creative process.** When you find yourself comparing yourself to others do a "Frank"* and do it your way. You have a unique approach.

7. **Let the process be non-linear** with stops and starts, lulls and chaos, tangents and associations. Just stay with it... keep going. When you stay in action, the process is alive with surprises.

Frank Sinatra "I did it MY way."

14

You Are Entering the Monthly and Daily Pages

The Months are in their usual order

AWe-Manac Crop Information

January: Coffee Crop

February: Bird Crop

March: Laughter Crop

April: Poet Crop

May: Dancer Crop

June: Aquarium and Pest Control Crop Duo

July: Ice Cream Crop

August: Shoe Crop

September: Book Crop

October: Clocks

November: Gratitude Crop

December: Holiday Stress Management Crop

This AWe-Manac is Perennial.
You can use it year after year after year.

Welcome
to the Monthly and Daily Pages

All the months
and days
are in order
for your convenience

Make the journey
with an open heart
and wonder will be
your companion

Hydrate.

ENTRY WAY TO JANUARY

There is a spiritual realm that is available to all who find its many entrances.
—James Melvin Washington

It is International Coffee Gourmet Month so if you were to percolate a robust beginning you would be ever so on-theme. For a different blend of year beginnings, abolish New Years resolutions; instead, simply review what went well last year. Target what thoughts and actions served you most and then resolve to continue to brew those modalities into a full-bodied operation this year. Open the door to a New Year: January was in fact named for the Roman god, Janus, protector of gates and doorways. Janus is depicted with two faces, one looking into the past, the other looking to the future (don't try this at home). But do figuratively look into the past and savor all you have achieved and look into the future believing that it is about to serve realities unsurpassed by mere expectations.

At January's Doorway:

This is a month of Capricorn and Aquarius, bread and radios, coffee and tea. It's a month of books, hobbies, prunes, and diets. There is soup this month. January is bakers, oatmeal, dried plums, and eggs. It's about awakening to connections, courageously splashing paint on a blank canvas, words on a vacant page, and new twirl-leaps on a vacant dance floor. It's about eating.

It's National Diet Month, Prune Breakfast Month, National Soup Month, Fat-Free Living Month, Dried Plum Breakfast Month, Bread Machine Baking Month, National Egg Month, National Retail Bakers Month, Wheat Bread Month, National Hot Tea Month, Oatmeal Month, and it's National Be On Purpose Month, National Hobby Month, National Book Blitz Month, National Radio Month, National Yours Mine and Ours. The second Wednesday is Make Your Dreams Come True Day and the 3rd Monday is Martin Luther King Jr. Day.

Wake up and live. Bob Marley

Awe-manac's Invented Event: January 22 Cat Appreciation Day

A Few Ways to Embody January Happenings

1. How many different words can you make from the two words, "It's January" after you've had a cup of coffee? Here are two to get you started: yarn and Saturn.

2. National Hobby Month: Take two more tiny steps to improve skills for your hobby. (Tiny steps: that's 1 to 5 minutes at a time).

3. National Oatmeal Month: Dress your oatmeal with toasted almonds, dried cherries and steamed milk.

Astrological Spells For a January Moment

Aries: Check yourself out in a window reflection but imagine yourself with wings.

Taurus: Quiet your mind and breathe, discover the breath within the breath.

Gemini: Open any book in a bookstore and find a message for you on page 56. It's there.

Cancer: Savor the feel of clean sheets and comfortable PJs as if it were something you all of a sudden appreciated 10 times more.

Leo: Do a favorite stretch, and with undivided attention and notice how good that feels.

Virgo: Look for someone smiling and imagine that their smile was in a deep way because of you.

Libra: Lie on your back on a comfortable floor, imagine any of your struggles melting into the ground and nourishing the roots of a rose bush.

Scorpio: Listen to a song with the intention of singling out instruments and then take turns listening to them as if you were pointing at the musicians. (Have the musicians nod at you when you point at them.)

Sagittarius: Take a morning walk with a sensuous flair, think Marilyn Monroe.

Capricorn: Design a miracle with your imagination right now and write it down as if you were its director.

Aquarius: Look around for a sign that tells you what project your intuition wants to direct you to next.

Pisces: Make a hot beverage a meditation of simplicity, release the past and the future, and steep only the "now."

18

Tides:

Ebbing: what will you release 5 percent of this month?:

_____

Flowing: what will you increase 5 percent?

_____

Vessel of strength: (What self-talk will keep you afloat?)

_____   _____

_____

Gardening Information

Flower: Carnation.

Monthly Awe-manac Crop: Coffee

Growing Tips: Plant grounded coffee beans in fertile filters before going to bed for a robust, mountain-grown flavor ignited at sunrise or 7am-ish. Watch for ideas that bloom from caffeinated highs, and cultivate.

Coffee Crop

january

Today I get to _____
_____

Daily Soul Vitamin

There is no way I can anticipate all the good things that are going to happen today.
~Brian Narelle

Toast of the Day

Lift your cup of hot tea to the sky and declare "Let the wonders begin."

Awe-servances

Happy Birthday to:
J.D. Salinger, 1919, author of *The Catcher in the Rye*.
B. Kliban, 1935, cartoonist famous for his cat cartoons.

A Universal Hour of Peace is observed at noon GMT.

Aha-phrodisiacs

For the New Year: pick a new thought you want to think and practice that new thought in 15 second increments whenever you remember.

Make a list of things that worked for you last year; make one of them a New Year's resolution (optional: resolve to do it 5 percent more a week if you would like to try something that might work).

J.D. Salinger Starter Fluid from *The Catcher in the Rye*: "If you really want to know about it...."

Use Kliban's title to spark some writing: *Two Guys Fooling Around with the Moon*.

Journal Juju

Write on the first page of a brand new journal: "There is no way I can anticipate all the good things that are going to happen this year," and then imagine what it feels like in the body to really believe that.

Dose of Mirth

Coffee isn't my cup of tea. ~Samuel Goldwyn
Coffee: creative lighter fluid. ~Floyd Maxwell
I think if I were a woman I'd wear coffee as a perfume.
~John Van Druten
There's too much blood in my caffeine system.
    ~Anonymous

New Year's Day is every man's birthday.
—Charles Lamb
Happy Birthday

♪ Note to Self: Gently steel into the new year.

Name Today _____

Daily Soul Vitamins
I write for the same reason I breathe –
because if I didn't, I would die. —Isaac Asimov

A cat is a lion in a jungle of small bushes.—Indian saying

Toast of the Day
Here's to the calm presence of a sitting cat.

Aweservances

Happy Birthday to
Isaac Asimov,1920, prolific author of science fiction and professor of biochemistry. Today was named National Science Fiction Day because Asimov wrote some awe-some stuff.

Today I get to

_____

_____

It's also Happy Mew Year for Cat's Day and National Cream Puff Day.
1842 The first wire suspension bridge was opened to traffic in Fairmont, PA.

Aha-phrodisiacs
Write a list of why you write or do art or why you want to; then pick one of those and write at length about it, getting deep into it even if it doesn't seem to make sense.

Write down some event that happened recently. Now recount it adding a few otherworldly powers and characters, reactions that might happen by way of science fiction, maybe a robot, maybe a cat with psychic abilities, maybe warp speed.

Write, doodle or collage a list of "mew year" resolutions that a cat might write.

Journal Juju
Is there a metaphor of a cream puff in your life for poem purposes? If not, consider popcorn, Jell-O or chewing gum. Use a wire suspension bridge as a metaphor for crossing from one point to another in your life: Write as if you were walking over to where you want to be or from where you were to where you are (if it has already happened). What do you see? How does it go? What helps you?

Dose of Mirth
Dogs come when they're called; cats take a message and get back to you later.
~ Mary Bly

A Question Brought to You by the Kindness Potion
What is one small way that you can be kind to yourself today?

Daily Soul Vitamin

If more of us valued food and cheer and song above hoarded gold, it would be a merrier world. ~J. R. R. Tolkien

Today I Get to
_____

Hobbit in a Hammock

Awe-Servances

Happy Birthday to J. R. R. Tolkien 1892, author of *The Hobbit* and *The Lord of the Rings* trilogy.

It's also The Festival of Sleep Day: A favorite holiday to catch up on a little sleep.

Toast of the Day
Here's to a refreshing Midday Nap.

Aha-phrodisiacs

Begin with this sentence: I have arrived home and there is a hobbit asleep in my bed. Repeated completions: "To sleep is to_____".

Word Pool: wherever he went, shoe, play, cheer, song, responsibility, handles, purple ribbon, poem, lit, snore, things I remember, noon, poetry, one of the few times, chair, road, zzzzzz, sidewalks, inevitable, life, rings, meander, just not sure.

Use the title *Festival of Sleep* for collage, drawing, painting or doodling

Journal Juju

List 3 things you're glad you did already this year. Use this as a title for a journal entry: *A Short History of My Sleep Life*. Optional: Make a list of possible chapter titles as if this were a book, tongue-in-cheek or serious. Write short blurbs under each title heading.

Dose of Mirth

It's a job that's never started that takes the longest to finish. ~J. R. R. Tolkien

Message from Awe-wakened Moment Potion:
Savor a nap.

Daily Soul Vitamin

I was like a boy playing on the seashore, and diverting myself now and then finding a smoother pebble or a prettier shell than ordinary, whilst the great ocean of truth lay all undiscovered before me. ~Isaac Newton

Awe-servances

Toast of the Day
Here's to having a fresh view take you by surprise.

Happy Birthday to:
Sir Isaac Newton, 1643, physicist, mathematician, astronomer, natural philosopher, and alchemist, science icon, discoverer of the law of gravity.

It's also: Trivia Day. Speaking of trivia, did you know the word "trivia" is another name for the Roman goddess Diana? Get Out of Your Boxer Shorts Day.

Aha-phrodisiacs

Describe how life operated before gravity was discovered. Write about a day without gravity. Write a dialog with gravity. Have some gravity.

Free associate, write a poem, or doodle about boxer shorts. What design would you put on boxer shorts?

Journal Juju

Write as if you are the goddess, Trivia; what would she write in her journal? Pick one and write about it in detail.

Dose of Mirth

You can't blame gravity for falling in love.
~Albert Einstein

Note to Myself

I've never written about boxer shorts before. I think I'll use this as an occasion to get a new pair.

Name Today

Soul Vitamin

"Nothing is more beautiful than the loveliness of the woods before sunrise." ~George Washington Carver

Awe-servances

Toast of the Day
HERE'S TO THE SIMPLE GROUNDING PLEASURE OF SITTING UNDER A TREE.

Birthdays:
Umberto Eco, 1932, philosopher and novelist.
George Washington Carver, 1864, botanical researcher.

Aha-phrodisiacs

Use Eco's title *The Island of the Day Before* for writing, collage, doodle or watercolor painting. Visit it in your imagination first: What kind of breezes does it have? Any signs about today on the island? What does the sky look like? What message is in the air? Do you hear any mumbling?

Dose of Mirth

"When in charge ponder. When in trouble delegate. When in doubt mumble." –unknown

Journal Juju

George Washington Carver said, "If you love it enough, anything will talk with you." Make a list of things you love. Pick one or more and have it or them write you a letter. What does it need from you? What advice would it give you? What small conversation would it share? What are its thoughts about dust?

Message Brought to You by the Body Temple

Here's a breathing practice that will ground you in your body. Breathe in halfway and hold. Breathe in again and hold. Breathe out halfway and hold, breathe out again and hold. Then for the third time, exhale pressing all your air out by pressing the abdomen in toward your spine and hold. Breathe in halfway and hold and then release the control of the breath and savor the soothing feeling of a breath uninterrupted. Exhaling deeply creates a more effective inhale.

Name Today
_____

Double Dose Daily Soul Vitamin

Poetry is a deal of joy and pain and wonder
with a dash of the dictionary. ~Khalil Gibran
Poetry is a packsack of invisible keepsakes.
~Carl Sandburg

Toast of the Day

Here's to reading something you really like and realizing you wrote it.

Happy Birthday to:
Khalil Gibran, 1883, artist, poet and writer, best known
for *The Prophet.*
Carl Sandburg, 1878, poet, historian, novelist, balladeer,
and folklorist.

Aha-phrodisiacs

Begin with one of Khalil Gibran's quotes and keep going with your own writing:
"All our words are but crumbs that fall down from the feast of the mind," or "Sadness
is but a wall between two gardens." Or portray one or both of the above quotes in
collage, doodles, a painting, or a rough sketch.

What's your purpose in life? Invent one. Write some poetry on purpose.

Dose of Mirth

There are two seasonal diversions that can ease
the bite of any winter. One is the January thaw.
The other is the seed catalogues.
~Hal Borland

Journal Juju

Make a list or a collage of the invisible keepsakes in
your packsack made visible. What essences, qualities,
strengths, tools, objects or thoughts would you keep in a packsack you carried?

Since it is January 6, give yourself credit for six small things you are already glad
you have done this year.

Notes to Self: Breathe consciously. Breathing is freeing.
Extraneous thought: Gibran was a cool guy.

Daily Soul Vitamin

Although it may be terrifying to get out of your comfort zone, it's very exciting to start a new chapter in your life. ~Katie Couric

Toast of the Day
Here's to the amazing convenience of talking to someone on a long-distance phone call.

Awe-servances.

Happy Birthday to: Katie Couric, 1957, first woman to solo-anchor the weekday evening news.

It's also: National Pass Gas Day (I didn't make this up). On this day in 1785, Balloonist Jean Pierre Blanchard successfully made the first solo crossing of the English Channel from the English coast to France.
In 1927 Intercontinental long-distance phone service began between New York & London. There were 31 calls made the first day.

Aha-phrodisiacs

Write a dialog that might have taken place on one of the first intercontinental calls.
Write a journal entry about Jean Pierre's experience on his balloon trip or doodle, collage, or draw what that might have looked like.
Write a poem about National Pass Gas Day and pass it on. Combine any or all of the above.

Journal Juju

List 3 things you're glad you did already this year. Use this as a title for a journal entry: _A Short History of My Sleep Life._ Optional: Make a list of possible chapter titles as if this were a book - tongue-in-cheek or serious. Write short blurbs under each title heading.

Dose of Mirth

Passing gas is just plain funny; I don't care how old I get. ~Ann, from a blog

Brought to You by Body Temple Potion

Yoga is one of the most effective practices to sustain or regenerate youthfulness and defy some of the difficulties of the aging process. Savasana (lying on the floor and allowing all the muscles to relax, and the mind to empty) can turn around a stressful day.

January 8
It's National Bubble Bath Day

Daily Soul Vitamin
When things go wrong, don't go with them —Elvis Presley

Toast of the Day
HERE'S TO THE SMELL OF
a SOOTHING baTH SalT

Happy Birthday to:
Elvis Presley, 1935, singer, musician, actor, and pop icon.

It's Also: Show and Tell Day at Work
(Since children have show and tell, adults should get to do the same)
and National Bubble Bath Day

Aha-phrodisiacs
Write a super short story about taking something odd to work for show and tell. Develop a new character first—with personality characteristics, an occupation, desire and conflict, then determine what that character might take to work.
Water can be therapeutic in so many ways. Climb inside a tub of nurturing warm water.
   Elvis Presley: Title Wave: Easy Come, Easy Go, Echoes of Love, Everybody Come Aboard, Fairytale, Find Out What's Happening, First In

Journal Juju
Use the Elvis title *Edge of Reality* or any of the above titles as your journal title and see what it inspires you to write.

Reality is that which, when you stop believing in it, doesn't go away.
~ Philip K. Dick

Today I get to

_____

_____

Name Today
_____

Daily Soul Vitamin

I wish that every human life might be pure transparent freedom.
~Simone De Beauvoir

Toast of the Day
Here's to towels just out of the dryer on a cool day.

Awe-servances

Happy Birthday to:
Simone De Beauvoir, 1908, author and philosopher.
Joan Baez, 1941, folk singer and songwriter known for her highly individual vocal style.
Dave Matthews, 1967, vocalist and guitarist.
It's Dotty Day!

Aha-phrodisiacs

Use this Dave Matthew song title as Starter Fluid for writing, doodling, painting, movement or in a collage: "The Space Between."

For Dotty Day, use dots as a trigger for your art. Make large dots and fill them in with favorite quotes or see how adding dots can add interest or whimsy to a piece or a collage. Or take someone named Dotty to lunch.

Journal Juju

Joan Baez said "Action is the antidote to despair." What kinds of activities, people, things, quotes or songs keep the blues away from you? Make a list or write in depth about one. In your journal depict what pure freedom looks like with words, collage or art.

Dose of Mirth

A line is a dot that went for a walk.
~Paul Klee

dot, dot, dot.

Notes to self: Continue perfecting the yoga pose savasana. Savasana is said to be better than sleep...

stilllife laying in Savasana

January 10

Daily Soul Vitamin

It is only a little planet, but how beautiful it is.
~Robinson Jeffers

Toast of the Day

Here's to our capacity to feel this delight and our beautiful little planet.

Happy Birthday to:
Robinson Jeffers, 1887, poet.
Rod Stewart, 1945, singer.

Also: Peculiar People Day and National Bittersweet Chocolate Day.

Aha-phrodisiacs

In honor of Rod Stewart's birthday write what happened to Maggie Mae. For example: "Maggie Mae does manicures six days a week down at Dot's, bowls on Tuesdays, lives in a single-wide trailer, and spends most nights drinking at the Rolling.... At home alone, she hangs up her clothes, feeds the cat, picks up a pen and puts an X through today's date on her kitchen calendar." ~Victoria Mellekian

Write a bittersweet chocolate haiku (5-7-5 syllables), poem, or ode, and/or eat some with undivided attention.

Dose of Mirth

My inferiority complex is not as good as yours. ~Unknown

Journal Juju

Purge on the page: List five things that frustrate you, then wipe their energy off your body (like wiping off cat hair) and write about anything about these things that might make you stronger. Or simply write "SO THERE. I release that energy and focus it on something more joy-filled."

Notes to self
Breathe deep when frustrated. Breathe deep now.
Don't hide bittersweet chocolate so well.

Today I Get to

Daily Soul Vitamin
You can't tell how deep a puddle is until you step in it.
—Unknown

Toast of the Day
Here's to receiving an unexpected expression of appreciation.

Awe-servances

Doodle Here

1963 Whiskey-A-Go-Go, America's first discotheque opened on Sunset Boulevard in L.A.
National Step-in-a-puddle day.
Use-more-of-your-mind day.

Aha-phrodisiacs
Write a poem about Whiskey-a-Go-Go or one of your favorite establishments.
   Write a memory about puddles. Play with the word puddle, give it different meanings, or write a piece that has puddle and a bunch of other "p" words in it.

Journal Juju
There is a proverb that reads, "every path has its puddle."
Write a thank-you note to yourself for getting yourself through the metaphorical puddles on your path. Get specific. doodle a picture of a few puddles you've gone through and label their meaning. Label the boots that helped you splash through them.

Subliminal Message brought to you by the inner Awe-lixir Potion.
"Take those precious moments when your brain feels blank to stay there. When you are granted the gift of being present without thoughts running through your head look at that as a moment of meditation." ~Tim Badonsky

Today I get to.... _____

January 12
It's National Soup Month

Daily Soul Vitamin

You can't wait for inspiration. You have to go after it with a club.
~Jack London

Toast of the Day

Here's to those pens that make your handwriting look better than it usually looks.

Happy Birthday to:
Jack London, 1876, author of *The Call of the Wild*.
John Singer Sargent, 1856, portrait and landscape painter.

Also: National Handwriting Day, Feast of Fabulous Wild Men, Lift Every Voice and Sing Day.

Aha-phrodisiacs

Google Sargent's work and choose a portrait or landscape to write about. Write in the first person about it, or choose two and write how the people are related or have a dialog between them.

  You have permission to sing in the shower, in the car, or incognito. Lift your voice above the din.

Dose of Mirth

A portrait is a painting with something wrong with the mouth.
~John Singer Sargent

Journal Juju

Use your handwriting to illustrate various emotions in your journal.

  Write about the call of your wild. Write a letter to yourself from the wild. Write to a fabulous fictional wild man. Have lunch with one.

  John Singer Sargent said, "You can't do sketches enough. Sketch everything and keep your curiosity fresh." Sketching creates an intimate connection with your subject even if you're not a skilled artist. Practice with permission to be imperfect. Do quick sketches when you travel and you will notice the quality of your experience will deepen.

Today I Get to _____

_____

Soup

January 13

Name today _____

Daily Soul Vitamin

Romance is the glamour which turns the dust of everyday life into a golden haze.

~Amanda Cross

Toast of the Day

Here's to choosing to the sound of wind chimes on an otherwise silent morning.

Happy Birthday to:

Anthony Faas, 1854, patented the accordion.

Alfred Fuller, 1885, founder of the Fuller Brush Company.

Carolyn Gold Heilbrun, 1926, author, wrote mystery novels under pen name of Amanda Cross.

It's also Change of Style Day.

Aha-phrodisiacs

What would accordion music look like if you could doodle, collage, or paint it?

Write about a character who is a Fuller Brush Man. What are his hobbies, opinions, or day like?

Write a poem about various Dr. Seussian things a Fuller Brush Man might sell. Write about a Fuller brush item that might also play accordion music.

Dose of Mirth

A gentleman is a man who can play the accordion but doesn't. ~Unknown

Journal Juju

Amanda Cross said, "Odd, the years it took to learn one simple fact: that the prize just ahead, the next job, publication, love affair, marriage always seemed to hold the key to satisfaction but never, in the longer run, sufficed." Wanting what we have is one of the "secrets" to life. Write a list of things you want but make them things you already have.

Message Brought to You by Arpeggio:

Play a song for yourself as if you were giving yourself a gift or as if the band or person singing the song were singing specially to you. If that's hard to do, imagine what it would be like.

January 14

Name today _____

Today I get to _____

Daily Soul Vitamin
I've learned... that life is tough, but I'm tougher....
~Andy Rooney

Toast of the Day
Here's to having a friend you can be goofy with.

Awe—servances
Happy Birthday to:
Albert Schweitzer, 1875, Alsatian theologian, musician, philosopher,
  and physician
Andy Rooney, 1919, *60 Minutes* journalist, humorist, commentator.
It's also Fire the Boss Week and National Dress Up Your Pet Day.

Aha—phrodisiacs
Albert Schweitzer said "Compassion, in which all ethics must take
root, can only attain its full breadth and depth
if it embraces all living creatures and does not limit itself to
mankind." I think what he's saying is don't dress up
your pet.
   Use the word "compassion" to write an acronym. Develop compassionate characters and then have them talk to you.

Dose of Mirth
Never wear anything that panics the cat. ~P.J. O'Rourke

Journal Juju
Write a repeated completion starting with "I've learned...
" and going fast, not worrying about punctuation or if
it even makes sense.
   If you need to, write an UNSENT memo to fire your
boss. (Not while at work.)

Question to Self
What's one small way I can be compassionate with myself today?

January 15

Name today _____

Today I Get To _____

Daily Soul Vitamin

Take the first step in faith, you don't have to see the whole staircase just take the first step. ~Martin Luther King Jr.

Toast of the Day
Here's to taking one more step.

Awe~servances

Happy birthday to:
Martin Luther King, Jr., 1929 black civil rights leader and Nobel Prize recipient.

1892 *Triangle* magazine in Springfield, MA published the rules for a new game which used a peach basket attached to a suspended board. It is known today as basketball.

Aha-phrodisiacs

Pick one or more of these Viewfinders and see what new approach you can have to continuing with the incomplete sentence "I have a dream…" (exuberant, courageous, imaginative, detailed oriented, magic oriented, kidlike, suspicious, republican, democrat, heroic, insecure).

In honor of basketball day, write about what the owner of the peach basket had to say.

Dose of Mirth

He felt that his whole life was some kind of dream and he sometimes wondered whose it was and whether they were enjoying it. ~Douglas Adams

Journal Juju

Write your creative dream as if it were happening in the present moment: write what you see, feel, touch, smell, hear, and sense. Or write poetry, prose, or a rough idea about who is dreaming your life.

Note to Self

Check the back of my mind, the back burner, any back orders, the back of a book and see if there are any ideas lurking in those places with which I can take a small step.

16
National Nothing Day

Daily Soul Vitamin

How beautiful it is to do nothing, and then rest afterward.
~Spanish Proverb

Toast of the Day
HERE'S TO NOTHING.

Two Sarvances

how nice is nothing

National Nothing Day. Anniversary of the event created by newspaperman Harold Pullman Coffin and first observed in 1973, "to provide Americans with one national day when they can just sit without celebrating, observing, or honoring anything "

Aha-phrodisiacs

Write about nothing. Those of you who usually write nothing, write something. Word Pool: sparkling, sidewalk, nothing, whisper, lunatic, hiding, bar, dumbstruck, crafted, bump, wields, unceasing, entire, weaves, primitive, discovery, tunnel, sneaker, Chevy.
   Keep going with Douglas Adams' Dose of Mirth below.

Journal Juju

Repeated Completions: "There's nothing I..."
"Sun sparkles on my upturned face Ocean breeze slithers over my body
Eyes closed / I discover my breath/ In and out
I discover my heart / And feel the music of the earth within me
Without me/ A part of me / Apart from me / And I realize/ I am nothing
I am everything." ~Jenn Simpson

Dose of Mirth

For a moment, nothing happened. Then, after a second or so, nothing continued to happen. ~ Douglas Adams

Name Today _____

Daily Soul Vitamin

The Muses love the morning. ~Ben Franklin

Toast of the Day
Here's to the sound of children singing.

Happy Birthday to:
Benjamin Franklin, 1706, founding father and
inventor of the Almanac.
William Stafford, 1914, poet and pacifist.
Vidal Sassoon, 1928, a father of modernist style.

Aha-phrodisiacs

William Stafford said, "I have woven a parachute out
of everything broken." Make a collage of a parachute
using different magazine pieces like a mosaic.

Journal Juju

Write about your various relationships with your hair.
  What would your metaphorical parachute contain that would come to
keep you from landing too hard? What sayings, people, or philosophies
have kept you from hitting the ground?

Dose of Mirth

*If truth is beauty, how come no one has their hair
done in a library?* ~Lily Tomlin

Pay attention to your body.

Desires for change, intuitive
validation, clear direction:
all show up in your body's energy.

January 18

Name today _____
I get to _____

Daily Soul Vitamin

We write to taste life twice. ~ Anais Nin

Toast of the Day
HERE'S TO THE ALTERED STATE OF JAZZ.

Happy Birthday to:
Peter Mark Roget, 1779, physician, author of
Roget's Thesaurus of English Words and Phrases.

It's also: Jazz, Day and Maintenance Day.

Aha-phrodisiacs

Write about a maintenance man or woman; use first or third person.
   Use the word "maintenance" to associate ideas that spark some writing
Replace some of the following words using a thesaurus and then use them for
a word pool: grow, sneak, bombard, elbow, borrow, put, time, elevate, decanter, pinch.

Dose of Mirth

"What's another word for Thesaurus?" ~ Steven Wright.

Journal Juju

What's another word for you today?
   Thinking maintenance: Write some positive thoughts that would serve you to
embody them. Remind yourself of some tools, approaches, or thoughts that have
worked for you in the past or recently. Remind yourself of one of your strengths
or recall a compliment or five.

A Message from the Potion Awakened Inner Messages

Bringing to mind what has worked in the past week or year empowers our common
sense. Common Sense can propel us fruitfully forward in many areas of our life.

Question to Myself

What has worked for me in any area or all areas of my life in the past week or year or
lifetime, for that matter?

January 19
It's National Oatmeal Month

Name today _____

Today I get to _____

Daily Soul Vitamin

When I'm inspired, I get excited because I can't wait to see what I'll come up with next. ~Dolly Parton

Toast of the Day
Here's to enjoying our own inspirations.

Happy Birthday to:
Edgar Allan Poe 1809, poet, short story writer, playwright.
Paul Cezanne, 1839, painter.
Dolly Parton, 1946, award-winning country singer, author, actress and philanthropist.
Brew a Potion Day.

Aha-phrodisiacs

Search online for Cezanne images, pick a painting, and write what happens in it next or write a poem that goes along with it.

Make up your own antigravity, antiaging, antidulling potion. What metaphorical ingredients would you put in it? What spell would it put you under?

Make an Oatmeal Potion: put steamed milk, toasted and slivered almonds, dried cherries and a little brown sugar on your oatmeal.

Dose of Mirth

I was the first woman to burn my bra - it took the fire department four days to put it out. ~Dolly Parton

Journal Juju

Edgar Allan Poe wrote: "I wish I could write mysterious as a cat." Repeated completions: "I wish I could write..." or "I wish I could ..."

Brought to you by Inner Awe-lixir Potion

Bruce Lee said "Empty your mind, be formless, shapeless like water. Now you put water into a cup, it becomes the cup, you put water into a bottle, it becomes the bottle, you put it in a teapot, it becomes the teapot. Now water can flow or it can crash. Be water, my friend."

January 20

Name today

Today I Get To _____

Daily Soul Vitamin

In order to attain the impossible,
one must attempt the absurd.
~ Miguel de Cervantes Savedra

Toast of the Day
Here's to the absurd.

Awe-Servances

Happy Birthday to:
Director David Lynch, 1946, filmmaker.

It's also Hat Day and on this day in 1885, the roller coaster was
patented by L.A. Thompson of Coney Island, NY.
Aquarius begins.

Aha-phrodisiacs

David Lynch said, "I like darkness and confusion and absurdity, but I like to know that
there could be a little door that you could go out into a safe life area of happiness."
Write as if there were a little door you could go through into a safe life area of happiness.
What does the door look like? What does it feel like to go through the door? Make the
door and/or the other side of it into art.

Dose of Mirth

It's a small apartment, I've barely enough room to lay my hat and a few friends.
~Dorothy Parker

Journal Juju

In honor of the roller coaster, write a summary of your metaphorical highs and lows this week and then scream.
   Aquarius is individualistic, altruistic, visionary, perceptive,
intellectual, ingenious, unpredictable, friendly, and scientific.
Pick at least three Aquarian characteristics and use each as a
heading. Under each heading write one or two small actions you
can take to manifest these adjectives into your life during Aquarius (Jan 20 – Feb 19),
even if this is not the sign you were born under.

January 21

Name today _____

Today I Get To _____

Daily Soul Vitamin
With a few flowers in my garden, half a dozen pictures and some books, I live without envy. ~Lope de Vega

Toast of the Day
Here's to the moments when you realize the simple things are wonderful and enough.

Awe~servances

It's National Hugging Day, National Creative Frugality Week, and National Granola Bar Day.

Aha-phrodisiacs
From the character of a frugal artist write in detail about one of these topics: your garden, your next art project, the sky, area rugs. Paint, collage or doodle the garden of a frugal artist.

Enjoy yourself enjoying a granola bar with a little more present awareness today. Choose your favorite, or be dangerous and try something new.

Dose of Mirth
I'm living so far beyond my income that we may almost be said to be living apart. ~e. e. cummings

Journal Juju
Write about "envy"—what associations does the word bring up for you?

Write about what people might envy you for. Then write a list of associations to the word contentment. Write about where you assign daily disappointment. Then do a credit report: make a list of things you're glad you did, no matter how small.

Note to Myself Breathe

January 22
Cat appreciation day

Name today ————————————————

Daily Soul Vitamin
I believe cats to be spirits come to earth. A cat, I am sure, could walk on a cloud without coming through. ~Jules Verne

Toast of the Day
Here's to the grace of a cat walking through the room and the comedy of kittens in monster drills (you know, when they run around the house seemingly for no reason at all).

Awe—Servances
Happy Birthday to:
Francis Bacon, 1561, philosopher, statesman and essayist.
Joseph Wambaugh, 1937, writer known for his fictional and non-fictional accounts of police work in the U.S.

It's also: Answer Your Cat's Question Day and Celebration of Life Day.

Aha—phrodisiacs
Write a list of questions a cat might have. Have a dialog on paper with a cat.
Write a poem, haiku, laundry-list, or song to celebrate life.
Make a collage that is a celebration of life. Celebrate life with a cat—share some salmon.

Journal Juju
Write a journal entry using Joseph Wambaugh's book title, *Lines and Shadows* as your title and invite associations, metaphors and scribbles to emerge. If you're stuck, make a

list of your associations to the word "lines" and another one to the word "shadows" and then weave the words, phrases, and sentences together like a word pool. Or write about the lines of the cat in the shadows of the house.

Francis Bacon said, *"A wise man will make more opportunities than he finds."*
What opportunities can you make this week?

January 23

Name today _____

Daily Soul Vitamin

Still life is the touchstone of the painter. ~Manet

Aweservances

Toast of the Day
Here's to Feet and all they do for us.

Happy Birthday to:
Édouard Manet, 1832, painter, a pivotal figure in the transition from Realism to Impressionism.

On this day in 1896 X-rays were discovered and it's Measure Your Feet Day.

Aha-phrodisiacs

Go to Wikipedia or search Google Images for Manet's painting *Luncheon on the Grass* and write from one or all of the characters' points of view. Make a collage of your own *Luncheon on the Grass*. Eat lunch on a blanket ... on the grass.

In honor of X-rays, write about being able to see through things: metaphorically or supernaturally. What if you could see through galaxies, mystery, scratch-off lottery tickets, lies, facades, masks, or the walls of people's houses?

Instead of measuring your feet, massage them. Now for just 30 seconds.

Dose of Mirth

Never test the depth of the water with both feet. ~Unknown

Journal Juju

Edouard Manet said "It is not enough to know your craft, you have to have feeling. Science is all very well, but for us, imagination is worth far more." Imagine how you would like to feel about your craft and write about it as if you already felt that way. Imagine your craft evoking feelings: what would they be?

Today I get to _____

JANUARY 24
It's National radio MONTH

Name today _____

Today I Get To _____

Double Dose Daily Soul Vitamin

"I can live for two months on a good compliment." ~Mark Twain

Toast of the Day
Here's to the Feeling of receiving a genuine compliment.

Awe—Servances

Happy Birthday to:

Neil Diamond, 1941, singer and songwriter.

It's also National Compliment Day and National Peanut Butter Day.

Aha—phrodisiacs

Neil Diamond Title Wave: Angel Above My Head, Play Me, You're So Sweet, Don't Know Much, Wrong Number, You Never Can Tell (Extra credit: Use one title as a Repeated Completion).

Write a piece that involves compliments. Try focusing on using one letter for alliteration. (e.g. : It's come to my attention to appropriately appreciate the amazing attitude you've added at the Appleton PTA…)

Write an ode to peanut butter. Have a peanut butter and green olive sandwich.

Make a few quick, rapid-fire collage or watercolor cards and write genuine compliments inside them. Send or deliver them. (Extra credit: do it anonymously.)

Listen to the radio and pretend there's a message broadcasting to you that will help trigger a new idea for a character, a subject to write about, or art (doodles included).

Dose of Mirth

"Marge, you're as pretty as Princess Leia and as smart as Yoda."
~A Complimenting Homer Simpson

Journal Juju

You have permission to collect and review compliments to fortify the confidence vital to creative success. Dare to believe they are true. Put them in a box designated for this special ritual or in a specially named file in your computer.

Note to Self
Nice job on that thing you did today. You know, that *thing.*

January 25

Name today _____

Today I Get To _____

Daily Soul Vitamin

Arrange whatever pieces come your way.
~ Virginia Woolf

Awe-servances

Virginia Woolf, 1882, chief modernist literary figures of the twentieth century.
It's also Observe the Weather Day and Opposite Day.

Aha-phrodisiacs

Revisit today's Soul Vitamin. Write a list of things that you associate with the word "pieces"; don't stop to analyze or ponder whether it is logical or makes sense. Now arrange those pieces (or words) adding more. You can also arrange pieces by making a collage and then giving it a title. Cut out squares of different pictures, patterns, and designs and arrange them according to your intuition.

   Virginia Woolf is famous for saying, "A woman must have money and a room of her own if she is to write fiction." Write about having a room of your own from different attitudes (vague, cunning, secretive, pensive, absentminded, careless, oppositional) or the attitude you are in today.

Dose of Mirth

The coldest winter I ever spent was a summer in San Francisco. ~Mark Twain

Journal Juju

Make a list of opposites: opposite ways you are feeling today, opposite things you would like to do, opposite things you would say. This exercise can help you discover some fresh thinking.

Brought to You by Awe-wakened Moment Potion and Jeff Doucette

When you find yourself tightening; a knot in the stomach, a clenched jaw, tightened shoulders, you are living in a moment of fear and separation. Gently pull yourself back into the moment by connecting to something real in the moment; that flower, that ceiling fan, the rush of the traffic, the breeze gently blowing across your skin. Let all of it in without judgment. Be the I Am with What Is. Become the "I Am" observer of your "What Is" reality.
~Jeff Doucette, Actor, Workshop Leader

January 26

Name today

Today I Get To

Daily Soul Vitamin

*I realized that if I had to choose, I would rather have
birds than airplanes.* ~Charles Lindbergh

Toast of the Day
Here's to creatively quirky humor.

Awe-Servances

Happy Birthday to:

Jules Feiffer, 1929, Pulitzer Prize-winning cartoonist and author.

Ellen DeGeneres, 1958, actress, stand-up comedian, talk show host, philanthropist.

Also: In 1784 in a letter to his daughter, Benjamin Franklin expressed his unhappiness over
the choice of the eagle as the national bird instead of the turkey.

Aha-phrodisiacs

Jules Feiffer Title Wave: Room with a Zoo, The House Across the Street, By the Side of the
Road. Use these titles to trigger writing or art. Write about a room with a zoo in the house
across the street.

  Start some writing with: "Anyway, I was getting some corn chips out of the vending machine at work and someone came up and said 'You're it!' and ran away."

Dose of Mirth

Just go up to somebody on the street and say 'You're it!" and just run away.
~Ellen DeGeneres

Journal Juju

Make up a bird to represent your household,
your work, your creativity, or an attitude.
Write about it: what bird, why, what would
you feed it? Collage, draw, or paint that bird.
Write from a bird's point of view. What
kind would you be? Fly around the room
but watch the chandelier—it could poke
your eye out.

Merrily, Merrily, Merrily, Merrily
Life is But a Steam

January 27

Name today _____

Today I Get To _____

Daily Soul Vitamin

"The essence of all art is to have pleasure in giving pleasure."
~ Mikhail Baryshnikov

Toast of the Day

Here's to a bite of impossibly delicious chocolate cake.

Awe-Severances

Happy Birthday to:

Wolfgang Amadeus Mozart, 1756, pretty popular prolific
  composer of the Classical period.

Mikhail Baryshnikov, 1948, ballet dancer icon with a gig as Carrie's
  boyfriend on *Sex and the City*.

Charles Lutwidge Dodgson (Lewis Carroll), the creator of *Alice in Wonderland*, known
  by some as the master of nonsense.

National Chocolate Cake Day

Aha-phrodisiacs

Nonsense can be liberating in writing and art and can lead to brilliance. Write a poem
in honor of Lewis Carroll making up a number of your own words. Make a collage or
doodle and integrate nonsense words into the picture (Optional: while listening to
Mozart).

  Write a Lewis Carrollesque ode to chocolate cake. Have a chocolate cupcake or
deliver one to someone in chocolate-cupcake need. Have a Mad Hatters's Tea Party and
serve upside down cupcakes. Clean the Cheshire cat litter box.

  Tomorrow is National Blueberry Pancake Day so you might want to buy ingredients
  or invite a friend to a pancake house to celebrate tomorrow.

Dose of Mirth

*The Queen of Hearts said, "Sometimes I've believed as many as
six impossible things before breakfast."* ~Lewis Carroll

Journal Juju

Write down 2 impossible things you can believe before dinner tonight. Have chocolate
cake for dessert (small piece). Make Mozart's name into an acronym.

January 28

Name today

Today I Get To _____

Daily Soul Vitamin

The creative is the place where no one else has ever been. You have to leave the city of your comfort and go into the wilderness of your intuition.
~Alan Alda

Toast of the Day

HERE'S TO THE WILDERNESS OF CREATIVITY AND THE WISDOM OF INTUITION.

Happy Birthday to:
Sidonie-Gabrielle Colette, 1873, French novelist whose pen name was Colette.
Alan Alda, 1936, award-winning actor.
Sarah McLachlin, 1968, musician, singer, and songwriter.

Also: National Kazoo Day and Blueberry pancake day.

Aha-phrodisiacs

Make blueberry pancakes.

Colette said that "Writing only leads to more writing." After the blueberry pancakes, start with one of these sentences: "I might as well write ...," "The reason I'm not going to write today is...," "I'm only a character in a novel but ..."

Sarah McLachlan's Title Wave: Possession, Wait, Plenty, Good Enough, Elsewhere, Solace, Drawn To The Rhythm, Into The Fire, The Path Of Thorns, Lost, Fear, Full Of Grace, Blue, Drawn To The Rhythm, Shelter, As The End Draws Near.

Dose of Mirth

What if the hokey-pokey really is what it's all about? ~Unknown

Journal Juju

Colette also said, "What a wonderful life I've had! I only wish I'd realized it sooner." Let this be permission to enjoy your life now. Make a permission slip, list all the things you are enjoying, allow 5 percent more enjoyment than usual in and practice this skill. Or write about the wilderness of your intuition… describe what you discover.

Notes to Self

My foolish ways are filled with writing potential. That Colette chick was really wise.

January 29

Name today _____

Today I Get To _____

Daily Soul Vitamin

"The more you praise and celebrate your life, the more there is in life to celebrate."
~Oprah Winfrey

Awe, Awe!

Toast of the Day
HERE'S TO THE SMELL OF CARNATIONS.

Awe-Servances

Happy Birthday to:
Oprah Winfrey, 1954, award-winning TV host, actress, philanthropist.
It's also Carnation Day and on this day in 1845 "The Raven" by Edgar Allen Poe was published for the first time in the *New York Evening Mirror*.
1987 The famous smile of *Mona Lisa*, according to *Physicians Weekly* was caused by a "...facial paralysis resulting from a swollen nerve behind the ear."

Aha-phrodisiacs

Go buy yourself, smell, or doodle some carnations. Or just visit some in the store.
   Write a haunting poem about another bird. (The Canary, The Hawk, the Parrot) – Have a repeating refrain like "The Raven" (or not).

Journal Juju

Oprah said, "Turn your wounds into wisdom." Let some of your emotional and physical wounds talk to you about the wisdom they would like to share. Feel free to ask questions (use your non-dominant hand to answer).

Dose of Mirth

Write about a character that has a certain expression stuck on his or her face because of a facial paralysis. What experiences would this character have because of that expression? Write in first or third person.

Notes to Myself

I'm doing better than I thought. Every day is getting more fabulous. I'm glad I get to be alive.

January 30

Name today

Today I Get To _____

Daily Soul Vitamin

Happiness lies in the joy of achievement and the thrill of creative effort.
~Franklin D. Roosevelt

I enjoy being purple

Toast of the Day
Here's to Feeling Free to express opinions.

Happy Birthday to:
Gelett Burgess, 1866, humorist and novelist. He wrote "I Never Saw a Purple Cow."
Franklin D. Roosevelt, 1882, the 32nd U.S. President.
Shirley Hazzard, 1931, novelist and short-story writer.
Phil Collins, 1951, award-winning musician, singer, and song-writer.

Awe-servances

Aha-phrodisiacs

Phil Collins title pool: Only You Know And I Know, I Don't Wanna Know, One More Night, Don't Lose My Number, Who Said I Would, Inside Out, Take Me Home.

Dose of Mirth

If in the last few years you haven't discarded a major opinion or acquired a new one, check your pulse. You may be dead. ~Gelett Burgess

Journal Juju

Shirley Hazzard said of writing, "It's a nervous work. The state that you need to write is the state that others are paying large sums to get rid of." Choose an uncomfortable state you experience and list its creative potential. Or get into an uncomfortable state and describe it like a real estate agent might describe a house, a chef a recipe, or a tour guide a monument.

Brought to You by Arpeggio Potion

Consider the rhythm of your heart's beating. It beats without any effort on your part and it keeps the beat through all sorts of life's deliveries. It's a beautiful song.

January 31

Name today

Today I Get To

Daily Soul Vitamin

Art enables us to find ourselves and lose ourselves at the same time.
~Thomas Merton

Toast of the Day
Here's to getting lost in hypnotic music.

Happy Birthday:
Norman Mailer, 1923, novelist, journalist, playwright, screenwriter, and film director.
Thomas Merton, 1915, acclaimed theologian, poet, author, and social activist.
Philip Glass, 1937, composer of minimalist or
theater music often repetitiously hypnotic.

Still Life and Being Lost

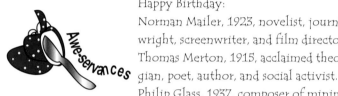

Awe-servances

Aha—phrodisiacs

One of Norman Mailer's books is titled *Advertisements for Myself*. Write an ad for
creative works you have done or would like to complete as if they were completed.
Or make a list of your greatest "hits."

In honor of Phillip Glass's birthday write poetry or prose, or do a collage or painting
with the same title as one of his works: *Mad Rush*. See if you can incorporate a
repetitive element.

Dose of Mirth

Appreciate me now, and avoid the rush. ~ Ashleigh Brilliant

Journal Juju

For a number of days write daily about the same walk you take or other routine you
carry out—but approach it from a different attitude or point of view each time you
write about it.

Message from Body Temple Potion

Walk often. Vary your theme: have a meditative walk, an energetic walk, a talk or hum
out loud walk, a notice everything the color blue walk, a walk to further an idea, a walk
in a different locale, a walk asking questions, a walk totally in the present as if on earth
for the first time. If these themes are hard for you, try just 5 percent of their spirit for
30 seconds or imagine what they might be like.

The AWe-MaNac is Brought to you by:
The Nine Anti-Aging potions (And a Spot Remover)

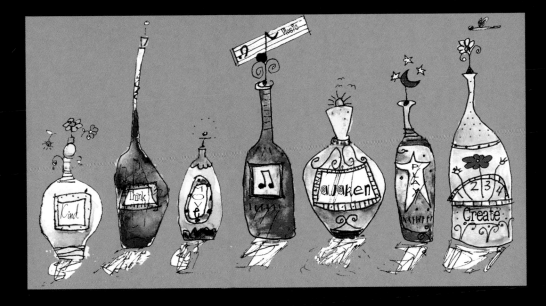

The potions are Filled With anti-dulling agents For creative brilliance, anti-gravity agents For a lift in every aspect of the Word and anti-aging agents For Well ... anti-aging. Included With Specially Marked potions is a Spot-Remover With powerful ingredients that eliminate lurking dismay.

(Warning: Cheap imitations result in inexpensive Substitutions.)

ENTRY WAY TO FEBRUARY

I planted some bird seed. A bird came up. Now I don't know
what to feed it. —Steven Wright

February is from the Latin words, *februarius mensis*, meaning month of purification. What needs purification in your life? Five minutes of clutter control? Tossing out three of the science projects in the fridge? Awareness of what thoughts are clogging up your higher purpose? Well, at least wash your sheets. Clean flannel sheets and a favorite pillow that soothes a day's tension can be the meaning of life on a cozy winter night. Train your mind to understand the pleasure possible in small things at least 2 percent more every time your head hits your pillow. Sleep well.

Some Celebrations at February's Door

February 1-7 is Solo Diners Eat Out Week. But wait there's more: February is National Bird Feeding Month, National Cherry Month, National Wedding Month, AND Return Shopping Carts to the Supermarket Month. I am not making this up. If you're planning on getting married this month have a wedding cake with a cherry on top. Have your guests throw bird seed at you as you walk out of the chapel. Ride off with your loved one in a shopping cart. And if the marriage doesn't work, return your spouse to the supermarket and go out to eat by yourself.

      Other Things: Groundhogs Day, American Heart Month, Plant the Seeds of Greatness Month, Black History Month, International Boost Self-esteem Month, International Embroidery Month, International Expect Success Month, Library Lovers' Month, National Snack Food Month, Potato Lovers Month, Responsible Pet Owners Month, Wise Health Consumer Month, 3rd Monday President's Day, 2nd New Moon after Winter Solstice Chinese New Year Day before Ash Wednesday (also 46 Days Before Easter) Mardi Gras. February begins with the sun in the sign of Aquarius and ends in the sign of Pisces.

Awe-manac Invented Events:
February 8: Be A Kid Day
February 18: Mistake Day

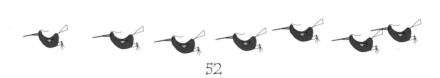

Suggested Ways to Celebrate

Sometimes I sit alone in restaurants, listening for and writing down whatever words or phrases I can hear from surrounding humans, then take those words and write a piece from them. If eating alone does not appeal to you, fill your grocery cart and eat at home (then return the cart). Write an ode to shopping carts. Write from a shopping cart's point of view, perhaps it is a cart hijacked by a person on the street, what worldly possessions does it carry around? Buy chocolate covered cherries as a Valentine's gift. Eat fresh cherries alone or with a bird. Doodle cherries in a doodled still life. Create a picture called *Still Life and Grocery Cart*. Doodle a grocery cart being carried away by birds. Make a bird feeder or fill the one that's been empty in your backyard for the last five years, attend a bird wedding—I don't know, it seems to me like the possibilities are endless.

Astrological Word-Spells for February

Aries: "Wild playful energy," choose someone to share it with.

Taurus: "Slow motion bliss." Meditate on it in your imagination.

Gemini: "Clever banter." Call a favorite person 3 times this month (3 different people can be substituted).

Cancer: "Edging toward authenticity." Buy a new welcome mat that is more YOU and feel more welcomed.

Leo: "Surreptitious generosity." Make a valentine, put a gift certificate in it, send it anonymously.

Virgo: "Unpredictable amusement in a moment of spontaneity." Watch for it.

Libra: "Inner/outer well-being." Try a yoga pose or a new one if you already practice it.

Scorpio: "Set it free." Let go of something you don't need this month (for extra credit - let go of two things).

Sagittarius: "Believe in connections." Open one of your books, see a truth waiting for you.

Capricorn: "Deliciously appreciative pause." Take the month off from self-help-appreciate yourself for who you are now.

Aquarius: "Fascinate on your focus." Concentrate your attention on something you are working on as if you are 5 times more fascinated with it. Start out one minute at a time.

Pisces: "Discover the treasure already there." Increase or begin meditating on everything that is already wonderful in your life.

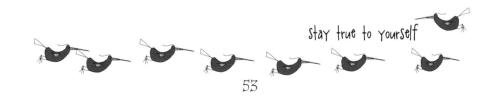

stay true to yourself

Tides:

Ebbing: (just a little bit)

_____

_____

Flowing: (just a little bit)

_____

_____

Vessel of strength: (words to keep you afloat) _____

_____

Gardening Information

Flower: Violet

Monthly Awe-manac Crop:: Birds

Planting Tips: Plant birdseed and when the birds come up, feed them little candy hearts that say "ohhh Baby" on them.

Soul Vitamin

*Hold fast to dreams for if dreams die
life is a broken-winged bird that
cannot fly.*
~Langston Hughes

Toast of the Day

Here's to appreciating everything that
Feels good about your body today

Awe-servances

Happy Birthday to:
Langston Hughes, 1902, poet, novelist and
  playwright.
It's also Women's Heart Health Day.
And Freedom Day. Anniversary of President Lincoln's
approval of the 13th amendment to the
US Constitution which abolished slavery.

Aha-phrodisiacs

Langston Hughes Word Pool: I wonder, laughter, the sun, move, dream variations,
heart melodies, that, may, wrap them in a blue cloud-cloth, wander, do, bring.

Journal Juju

What habits or thinking patterns might you be a slave to? Write them down
simply to unleash the power awareness can bring. Write an entry in your journal
as if you were presently doing what you would be doing if you were not a slave to
your currents habits - but make sure this is an awareness exercise - just
observational, without judgment or pressure.

Dose Of Mirth

I'm just trying to make a smudge on the collective unconscious.
~David Letterman

Notes to self

Today I get to _____

_____

2
Here's to the wisdom of the heart
⋆ ⋆ ⋆ ⋆ ⋆ ⋆ ⋆ ⋆ ⋆ ⋆

Name Today

Daily Soul Vitamin

If I create from the heart, nearly everything works; if from the head, almost nothing. ~Marc Chagall

Awe—Servances
Happy Groundhog Day.
Happy Birthday to:
Liz Smith, 1923, journalist and gossip columnist.

A ha phrodisias

For Groundhog's Day let your shadow write about you today. Starter Fluid: "It's not easy being your shadow..." or In one column write the steps decided from your head in another column write the steps your heart might take.
     Watch Bill Murray's *Groundhog Day.*

Journal Juju

Liz Smith said, "Begin somewhere; you cannot build a reputation on what you intend to do." Let your heart write about beginnings.
   Choose a Repeated Completion: "Before I begin...", "I begin...", "In this moment, I..." Or if your shadow could write about you, what would it say? Have your shadow tell you what it needs from you and what its gift is to you. "As your shadow I'd like to tell you ..."

Q. What do you call a groundhog's laundry? A. Hogwash.

Today I get to

Note to self: Think this— I am compassionate with the shadow aspects of myself. I'm only human but that's better than being a groundhog.

Soul Vitamin

I love writing. I love the swirl and swing of words as they tangle with human emotions.
~James Michener

Toast of the Day
Here's to smiles inspired by puppies

Awe-servances

Happy Birthday to

Gertrude Stein, 1874, writer and a catalyst for modern art and literature.

Norman Rockwell, 1894, artist and illustrator icon.

James Michener, 1907, author of more than 40 titles.

45 days of winter have elapsed before the Spring Equinox - halfway through.

Aha-phrodisiacs

Write about being "halfway" to anything. Repeated completion: "I am halfway..."

Gertrude Stein said, "I like a view but I like to sit with my back turned to it."
Write what you think she is saying as if you wrote the quote, - use it
metaphorically, literally or comically.

Dose Of Mirth

If a picture wasn't going very well, I'd put a puppy in it. ~Norman Rockwell

Journal Juju

If your day is not going well, what could you put in it, real or imaginary? A
puppy? A song? A yoga pose? A new soft washcloth to wash away the
not-going-wellness? An imaginary tropical beach? Write about it, draw it, collage,
or pin it to your shirt.

Gertrude Stein also said, "We are always the same age inside." What age are you
inside and what do you like about that age?

"Everybody who writes is interested in living inside themselves
in order to tell what is inside themselves. that is why writers
have to have two countries, the one where
they belong and the one in which they live really."
~Gertrude Stein

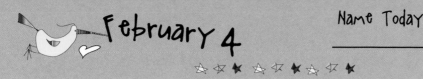
Daily Soul Vitamin

It is the greatest shot of adrenaline to be doing what you have wanted to do so badly. You almost feel like you could fly without the plane. ~Charles Lindburgh

Toast of the Day
Here's to the Weightlessness that Happens When you are engaged in doing something you love.

Awe-servances

Happy Birthday to:

Charles Lindbergh, 1902, the first to fly solo and nonstop over the Atlantic Ocean.

Alice Cooper, 1948, rock singer, songwriter, and musician.

1824 J.W. Goodrich introduced rubber galoshes.

It's also Cardiac Rehabilitation Week.

Aha-phrodisiacs

Write some tips for heart repairs or keep going with "In order for a broken heart to repair, one ... Alice Cooper Title Wave: Welcome to My Nightmare, Give It Up, Under My Wheels, Caught in a Dream

   Write a poem, song or story inspired by rubber galoshes.

Journal Juju

Charles Lindbergh said, "Isn't it strange that we talk least about the things we think about most?" Journal about the things you think about the most. Fresh approach: write about yourself in the third person. "He/She thought mostly about ..."

Dose of Mirth

Flying a plane is no different from riding a bicycle. It's just a lot harder to put baseball cards in the spokes. ~ Captain Rex Kramer, in the movie *Airplane.*

Note to Myself

Make time to do things I love. I'm a better person for others when I do. I fly when I'm creative.

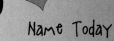

5

Name Today _____

Daily Soul Vitamin

The desire to be singular and to astonish by ways out of the common seems to me to be the source of many virtues. ~Marie de Sévigné

Awe-servances

Happy Birthday to:

Marie de Sévigné, 1626, Parisian writer
  famous for writing letters.
On this day in 1981 the largest Jell-O was made in Brisbane, Australia.
  It was 9,246 gallons of watermelon-flavored Jell-O.

Toast of the Day
Here's to Food that Wiggles.

Aha-phrodisiacs

Write an ode, haiku, poem, or song about Jell-O. Do some Jell-O movements during your break.

  Word Pool: merely, window, extraordinary, sometimes, underneath, drawn, opinion, circle, wince, suffer, Jell-O, heckle, brighten, notorious, mailman, wave, wily, further, happenstance, belly, dangerous

  Starter Fluid: "It was close to 2 am and in the neon lit night outside of Joe's ...."

Dose of Mirth

Ice cream is not sexy. It's not wiggly and jiggly.
~Utah Senator Gene Davis, upon naming Jell-O as the state's official snack.

Journal Juju

Marie de Sévigné said, "There is no person who is not dangerous for someone."

  To whom are you dangerous? Write about it, exaggerate it, make it up if you need to.

  Whom or what is dangerous to you? Write a letter that shows or talks about danger.

Repeat Advertisement from Awe-wakened Inner Messages Potion

You are singular and remarkable. You ARE singular and remarkable.
YOU are singular and remarkable.

Note to Myself

I am singular and remarkable. I'm also single and marketable.

Name Today _____

Daily Soul Vitamin

Man is a universe within himself. ~Bob Marley

Toast of the Day

HERE'S TO A LONG HOT SHOWER AS A UNIVERSE OF ITS OWN.

Note to Myself

What's one five-minute step I can take that might be a small part of planting a seed of greatness?

Awe-servances

Happy Birthday to Bob Marley, 1945, reggae singer, songwriter, and political activist.
Natalie Cole,1950, singer of "Unforgettable" among many others
It's also Pay a Compliment Day and National Self Esteem Month.

Dose of Mirth

My roommate says, I'm going to take a shower and shave, does anyone need to use the bathroom? It's like some weird quiz where he reveals the answer first.
~ Mitch Hedberg

Seeds of Greatness

Aha-phrodisiacs

Describe five ways to unlock a dreadlock (i.e. the feeling of daily dread).
Use the word "universe" as a trigger for writing or making art.
E-mail a compliment to someone, leave an anonymous compliment note somewhere.

Journal Juju

Write in detail about one event or person in your life that is "unforgettable."
Journal Titles:
A Few Compliments I'd Like to Hear,
A Few Compliments I'd Like to Give (myself and others),
A Few Unforgettable Compliments I've Had

Repeat Advertisement from A.wakened Inner Messages Potion

You are still singular and remarkable. What's one small thing for which you can give yourself credit?

☆ ✦ ★ ☆ ✦ ★ ☆ ✦ ★

Daily Soul Vitamin

You must live in the present, launch yourself on every wave, find your eternity in each moment. ~ Henry David Thoreau

Awe—servances

Happy Birthday to:
Charles Dickens, 1812, one of history's most famous novelists.
Today is also "Wave All Your Fingers at Your Neighbors Day" (not making this up).
No Talk Day.

Toast of the Day

Here's to a friendly wave, waving the fees on your overdue anything, an ocean wave's salty baptism, a wave of abundance.

Aha—phrodisiacs

Dickens Word Pool: (permission to write bad poetry today): shy, wave, twist, tale, two, cities, chimes, haunted, bleak, expectations, great, mystery, traveler, notes, bless, poor, past, sing, mutual, nobody, language, seven.

    Good writing has lots of images in it. We store abstract notions as images; when you look beyond the picture of the word in your head, what pictures do you see for the word "mystery"? I see a detective with a Sherlock Holmes hat on. List them and then stream them together in a mysterious tapestry. If mystery doesn't work for you try "city", ad-venture", nobody," or list images for all these.

Dose of Mirth

If you saw a heat wave, would you wave back?
~ Stephen Wright

Journal Juju

No talking in the journal today, just drawing pictures, doodles, scribbles, and cutting and pasting what you feel.

A Message from Body Temple and Awe-wakened Moment Potions

RUN FOR THE HILLS!

return renegade grocery carts this month

When engaged in the practice of yoga, the sensation of pleasura-ble stretch and inspired breathing gives mortals a calm, centered and restored mind. It is a definite asset in the art of being fully alive. Yoga is a wonder-making practice, it is simple and blissful and has transformed the lives of many a mortal from stress-ridden, nervous, unfocused zombies into a tranquil souls with body rejuvenated, spirit awake, and mind clear, centered, and open to the banquet of senses all around.

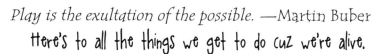

THINK LIKE A KID DAY

Play is the exultation of the possible. —Martin Buber

Here's to all the things we get to do cuz we're alive.

Happy Birthday to: Martin Buber, 1878, philosopher, translator, and educator. Jack Lemmon, 1925, one of the most award-winning actors of his generation.

Things to Play with

Write a list of ways you can make your job, relationship, or creative project more fun. Write a story or an entry in your journal using little doodled or cut out pictures for some of the words like in some kid magazines. Or use do-dads. Kids don't care if they're perfect or not.

Do-Dad Door to Door Salesman

Journal Thingy

Jack Lemmon said, "Failure seldom stops you. What stops you is the fear of failure." Write about where you are with the fear of failure or fear of success. Break down the steps to your dreams . Have the invincible power of a child's imagination as you do this.

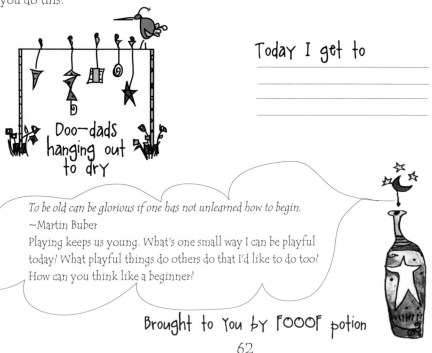

Doo-dads
hanging out
to dry

Today I get to

_____
_____
_____

To be old can be glorious if one has not unlearned how to begin.
~Martin Buber
Playing keeps us young. What's one small way I can be playful today? What playful things do others do that I'd like to do too? How can you think like a beginner?

Brought to you by FOOOF potion

62

Daily Soul Vitamin

Helped are those who create anything at all, for they shall relive the thrill of their own conception and realize a partnership in the creation of the Universe that keeps them responsible and cheerful. ~Alice Walker

Toast of the Day
Here's to the color purple and all the other ones too.

Awe–Servances

Happy Birthday to:

Mia Farrow, 1945, actress.

Alice Walker, 1944, Pulitzer Prize-winning author for *The Color Purple*.

It's also National Inventor's Day.

Aha–phrodisiac

Jonathan Schattke said, "Necessity is the mother of invention, it is true, but its father is creativity, and knowledge is the midwife." Who is the mother, father, and midwife of: the color purple, of a surprise, of blossoming of a day well spent? Go ahead, don't be concerned with being perfect, just make up anything, being perfect is not that interesting.

   Do something today with the color purple.

Journal Juju

Mia Farrow said, "I get it now; I didn't get it then. That life is about losing and about doing it as gracefully as possible...and enjoying everything in between." Explore in your journal where you stand with this quote. Or do this Repeated Completion: "Life is about ..."

Dose of Mirth

I think it pisses God off if you walk by the color purple in a field somewhere and don't notice it. ~ Alice Walker

Note to Myself

I REALLY like that Alice Walker quote at the top of the page. I'm going to read it often and maybe even memorize it. Maybe I'll be more responsible.

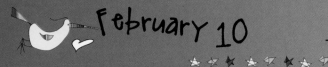

Name Today
_____

I get to

Daily Soul Vitamin

Don't let anyone rob you of your imagination, your creativity, or your curiosity. It's your place in the world; it's your life. Go on and do all you can with it, and make it the life you want to live. ~Mae Jemison

Awe-servances

Happy Birthday to:
Jimmy Durante, 1893, singer, pianist,
  comedian and actor.

Toast of the Day
Here's to the texture and taste of a toasted marshmallow.

Plus in 1863 the fire extinguisher was patented by Alanson Crane.
It's also Umbrella Day.

Aha-phrodisiacs

In honor of Jimmy Durante, write something and then add "cha cha cha" on the end.

  Write an ode or haiku about an umbrella. Make a collage of an umbrella under a rain storm of cha, cha, chas.

Journal Juju

Take a moment and write a list of subliminal messages you would like to receive regularly and then write some of them in the months ahead in your daily planner.

  Write about the fire extinguisher as a metaphor (what fire needs to be put out in your life?) or any experience you have with it in reality.

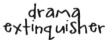

drama extinguisher

Message from A.I.M Potion

"Make it the life you want to live…" For 15 seconds think and feel from a quality that would make your life one you want to live. Feel 5 percent more courageous, free, uninhibited, motivated, energetic. Practice the thinking and feeling first and then notice that the doing is easier.

Daily Soul Vitamin

I haven't failed. I've just found 10,000 ways that won't work
~Thomas Edison

Toast of the Day
Here's to not taking for granted
the convenience of electricity.

Aw o—servanres

Happy Birthday to:

Thomas Alva Edison, 1847, invented 1,200 patents including the
light bulb, the phonograph, and the telephone so today is also Be
Electrific Day.

Sidney Sheldon, 1917, award-winning playwright, TV and movie
screenwriter, and novelist.

Sheryl Crow, 1962, nine-time Grammy-winning singer-songwriter.

Aha—phrodisiacs

Use Sidney Sheldon's book title, *The Stars Shine Down,* as your
title for poetry, prose, journal entry, collage, doodling, drawing with
your eyes closed, or rambling out loud in a random stream of
consciousness.

Write about what electrifies you.

Dose of Mirth

*When Thomas Edison worked late into the night on the electric light, he had to
do it by gas lamp or candle. I'm sure it made the work seem that much more urgent.*
~George Carlin

Journal Juju

Thomas Edison said, "I am not discouraged, because every wrong attempt discarded is another step forward." Draw a simple staircase and on the middle of
each stair write a wrong attempt you made and on the top of each stair write
why it is a step forward. Search your soul for the reason if it is not apparent.

I get to _____

Name Today
_____

✩ ✩ ✭ ✩ ✩ ✭ ✩ ✩ ✭

I get to _____

Soul Vitamin

It is not the strongest of the species that survives, nor the most intelligent; it is the one that is most adaptable to change. ~Charles Darwin

Toast of the Day

Here's to the saying "This too shall pass."
(Abe Lincoln often said this to himself.)

Awe-Servances

Happy Birthday to:

Charles Robert Darwin, 1809, author and naturalist.

Abraham Lincoln, 1809, the 16th President of the US, who endured many personal hardships with grace and courage.

Lost Penny Day. Donate all your pennies to a shelter or agency that assists the homeless. (Celebrated on Abraham Lincoln's birthday, as his likeness graces the penny.)

Aha-phrodisiacs

Write about the journey of a lost penny. Write about a girl named Penny who gets lost. Write about pennies for change... okay... that's silly.

Journal Juju

In honor of Darwin, write about something that has evolved in your life. Make a time line and show with little symbols and words the various stages of evolution. Ideas include the evolution of your journey to yourself, your creativity, your career, your relationship, your growth of wisdom, your view about being free from pressure, your ability to relax, etc.

Dose of Mirth

Why do you have to "put your two cents in" but it's only a "penny for your thoughts"? Where's that extra penny going to? ~Unknown

Message from Body Temple Potion

Even in the winter there are places you can walk. Walking keeps your spirits up. Or dance wildly in your living room; dress up for it.

❤ 13 ❤

You began to be irreplaceable to me long before I had ever heard of you.
~Roger Sale

Name Today _____

I get to _____

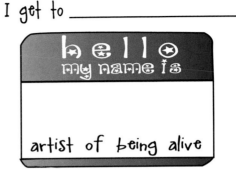

h e l l o
my name is
_____
artist of being alive

Daily Soul Vitamin
Words have meaning and names have power.
~ Unknown

Toast of the Day
Here's to the miraculous power of the computer and Internet.

Awe-servances
Happy Birthday to:
Grant Wood, 1892, the painter of *American Gothic*, (the man and woman farmers who weren't smiling).

Clean Out Your Computer Day.
Get A Different Name Day. A day to change a name you don't like.

Aha-phrodisiacs
Write about what happens next in the painting *American Gothic* or write what the man and woman are thinking. Google the painting for a review of what it looks like.

   Take 5 minutes and delete some things you don't need on your computer. It will clear the way for new ideas to be written.

Dose of Mirth
Always end the name of your child with a vowel, so that when you yell the name will carry. ~ Bill Cosby

Journal Juju
Play with the idea of changing your name even if you don't plan on it. What would you change your name to? Make a list of different possibilities. How would this change the way you feel about yourself?

Note to Myself
I don't really have anything to say today to myself... I think I'll just daydream a bit.

Daily Soul Vitamin

Life is short and we have never too much time for gladdening the hearts of those who are travelling the dark journey with us. Oh be swift to love, make haste to be kind. ~Henri-Frederic Amiel

Awe-servances

Happy Valentine's Day: According to English poet Geoffrey Chaucer, birds began choosing their mates on February 14.

Happy Birthday to:

George Washington Gale Ferris, 1859, inventor of the Ferris Wheel. Today is dubbed Ferris Wheel Day.

Jack Benny, 1894, comedian, vaudeville performer, and radio, television, and film actor.

It's also World Marriage Day and Birds Mating Season begins.

A haphrodisias

Send yourself a Valentines e-card or make one.

Ambrose Bierce said "Love is temporary insanity curable by marriage." Keep going with this quote as if you were an expert on the subject.

Make sure the birds in your neighborhood know Bird Mating Season begins; they've been waiting since January.

Journal Juju

Write a poem or haiku about Ferris Wheels. You have permission to write a really bad poetry. Here, I'll set the Ferris Wheel poetry "bar" low, so to speak: The Ferris wheel turns round and round/ High it goes, then close to ground/ I see afar when I'm at the top/ But it scares me and I'm not sure the whole thing is worth it.

In Hollywood a marriage is a success if it outlasts milk. —Rita Rudner

Name Today _____

Soul Vitamin

I've loved the stars too fondly to be fearful of the night.
~Galileo Galilei

Toast of the Day
HERE'S TO THE WAY a WARM car FEELS
ON a COLD day.

Awe—Servances

Happy Birthday to:

Galileo, 1564, physicist, mathematician, astronomer, and philosopher.

Susan B. Anthony, 1820, one of the first womens' rights activists.

Melissa Manchester, 1951, singer-songwriter and actress.

Matt Groening, 1954, award-winning cartoonist and the creator of *The Simpsons*.

Aha—phrodisiacs

Use Viewfinders in the back of the book to write about one or all of Melissa
Manchester's song titles:

Pick randomly or try free-spirited, boastful, paranoid, silly, compulsively tidy,
expansive, one of few words: Lucky Break, When I Look Down That Road ,
Where the Truth Lies

Journal Juju

In reference to the Galileo quote at the top, do this two-part repeated
completion: I've loved ___ too fondly, to be fearful of ____. (for example, I've
loved creativity too fondly to be fearful of what people think.

Dose Of Mirth

*Love is like racing across the frozen tundra on a snowmobile which flips
over, trapping you underneath. At night, the ice-weasels come.*
~Matt Groening

Today I get to _____

_____

_____

Subliminal message: My heart is mending and coming back
in the fullness and gracefulness of
compassion for myself and others

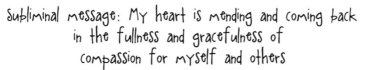

Feb 16

Daily Soul Vitamin
Action has magic, grace and power in it. ~Goethe

Toast of the Day
Here's to arriving home safe after a long trip.

Awe-servances
Happy Birthday to:
Edgar Bergen, 1903, entertainer and ventriloquist.

It's also Feast of Sticky Buns Day, Bumper Car Day, Mule Day, Annual Sit. and Spit Contest, National Almond Day, Do a Grouch a Favor Day.
The nation's first 911 emergency telephone system went into effect in
    Haleyville, AL, 1968.
France's longest traffic jam, 109 miles, occurred in 1980.

Aha phrodisias

There must be a story in the combination of the things above that are celebrated today - see if you can put them together (buns, bumper cars, mules, sit and spit, almonds, grouches).

Journal Juju
If you were a bumper car, who or what would you be bumping into? What would be your emotions, duties, thoughts, or dreams?
Permission to write in your journal in Grouch mode today.

Today I get to
_____
_____
_____
_____
_____
_____

Martini Birds Write a poem about them.

17

I get to _____ Name Today _____

Daily Soul Vitamin

*Yoga is not just another self-improvement craze....
It is a practice of self-acceptance, which is a very
different thing. You don't need to be fixed; you
simply need to ... remember who you truly are.*
~Gurmukh Khalsa

Crabs doing a Sun Salutation

Awe-servances

Happy birthday to:
Rene Theophile Hyacinthe Laennec, 1781, known as the
   "father of chest medicine." He invented the stethoscope.

It's also National Cafe Au Lait Day, Championship
   Crab Races Day and World Human Spirit Day.

Toast of the Day
Here's to the bliss
that comes from
holding a yoga pose
just long enough.

Aha-phrodisiacs

Using your imagination, make a list of other things the stethoscope can detect about
   a person. Write a story, a song, or a poem about them.
In honor of National Cafe Au Lait Day and Championship Crab Races Day,
   write about caffeinated crabs running a race.

Dose of Mirth

Today I met with a subliminal advertising executive for just a second. ~Steven Wright

Journal Juju

Gurmukh Khalsa reminds us to "remember who you truly are." Write some
adjectives that describe people you really admire. Now see yourself in the mirror of
those people, as often when we admire someone we have qualities like they have or
we have the energy to meet up with those qualities.

Subliminal Message Brought to You by Body Temple Potion

Yoga is one of the most effective practices to affect youthfulness and defy some of the
difficulties of the aging process. The shoulder stand can normalize a thyroid creating
havoc in mid-life, savasana can turn around a stressful day, and a simple forward fold
can dissolve feelings of being stuck.

Note to Myself

Do yoga today even if it's just for 5 minutes.

The 8-Teeenth
The Awe-Manac's Misstake Day

Daily Soul Vitamin

Do you ever make silly mistakes? It's one of my very few creative activities.

Toast of the Day
Here's to silly mistakes that turn into creative discoveries.

a box of rain

Awe-Servances
Happy Birthday to:
Len Deighton 1929, British historian and author.

On this day in 1979, Snow fell in the Sahara Desert
(by mistake?)

Aphrodisias

Write a poem, a haiku or a news report about snow falling in the Sahara
Desert. Explore surrealism, a juxtaposition of two unrelated realities; make
a collage about weird weather happening in an unexpected place like rain
in a closet, or sunshine in a coffee cup. A thunder storm in a refrigerator?
   Do art by mistake.

Journal Juju

Journal title: *Some of My Favorite Mistakes.* (Some mistakes are too much
fun to make just once). Or explore the nature of your mistakes. Or have
a mistake you made write you a letter of thanks or explanation.
   Write yourself a permission slip to make mistakes. Include one of these
quotes:
"He who hesitates because he feels inferior is being surpassed by he who is
   busy making mistakes and becoming superior." ~Henry Link
"Punishing honest mistakes stifles creativity." ~Ross Perot
"Mistakes are part of the dues one pays for a full life." ~Sophia Loren
"Just because you make mistakes doesn't mean you are one."
   ~Author Unknown

Dose of Mirth

interesting!

Never say, "oops." Always say, "Ah, interesting."
~Unknown

Today I get to
give myself permission to make mistakes

Daily Soul Vitamin

I live with the people I create and it has always made my essential loneliness less keen. ~Carson McCullers

Toast of the Day

Here's to wise older women who are not afraid to speak their minds.

Awe-Servances

Happy Birthday to:

Nicolaus Copernicus, 1473, astronomer and priest who stated that the sun, not the earth, is the center of the universe.

Carson McCullers, 1917, writer.

Smokey Robinson 1940, an R&B and soul singer and songwriter.

It's also Spunky Old Broads Day (not making this up).

Altered State of Telescope

Aha-phrodisiacs

Write about being the center of the universe.

Smokey Robinson Title Wave: Tears of a Clown, The Tracks of My Tears, You've Really Got a Hold On Me, I Second That Emotion

Make a list of things you would be doing today if you were a Spunky Old Broad.

Write a dialog between a spunky old broad and a meek little old lady or man.

Dose of Mirth

Every time we start thinking we're the center of the universe, the universe turns around and says with a slightly distracted air, "I'm sorry. What'd you say your name was again?"
~ Margaret Maron

Journal Juju

What is the center of your center of the universe? What if it started rotating around you? What characters would you create to keep you company if you could?

Subliminal Message Brought to You by the Kindness Potion

The Dalai Lama said, "My religion is very simple. My religion is kindness." What's one small way you can carry out the religion of the Dalai Lama today or tomorrow?

20

I get to _____   Name Today _____

Daily Soul Vitamin

The only things in my life that compatibly
exist with this grand universe are the
creative works of the human spirit. ~Ansel Adams

Awe-Servances

Happy Birthday to:
Ansel Adams, photographer 1902,
    famous for his black and white photos.
Pisces Begins.

Toast of the Day
Here's to FULL attention paid
to biting into the juicy meat
of a sweet orange.

Aha-phrodisiacs

Pisces is receptive, supersensitive, impressionable, peace-loving, serious, sympathetic, charitable, compassionate, artistic, creative, dreamer, dedicated, imaginative, psychic, shy, introverted, spiritual and reclusive. Invent a character with a few Piscean traits but show some traits in dialog or action rather than using any of the words. For instance artistic, charitable, shy, peace-loving and psychic might look like this: "I could sense George needed something special today so I painted a peace sign and left it anonymously on his front porch."

Dose of Mirth

I am two with nature. ~Woody Allen

Journal Juju

Pick three or four Pisces traits and write about where you are
with them in your life even if you're not a Pisces.

    Doodle a picture or take a photograph that illustrates being at
two with nature.

    Ansel Adams said, "There is nothing worse than a sharp image of a fuzzy concept."
Write about something sharp and something fuzzy in your life today. Title an entry:
Sharp Fuzziness.

Subliminal Message Brought to You by FOOOf

Enlightenment takes place when one lets his innocence emerge and sees nature and life with
a childlike awe and respect. The "why" of a child is repeated over and over, causing more
questions and the never-ending process of discovery. ~Charles DuBack

I get to _____

Daily Soul Vitamin
I am in a beautiful prison from which I can only escape by writing. ~Anaïs Nin

Awe-servances
Happy Birthday to:
Anaïs Nin ,1903, author, famous for her
   published diaries, as well as for her erotica.
Erma Bombeck, 1927, writer, humorist

Also: On this day in 1885 the Washington
   Monument was dedicated.
United Nations International Mother
   Language Day

Toast of the Day
Here's to the Freedom
that creativity gives
us in any
circumstance.

Aha-phrodisiacs
Put your last name in the middle of these two words:
The ... Monument. What would that monument look like and what about you would it
honor. Doodle its picture, collage it, paint it, do a short interpretative dance of it.
   In honor of United Nations International Mother Language Day, make up a few words
and write a little piece of prose, poetry or a news report using them.

Dose of Mirth
*Housework is a treadmill from futility to oblivion with stop-offs at tedium and counter-produc-
tivity. Housework, if you do it right, will kill you.* ~Erma Bombeck

Journal Juju
Anaïs Nin said, "I postpone death by living, by suffering, by error, by risking, by giving,
by loving." The mind loves repetition in the process of writing. Using "by" several times
creates a rhythm and a natural conduit for words volunteered from the subconscious. Do
your own repetitive rhythm by doing a similar quote but start with "I live deeply by ...
by ... by ..." or "I deny my reality by ... by ... by ..." or, I procrastinate by ..., by ... by ...

Note to Myself
Write, no matter how good it isn't or is. Writing is liberating. Stop reading books about
writing ('cept this one) and just start now.

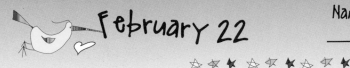

February 22

_____

Daily Soul Vitamin

True friendship is a plant of slow growth and must undergo and withstand the shocks of adversity before it is entitled to the appellation. ~George Washington

Toast of the Day

Here's to the feel of a quaint store.

Awe—servances

Happy Birthday to:
George Washington, 1732, first US President.
Drew Barrymore, 1975, actress and film producer.

On this day in 1879, the first five and dime chain store, Woolworth's, opened in Utica, NY.

Aha—phrodisiacs

Drew Barrymore said, "I want to kick down the walls and explore this life!" Use this to begin a piece of writing or use the quote to inspire a painting, doodle or collage of what is on the other side of the walls.
Write about your memories of five and dime stores in prose, poetry, ode or an essay.

Dose of Mirth

My heart has been broken so many times, it jingles when I walk. ~Garrison Keillor as his Guy Noir character.

Journal Juju

Make a list of the qualities of a friendship you have and then weave them together like a tapestry of poetic verse, adding words as you are inspired or arranging them in such a way that they sound like a poetic friendship poem.

Note to Myself

Kick down the walls and explore this life.

Today I get to _____

_____

feb

♥ 23 ♥ ♥
Name Today _____

I get to _____

Daily Soul Vitamin
Whether I was in my body or out of my body as I wrote it, I know not. God knows.
~ George Frideric Handel

Awe-Servances
Happy Birthday to:
George Frideric Handel, 1685, Baroque composer.
Samuel Pepys, 1633.
"As far as we know, Pepys was the first Englishman to fill his diary with descriptions of his most personal and ordinary experiences: his aches and pains, what he liked to eat, going to the bathroom, his marital love life, and his extramarital affairs, graphic details that novelists wouldn't start incorporating into their work for more than 200 years."
~ Writers Almanac with Garrison Keillor

Aphrodisias
Word Pool: uncover, live, original, start, can opener, chopsticks, turn, snap, special, appear, startling, watch, warn, corner, suspicious, peek, partial, window, clock, please, puzzle, music, stir, fragile, Baroque

Journal Juju
To celebrate the birth of one of the greatest diarists in the English language, spend some quality time with your journal today. As did Samuel Pepys, use the journal in an original way. Some ideas: 1. Make a list of nouns from yesterday (or today if it is the evening), then adjectives, then verbs, then construct verse or poetry. 2. At the end of the day use this as a repeated completion: *It was a day of* … 3. Strike an out-of-body point of view and do stream of consciousness writing starting with "I'm going to tell you the truth …"

Dose of Mirth
A guitarist was so Baroque, he robbed a music store and ran off with the lute. ~from www.badpuns.com

Question from Arpeggio Potion
How would it feel to be immersed inside of Baroque or any other music? Imagine it as you listen to some today.

♥ 24 ♥
Name Today _____

I get to ☆ ☆ _____

Daily Soul Vitamin
The Sun will not rise, or set, without my notice and thanks.
~Winslow Homer

Toast of the Day
Here's to doing a double-take when your eye just happens to catch a majestic sunset.

Awe-servances
Happy Birthday to:
Winslow Homer, 1836, landscape painter and printmaker.
Rupert Holmes, 1947, composer, songwriter and author of
plays, novels and stories.
Steven Jobs, 1955, Apple Computer founder.

Bottle with Winslow Homer quote in it

Aha-phrodisiacs
Rupert Holmes is best known for his number one pop hit "The Pina Colada Song."
Use the word "escape" as a trigger for art, writing or dance.

Dose of Mirth
8 examples for saying "No." I'd love to, but...
1. *I want to spend more time with my blender.*
2. *I've been scheduled for a karma transplant.*
3. *I'm staying home to work on my cottage cheese sculpture.*
4. *I did my own thing and now I've got to undo it.*
5. *I'm doing door-to-door collecting for static cling.*
6. *My crayons all melted together. ~Unknown*

Journal Juju
Steve Jobs said, "It comes from saying 'no' to 1,000 things to make sure we don't get on the wrong track or try to do too much." What are some things you need to say "no" to in order to help with the things to which your soul is saying "yes". Make a list. Then write NO by them. Then make a YES list. Do not feel pressure to do these things. The first step is awareness.

Note to Myself
It's okay to say "no" to the things that do not enrich my life experience, especially as I get older.

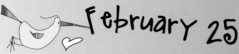

February 25

Name Today
_____

I get to _____

Daily Soul Vitamin

Love one another.
~George Harrison's last words

Toast of the Day

Here's to old Beatle songs.

Awe-servances

Happy Birthday to:

Pierre-Auguste Renoir, 1841, leading artist in the development of the Impressionist style.

George Harrison, 1943, award-winning singer, songwriter, author with The Beatles.

Jack Handey, 1949, humorist, author.

Still Life Galaxy Drawn by a Kid

Aha-phrodisiacs

Renoir advised, "Paint like a child." Paint a guitar gently weeping like a child might paint it; use inexpensive paint and paper. Cut it out and use it as part of a collage. Or draw it or anything with your non-dominant hand.

Journal Juju

Renoir said, "An artist, under pain of oblivion, must have confidence in himself, and listen only to his real master: Nature." Let nature write you a letter encouraging your confidence. What might the trees, the wind, or the waterfall say? Journal amidst nature.

Brought to you by Awe-wakened Moment Potion

Most people are carrying the burden of the past, anticipating the future, while missing life in the present. Melt into the present... Try right now, even if it's just 5 percent more or imagine what it might be like. For 10 seconds, whenever you think of it, practice melting into what feels good about the moment.

February 26

☆ ☆ ✸ ☆ ☆ ✸ ✸ ☆ ✸ ✸

I get to _____

Daily Soul Vitamin

You build on failure. You use it as a stepping stone.
Close the door on the past. You don't let it have any of
your energy, or any of your time, or any of your space.
~Johnny Cash

Aha-phrodisiacs

Happy Birthday to:

Christopher Marlowe, 1564, dramatist, poet, and translator.

Victor Hugo, 1802, poet, novelist, playwright, essayist,
   visual artist, human rights campaigner.

Johnny Cash, 1932, award-winning rock and roll
   singer and songwriter icon.

National For Pete's Sake Day.

Toast of the Day

Here's to cloud
sculptures
floating large,
changing in
slow motion
in sculpture-
garden skies.

Aha-phrodisiacs

Christopher Marlowe said, "I am Envy. I cannot read
   and therefore wish all books burned."

Continue with this shadow exercise of envy using the absurd nature of it to justify the opposite of what you
write. "I cannot sing therefore I wish all singers hoarse-
ness." "I cannot fly therefore I wish all birds to ride bikes."
You may come up with some interesting images or ideas.

Dose of Mirth

Use what talents you possess: the woods would be very silent if no
birds sang there except those that sang best. ~Henry Van Dyke

Journal Juju

Victor Hugo said, "Be as a bird perched on a frail branch that she feels bending beneath
her, still she sings away all the same, knowing she has wings." Apply this metaphor to
your life. What is the frail branch that is bending? What is the activity you continue to
do or the song you sing as the branch bends? Affirm that you have what it takes to
relax and trust the process.

Starter Fluid: "It was the summer I turned sixteen".

Daily Soul Vitamin

I have come to believe that a great teacher is a great artist and that there are as few as there are any other great artists. Teaching might even be the greatest of the arts since the medium is the human mind and spirit. ~John Steinbeck

Awe~servances

Happy Birthday to:
Henry Wadsworth Longfellow, 1807, a legendary poet.
John Steinbeck, 1902, Nobel-Prize winning novelist.

老师

Chinese Symbol for Teacher

Toast of the Day
Here's to great teachers and the memories of their encouragement.

A ha phrodisias

In reference to growing older, Henry Wadsworth Longfellow said, "And as the evening twiligtht fades away / The sky is filled with stars, invisible by day." Loosly associate what becomes clearer as we grow older.

Dose of Mirth

Ideas are like rabbits. You get a couple and learn how to handle them, and pretty soon you have a dozen. ~John Steinbeck

Journal Juju

Make a list of teachers or other people who have had an influence on you and beside their name write a word or two of how they inspired or helped you.

Message from Mind Solution

Memorize a quote or poem you like. Keeping the mind active has been shown to compensate even when Alzheimer's disease is present.

81

Multiple Soul Vitamins

The best way to have a good idea is to have a lot of ideas.
~Linus Pauling (born today)
*I recommend to you to take care of the minutes; for hours will
take care of themselves.* ~Lord Chesterfield
A work of art which did not begin in emotion is not art.
~Paul Cezanne

Toast of the Day
To varying the routine every
now and then
to keep life fresh, the spirit
spontaneous and the mind awake

Aha-phrodisiac

Starter Fluid for poetry, prose or monologue:
I Got Stars Shooting Out of My Head.

Journal Juju

Things I liked about this Feb: person of the
month, moment of the month, favorite
outing of the month, favorite book, movie,
and accomplishment.
What made this month different?

I get to

_____
_____
_____
_____
_____

February 29

☆ ⭐ ★ ☆ ⭐ ★ ☆ ★

I get to _____

Daily Soul Vitamin

Give me a laundry list and I'll set it to music.
~Gioacchino Rossini

Toast of the Day
Here's to a comfortable chair
in which to read or daydream.

Awe-servances

Leap Year: The Gregorian calendar, the current standard
calendar in most of the world, adds a 29th day to
February in all years evenly divisible by four, except
for centennial years.

Happy Birthday to:
Gioachino Antonio Rossini, 1792, Italian composer.

Laundry List

A haphrodisias

Include the term "laundry list" in poetry or prose. Take a laundry list and
make it into art, dance or poetry.

Play off of the word "fumble" in prose or poetry – just see where it takes you.
Start with an association to the word and then just keep going in whatever direction it
takes you.

Write an ode to the extra day in this year.

Dose of Mirth

*The most dangerous thing in the world is
to try to leap a chasm in two jumps.*
~David Lloyd George

Journal Juju

Make a laundry list of everything you are glad you did in the past few days. Make a
laundry list of wishes as you listen to Rossini or someone else.

Note to Self

Take a leap where I would have taken a small step just to see what happens.

"Now and then we had a hope that if we lived and were good, God would permit us to be pirates." -Mark Twain

"Thanks for letting me hang out here, God. Cool Planet."~Steven Smith~Comedian

"Creative individuals tend to be smart, yet also naive at the same time.   Creative individuals have a combination of playfulness and discipline, or responsibility and irresponsibility." ~Mihaly Csikszentmihalyi.

You have permission to be a pirate, host a cooking show in your own kitchen, be a detective in a grocery store, a Victoria's Secret Model who wears high tops backwards, a spy in a Laundromat, or a little kid in an adult's body just plain happy to be on the planet. FOOOF (with Laughing Gas) will help you discover the power of child-like energy to sweeten your adult existence. Serious stuffiness is hazardous to your creativity and longevity. The spirit of the child, inherent in this potion, is a force that can serve us for the rest of our lives with delight, perspective, wonder, and toys.

FOOOF!..
WITH LAUGHING GAS

Possible Effects:
Liberated playfulness that results in a relaxed, creative, uninhibited, very fun approach to life and all its stuff.

Warning: Consult your doctor if silliness is sustained longer than four hours and tug on his stethoscope. Side effects may include non-stop laughing - make sure you are hydrated. Caution: Do not play yard darts while on Fooof (with Laughing Gas) you might put someone's eye out!

ENTRY WAY to MARCH

March was originally the first month on the early Roman calendar. Its name honors Mars, the Roman god of war. To honor Mars, it's the Awe-Manac Month of Unleashing Your Inner Warrior On All Tormenting Thoughts And Unfulfilling Actions Keeping You Captive. Liberate yourself 5 percent more each week from these nuisances by striking a warrior pose and sounding a war cry when discouraging forces such are relentless self-judgment or any external sabotaging agents surface from their pits of destruction. Triumphant War Cry example: HEY, YOU CAN'T STOP ME FROM DOING MY CREATIVE STUFF. .

A Few Celebrations at March's Door:

It is Music in Our Schools Month. Music is one of the Anti-aging, Anti-gravity, Anti-Dulling Potions. Try this: use background music while reading *The Awe-manac* or any book. Background music can create mood, atmosphere, and more depth of enjoyment for reading. You can also find music to accompany your warrior spirit this month. When you are feeling in need of military action, turn up the volume on empowering music.

It's also Humorists Are Artists Month, International Ideas Month, International Listening Awareness Month, International Mirth Month, National Collision Awareness Month, National Craft Month, National Ethics Awareness Month, National Frozen Food Month, National Nutrition Month, National Social Work Month, National Women's History Month, Optimism Month, Small Press Month, Spiritual Wellness Month, Youth Art Month. March begins in Pisces and ends in Aries.

Awe-Manac Invented Events:

Month of Unleashing Your Inner Warrior on All Tormenting Thoughts and Unfulfilling Actions Keeping You Captive and Love Music More Month

Still Life Melody

March 10: A day to appreciate animals
March 13: Lull Day
March 14: Albert Einstein Day
March 18: Updike Day

Ways to Celebrate March

1. Love Music More Month:
Explore music or musical artists that you are not familiar with or simply haven't listened to that much - find some new tunes to add to your repertoire of music that make you feel good or that empowers you to stay true to your cause of fulfillment, creativity, kindness and world peace.

2. International Ideas Month:
 Write a list of ideas for how to celebrate International Ideas Month.

3. Save Your Vision Month:
Exercise to help reduce stress and fatigue on the eyes: a. Move your eyes like the movement of a clock or pretend you are watching a tennis match but just move your eyes, not your head. (Do not do this exercise while driving or during job interviews.) b. Close your eyes as tightly as you possibly can. Squeeze the eyes, so that the eye muscles contract. Hold this contraction for three seconds and then let go quickly. This causes deep relaxation of the eye muscles and is especially beneficial after the slight strain caused by the eye exercises. Blink the eyes a few times.

4. Collide with optimism, humor, and good nutrition.

5. Humorists Are Artists: Throughout March pages, observe the still-life art painted by our resident Awe-manac humorist.

Astrological Spells

Dried Still life and Blue Bird

Aries: Imagine a smile circulating inside of your cells.

Taurus: Purposely scan your car radio for some music you've never heard before and listen with an open mind.

Gemini: Make patience a new hobby you are terribly keen on perfecting.

Cancer: Buy a new houseplant and give it a name that amuses you; post the name by the pot.

Leo: Give yourself $25 to spend in a craft store however your child-spirit wants

Virgo: Discover a new, tasty way to prepare veggies and narrate making it as if you were on the Food Network.

Libra: In writing (optional: with rough illustrations), reinvent an event in your history as a more empowering one.

Scorpio: Take 15 to 30 seconds to feel a full-body, mind, and spirit sense of buoyancy.

Sagittarius: Place a cool washcloth on your eyes for 5 minutes sometime this month and sigh.

Capricorn: Spend some time with a specific tree this month, get to know it.

Aquarius: Take a day just for yourself this month, do anything as long as you include something you haven't done in a long time.

Pisces: Buy a coloring book and color it for relaxation for 15 minutes, and on the next day visit an aquarium or a pet store with tropical fish.

Tides

Ebbing: What are you letting go of this month? (just a little bit)

Flowing: Where are you expanding this month? (just a little bit)

Vessel of strength:

Gardening Information

Flower: Daffodil

Monthly Awe-manac crop: Laughter

Planting Tips: Plant each silly seed 150 feet apart (just kidding), plant in mounds or one big hill-arious, fertilize with an inside joke, stalk some beans (hee hee hee), and giggle with water continuously dripping out your mouth over the seeds. Smiles are 6 feet in width when full grown. Harvest by standing behind them with the upper part of your face showing and having someone snap your picture.

March 1

Name Today _____

Soul Vitamin

Most of my major disappointments have turned out to be blessings in disguise. So whenever anything bad does happen to me, I kind of sit back and feel, well, if I give this enough time, it'll turn out that this was good, so I shan't worry about it too much. ~*William Gaines*

Toast of the Day

Here's to noodles with a favorite savory sauce (in moderation).

Awe-servances

Happy Birthday to:

Sandro Botticelli 1445, Renaissance painter.

William M. Gaines, 1922 founder of *Mad* Magazine.

Harry Belafonte, 1927 Singer, Political Activist.

It's National Noodle Month.

Still life in Chair Except for Orange

Aha-phrodisiacs

Find Botticelli's *Primavera* in an online search, choose a figure and write from his or her point of view or write what could happen next in the scene if this were a scene in a movie or play.

Find a picture of a plate of noodles and reinvent it as something else in a collage: the hair of a noodle-headed person, a freeway system for words, a mound with flowers growing out of it.

Journal Juju

Harry Belafonte's Title Wave for journal writing: Streets I Have Walked, In My Quiet Room, Turn the World Around

Dose Of Mirth

The day after tomorrow is the third day of the rest of your life. ~ *George Carlin*

Today I get to

_____

_____

_____

Subliminal message from Awe-wakened Moment Potion

I breathe gently into each moment and each moment is gentler to me.

Soul Vitamin

There is no one alive who is Youer than You. ~ Dr. Seuss

Toast of the Day
Here's to memories of your first exposure to Dr. Seuss

March Humor Crop

Awe-Servances

Happy Birthday to
Theodor Seuss Geisel, Dr. Seuss, 1904, writer and cartoonist.
John Irving, 1942, award-winning novelist and screenwriter.

Aha-phrodisiacs

Pick a subject and write about it in the genre of Dr. Seuss. If you cannot think of a subject choose: a recent event, your thoughts about work, green pasta and ham, purple pansies.

   John Irving said "my capacity to be by myself and just spend time by myself hasn't diminished any. That's the necessary part of being a writer, you better like being alone." Take some time to be alone with your creative passion –anything from a few hours to a few weeks (or months if you can). Write about the whole concept of "you."

Journal Juju

Use Maya Angelou's quote below as Starter Fluid for writing, art, or collage.

   Dr. Seuss said, "Be who you are and say what you feel because those who mind don't matter and those who matter don't mind." Say what you feel that hasn't been said yet in your journal today or use this title: *Those Who Matter Don't Mind.*

   John Irving said "Good habits are worth being fanatical about." What are some good habits you would like to be fanatical about? Start one today for 2 minutes.

Dose Of Mirth

Life loves to be taken by the lapel and told, "I'm with you kid, let's go." ~ Maya Angelou

Subliminal question from Awakened Inner Messages Potion
What small thought, really small thought
can I think today that would open me to more joy?

Today I get to
_____

be alive

89

March 3

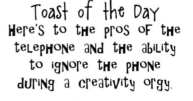

Name Today _____

_____

Daily Soul Vitamin

I don't answer the phone. I get the feeling
whenever I do that there will be someone
on the other end. ~Fred Couples

Awe—servances

Happy Birthday to:
Alexander Graham Bell, 1847, inventor of the telephone.

Aha—phrodisiacs

Write a phone conversation between two of your
   characters or you with the historical figure of your choice.
Make a collage of a phone conversation;
   let your imagination percolate on that one.

Dose of Mirth

The bathtub was invented in 1850 and the telephone
in 1875. In other words, if you had been living in
1850, you could have sat in the bathtub for 25
years without having to answer the phone.
~Bill DeWitt

Toast of the Day
Here's to the pros of the
telephone and the ability
to ignore the phone
during a creativity orgy.

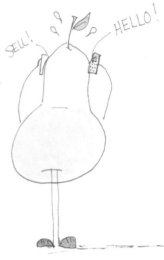

Journal Juju

Henry Miller said, "I'd rather sit down and write a letter
than call someone up. I hate the telephone."
Write about your relationship with the telephone.

A word from Aha—phrodisiacs Potion

Creativity Tip: Turn off the phone during your sacred creative time. Or if it's overdue,
call someone who makes you feel creative or rejuvenates you when you talk to them
or vice versa.

Today I get to _____

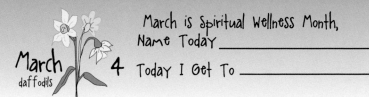

March is Spiritual Wellness Month,
Name Today _____
Today I Get To _____

Daily Soul Vitamin

Spring passes and one remembers one's innocence. Summer passes and one remembers one's exuberance. Autumn passes and one remembers one's reverence. Winter passes and one remembers one's perseverance. ~ Yoko Ono

Toast of the Day
Here's to listening to Vivaldi's "Four Seasons" over a delicious breakfast.

Awe-servances

Happy Birthday to:
  Antonio Vivaldi, 1678, composer, famous violinist.

It's also March 4 Yourself Day: march off to work, march off to school, or just march doing what you do.

Aha-phrodisiacs

Let the word "march" be a springboard of inspiration for poetry or prose in any of its forms.

  In honor of Vivaldi's *The Four Seasons*, divide a piece of paper into four sections and fill each section with one of the four seasons with a doodle, drawing, collage, or representation of color. Or fill each section with statements of what you want to have happen in those seasons as if it already happened. Or define four cycles you experience throughout the year and make images that represent those cycles.

Journal Juju

Write about where you march off to and why.

Still Life and
Last Supper

The Ideas of March

Name today _____

Today I get To _____

Daily Soul Vitamin

There are few hours in life more agreeable than the hour dedicated to the ceremony known as afternoon tea.
~ Henry James

Toast of the Day

Here's to ceremonies that exalt simple moments of delight.

Awe-servances

 Happy Birthday to:
Leslie Marmon Silko, 1948, Native American writer.

Also in 1872, George Westinghouse patented the air brake, which is
a conveyance braking system applied by means of compressed air.

It's Multiple Personalities Day.

Aha-phrodisiacs

Write a list of your associations about the word "ceremony." Then see what you are inspired to do with that list.

Make a collage, doodle, or painting titled *Ceremony*.

Dose of Mirth

I couldn't repair your brakes so I made your horn louder. ~Unknown

Journal Juju

Use "brake" as a metaphor in your life. Where do you need to put the brakes on? Where do you need to take your foot off the brake? Where do you need a lucky break?

And now a Question from Awe-wakened Moment Potion

In this moment right now, what are you enjoying mentally, physically or spiritually? Stop and breathe into it, imagine that feeling expanding ten times. Allow yourself to be fully in the moment of your pleasure.

Daily Soul Vitamin

A kiss is a rosy dot over the "I" of loving.
~ Cyrano De Bergerac

Awe—servances

Happy Birthday to:
Michelangelo, 1475, artist icon.
Cyrano de Bergerac, 1619, dramatist and
    duelist known for his large nose.
Elizabeth Barrett Browning, 1806, poet of
    the Victorian era.

Still life and Line Dance

Aha-phrodisiacs

E.B. Browning Starter Fluid, "What was he doing, the great god Pan / Down in the reeds by the river?" Write an ode to Michelangelo. Or keep going with today's Soul Vitamin.

Dose of Mirth

When I want any, good head work done; I always choose a man, if possible with a long nose.
~Napoleon Bonaparte

Journal Juju

Michelangelo said, "Faith in oneself is the best and safest course." For the next 30 seconds practice the feeling in your body of 5 percent more faith in yourself. Or imagine what that might feel like. What would you do with a little more faith in yourself?
  "Instinct is the nose of the mind." What does your mind's nose sniff out today?

Question Brought to You by the Kindness Potion

Can you dedicate whatever you are doing to a purpose higher than yourself, even if only you know about the dedication? When we do this, new forces enter in, to back and direct you.

Daily Soul Vitamin

What drives the creative person is that we see it all. ~Wanda Sykes

Toast of the Day

Here's to the arrival or impending arrival of spring weather.

Awe-Servances

Happy Birthday to:

Luther Burbank, 1849, botanist and horticulturist.

Willard Scott, 1934, weatherman.

Wanda Sykes, 1964, stand-up comedian and actress.

1933 The game Monopoly was invented.

Weather Plant

Aha-phrodisiacs

Referring to today's Soul Vitamin, what do creative people see? Write about it confidently as if you were an expert.

Write about the weather at Park Place in a Monopoly game.

Write a fictional account of being a weatherman, weaving weather metaphors into the day.

Dose of Mirth

Weather is a great metaphor for life, sometimes it's good, sometimes it's bad, and there's nothing much you can do about it but carry an umbrella. ~Pepper Giardino

Journal Juju

Luther Burbank said, "The secret of improved plant breeding, apart from scientific knowledge, is love." Write a letter to yourself from a plant who loves you and wants to share observations with you.

Brought to You by Body Temple Potion

When you explore the world of yoga class possibilities, keep in mind that it is important for you to find the right one for your unique needs. There is an entire spectrum of style,s and if you are a gentle yoga person and find yourself in an Ashtanga class you may dismiss yoga as too difficult and miss out on the magnificent mortal mood modifier that it can be.

March 8

Name today _____

Today I get To _____

Daily Soul Vitamin
Ah, music. A magic beyond all we do here!
~J. K. Rowling, Creator of Harry Potter

Toast of the Day
Here's to the Magic of Music
to inspire, connect
and accompany our lives.

Awe-servances

Happy Birthday to:
Carole Bayer Sager, 1947, lyricist, songwriter, and singer.

International (Working) Women's Day.
Learn What Your Name Means Day.
Uppity Women Day: Uppity women from around the world
unite in their ability to be themselves.

Aha-phrodisiacs
Carole Bayer Sager Title Wave: Don't Wish Too Hard, A
Groovy Kind Of Love, Home To Myself, Steal Away Again,
Shy as a Violet.

Do a doodle, collage or a painting of a mind stretched
by an idea.

Write about one or more of these subjects from the
point of view of an uppity woman: working, bras, tuna
casserole, music, names, staying young, trying to relax.

Write an uppity ode to working women.

Journal Juju
Isabel Allende said, "Write what should not be
forgotten." Good idea. Repeated Completions:
"I will not forget …"

Uppity Woman Doing Magic

Quotes Brought to You by Arpeggio Potion
If I ever die of a heart attack, I hope it will be from playing my stereo too loud. ~Anonymous
There is nothing in the world so much like prayer as music is. ~William P. Merrill

March
daffodils

Name Today _____

Today I Get To _____

Daily Soul Vitamin
The only rule is that there are no rules. ~Del Close

Toast of the Day
Here's to the delight of the quick-witted.

Awe-servances

Anti-panic Tea

Happy Birthday to:

Amerigo Vespucci, 1451, explorer; the Americas are named after him.

Del Close, 1934, one of the premier influences on modern improvisational theater.

It's also Panic Day. A day to run around in a panic and tell everyone you can't handle it anymore. (Not making this up).

Aha-phrodisiacs
Write or improvise in a panicked state about one or more of these subjects: dinner party, a dandelion, losing a sock, missing an exit, losing your mind, not being able to relax.

Make artwork to go with John Calvi's quote: "When I took the leap, I had faith I'd find the net; instead I learned I could fly."

Dose of Mirth
Peculiar travel suggestions are dancing lessons from God.
~ Bokonon, in Kurt Vonnegut's *Cat's Cradle*

Journal Juju
A week ago, we asked you if you could incorporate a good habit for 2 minutes a day for the next week: How did you do? And if you didn't do it, well, try it for another week.

Subliminal Message From Awe-Wakened Moment Potion:
I see beauty with 100 percent appreciative awareness.

Note to Self
Break a limiting rule today—as long as it has nothing to do with morals or safety.

Today I get to _____

March 10 It's Pet Appreciation Day

Daily Soul Vitamin

If having a soul means being able to feel love and loyalty
and gratitude, then animals are better off than
a lot of humans. ~ James Herriot

Any glimpse into the life of an animal quickens
our own and makes it so much the larger and
better in every way. ~John Muir

An animal's eyes have the power to speak a great
language. ~ Martin Buber

Until one has loved an animal, a part of one's soul
remains unawakened. ~ Anatole France

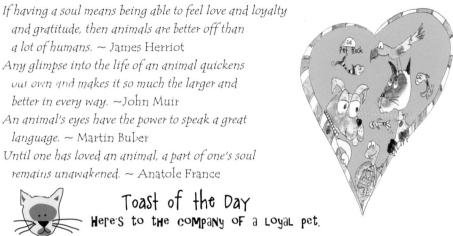

Toast of the Day

HERE'S TO THE COMPANY OF A LOYAL PET.

Awe—Servances

Happy Birthday to
James Herriot, 1916, veterinary surgeon, writer, and animal advocate.
The Awe-manac remembers him by making March 10th Pet Appreciation Day.

Aha—phrodisiacs

Make a donation to an organization that does some good for animals.
Make an animal collage. What are your spirit animals?
Write about your usual day from the point of view of the animal you
would be if you could be an animal.
Make a card of all you appreciate about your pet and post it.

Journal Juju

Write from your pet's point of view a list of things he or she appreciates about you.

Dose of Mirth

I think animal testing is a terrible idea; they get all nervous
and give the wrong answers. ~Peter Kayu

Daily Soul Vitamin

Any time that is not spent on love is wasted.
~ Tasso

Toast of the Day

Here's listening to a song that gets your
FULL attention and makes you smile.

Awe-servances

Torquato Tasso, 1544 Italian poet.

Bobby McFerrin, Jr., 1950, jazz-influenced
a cappella vocal performer and conductor.

Douglas Adams, 1952, author, comic radio
dramatist, and musician, best known for
The Hitchhiker's Guide to the Galaxy series.

Aha-phrodisiacs

Bobby McFerrin performs a song called "Windows". Use this title for
collage, doodling, or poetry. For poetry: make a list of all your associations for
window. Then see if you can find a thread to weave them
all together in free verse.

Dose of Mirth

*It is a mistake to think you can solve any major
problems just with potatoes.* ~ Douglas Adams

Journal Juju

Bobby McFerrin said, "When you're settled and still, that's the best way to create
because your best self makes your best stuff." Get settled and still, then listen.
Read something you think helps you get in touch with your best self (like a
Soul Vitamin that has resonated with you or a past journal entry), then write.

Message from Aha-phrodisiacs Potion

Bobby McFerrin also said, "I have to set a goal and a deadline or I won't get anything done. I have to come up with two or three ideas a day and finish them. I
don't have to like them, but I have to finish them because sometimes I won't
like an idea but a month later I'll like it a lot."

Daily Soul Vitamin

The only people for me are the mad ones. The ones who are mad to love, mad to talk, mad to be saved; the ones who never yawn or say a commonplace thing, but burn, burn, burn like fabulous yellow Roman candles exploding like spiders across the stars.
~Jack Kerouac

Toast of the Day
Here's to a balMy tropical NIGHT iN UNSPoiLed NatURe.

Awe—Servances

Happy Birthday to:
Carl Hiaasen, 1953, journalist and novelist.
Jack Kerouac, 1922, novelist, writer, poet, and artist of the Beat Generation.

It's also National Napping Day: Be aware of the health and productivity benefits of napping.

Aha—phrodisiacs

Stormy Weather is a Hiaasen title: Paint or collage a storm and feel free to make the storm something other than rain (flying transistor radios, lamp shades, clouds raining light bulbs, books, raining words, cats and frogs).
    Kerouac Starter Fluid: "My witness is the empty sky." Or make a collage, scribble, or painting to go with his quote above in Soul Vitamins.

Dose of Mirth

The first rule of hurricane coverage is that every broadcast must begin with palm trees bending in the wind. ~ Carl Hiaasen

Journal Juju

Yogi Berra said, "I usually take a two hour nap from one to four." Write about the art of napping: make up five main points that ensure an excellent napping experience.

Message Brought to You by Body Temple

A short nap in the afternoon is good for your heart and can result in little idea epiphanies.

Note to Myself: Be patriotic and celebrate National Napping Day today.

MARCH 13

Name Today _____

Daily Soul Vitamin

*Sitting quietly, doing noth-
ing, spring comes, and the
grass grows by itself.*
~ Zen proverb

Toast of the Day
Here's to letting go
of the process for
a day.

STILL LIFE IN hAMMOCK

Awe-servances

Take a break from it all. Glide.

Aha-phrodisiacs

Daydream. Appreciate yourself just the way
you are today. No self improvement.

Dose of Mirth

*Let not the sands of time
get in your lunch.*
-National Lampoon

Journal Juju
Listen to music
and scribble.

March 14

Daily Soul Vitamin

A table, a chair, a bowl of fruit and a violin; what else does a man need to be happy? ~Albert Einstein

Toast of the Day
Here's to the power of the imagination.

Awe-Servances

Happy Birthday to:

Albert Einstein, 1879, Nobel Prize-winning theoretical
   physicist, best known for his theory of relativity. 1999 *Time* magazine's
   "Person of the Century, Einstein is synonymous with *genius*.

Aha-phrodisiacs

Einstein Starter Fluid: "The only reason for time is so that every- thing doesn't happen at once." Or write about everything happening at once.

Dose of Mirth

Once you can accept the universe as matter expanding into nothing that is something, wearing stripes with plaid comes easy.
~ Albert Einstein

Journal Juju

Break the rules and invent a new emotion. E=?

Today I Get to

_____

_____

Note to myself

imagine what it would be like to be 5percent more engaged in my creative passion.

Our task must be to free ourselves ... by widening our circle of compassion to embrace all living creatures and the whole of nature and its beauty. ~Albert Einstein Our task must be to free ourselves ... by widening our circle of compassion to embrace all living creatures and the whole of nature and its beauty. ~Albert Einstein Our task must be to free ourselves .. by widening our circle ...

March 15
International Mirth Month

Soul Vitamin
Never take counsel of your fears. ~Andrew Jackson

Toast of the Day
Here's to finding a twenty dollar bill
in your pocket.

Awe-Servances
Happy Birthday to:
Andrew Jackson, 1767, the seventh US President.

It's also Rude Awakenings Day.

Aha-phrodisiacs
List five secret selves (e.g.: A cowgirl, a blues singer, a queen, a construction worker. Or make it fictional: a Disney character, a monkey. Or a character you would just like to explore: a tattoo artist, a sit-com actor). Pick one and do a guided writing timing your response for 2 minutes for each of the following unfinished sentences then moving on to the next.

Finish these sentences: I am ..., I am known for..., When nobody's watching I..., It makes me mad when..., My latest accomplishment is ..., I laugh when..., For breakfast I have..., My best friend and I..., In the spring I..., My next project is..., I just want to..., and I'd just like to tell the world...

Journal Juju
Any rude awakenings lately? List any you remember from the past and elaborate on at least one. Write the above Daily Soul Vitamin in your journal just to reinforce its wisdom, yes, I'm talking to you.

Dose Of Mirth
If you always take time to stop and smell the roses, sooner or later, you'll inhale a bee. ~Unknown

Today I get to ——————————————————————
————————————————————————————————————

AND NOW a Message From Inner Awe-Lixir: Close your eyes and for 20 seconds connect to a place inside undisturbed by anyone or anything

March 16 Lips Day

Soul Vitamin

While you are proclaiming peace with your lips, be careful to have it even more fully in your heart. ~ St. Francis of Assisi

toast of The Day
Here's to the touch of someone's lips

Awe-servances

Lips Appreciation Day. From Ruth and Thomas Roy, inventors of several nationally known quirky commemorations included in *The Awe-manac.* Check out more at www.wellcat.com

Dose Of Mirth

I used to kiss her on the lips, but it's all over now.
~Unknown

Aha-phrodisiacs

Judy Garland said, "It was not my lips you kissed, but my soul." Virginia Woolf said, "Language is wine upon the lips." Percy Bysshe Shelley said, "... a wild dissolving bliss / Over my frame he breathed, approaching near, / And bent his eyes of kindling tenderness / Near mine, and on my lips impressed a lingering kiss," What do you say about lips?

"Do something nice for your lips today. Buy a lip balm. Better yet, kiss somebody!"
~Ruth & Thomas Roy

Journal Juju

Write about your relationship with your lips. What do your lips have to say to you? Write a letter.

Two weeks ago, (March 2), on John Irving birthday we asked you to get fanatical about a habit 2 minutes a day, how'd that go? And if you didn't do it, well try it again for another week, just keep going, no need to be perfect, just persistent. When creativity becomes a habit, it becomes comfortable, desirable even, and resistance is less of an issue.

Today I get to ——————————————————

————————————————————————————————

Daily Soul Vitamin

St. Patrick's Day is an enchanted time – a day to begin transforming winter's dreams into summer's magic." ~Adrienne Cook

Toast of the Day
HERE'S TO THE MANY SHADES OF THE COLOR GREEN.

Awe–Servances

Happy St.Patrick's Day: The patron saint of Ireland, Bishop Patrick left his home in England and introduced Christianity to Ireland.

Happy Birthday to:
Nat King Cole, 1919, singer.

Happy St Patrick's Day

Aha–phrodisiacs

Write a limerick pertaining to a recent event in your life, green beer, or about someone who makes you laugh. A limerick is where the first, second, and fifth lines each have eight syllables and rhyme with each other, while the middle lines have only six syllables and a separate rhyme.

Dose of Limerick

A mathematician named Bath, Let x equal half that he hath.
He gave away y/, Then sat down to eat pi
And choked. What a sad aftermath. ~Unknown

Journal Juju

Nat King Cole said "Everybody who has a creative mind should sit down and try something new." What is something new you can do today in your journal? Write in it upside down? Write about your life in news story form? Write about yourself in the third person? Write about yourself in the seventh person? Make up what "in the seventh person" means? Write about your inner leprechaun?

Name Today _____

Daily Soul Vitamin

Creativity is merely a plus name for regular activity. Any activity becomes creative when the doer cares about doing it right, or better. ~John Updike

Toast of the Day
HERE'S TO ANONYMOUSLY GIVING SOMEONE SOMETHING creative.

Awe-servances

- Happy Birthday to:
  John Updike, 1932, novelist.

  It's Anonymous Giving Week, a time to celebrate the true spirit of giving by a random act of kindness or an anonymous contribution.

Aha-phrodisiacs

Make a little card with a Soul Vitamin in it or write a kind limerick and send it to someone anonymously.

Updike wrote "Each morning my characters greet me with misty faces willing, though chilled, to muster for another day's progress through the dazzling quicksand the marsh of blank paper." Have a character greet you in writing and tell you what he or she would like you to write next. Starter Fluid: "As I wade through the marsh of the blank page …"

Dose of Mirth

We do survive every moment, after all, except the last one. ~ John Updike

Journal Juju

John Updike said, "Perfectionism is the enemy of creation, as extreme self-solitude is the enemy of well-being." Write a permission slip on releasing perfectionism and do an assessment of your status with solitude.

Today I get to _____

March 19

Name Today _____

Daily Soul Vitamin

To be one's self, and unafraid whether right or wrong, is more admirable than the easy cowardice of surrender to conformity. ~Irving Wallace

Toast of the Day
Here's to the birds that make up our nature's background.

Awe-servances

Happy Birthday to:

Irving Wallace, 1916, bestselling author and screenwriter.

It's Also Swallows Day (traditional return to Capistrano).

March 19 is usually the last day of the winter season in the Northern Hemisphere, and the last day of the summer season in the Southern Hemisphere.

Aha-phrodisiacs

Irving Wallace Title Wave: Prize, Man, Three Sirens, Sunday Gentleman, Plot, Seven Minutes, Word, Fan Club, Pigeon Project, Second Lady, Almighty, Miracle, Seventh Secret, Celestial Bed, Golden Room, Guest of Honor

Write about the concept of "last" in whatever way you associate it.

Dose of Mirth

Imagine if birds were tickled by feathers. You'd see a flock of birds come by, laughing hysterically! ~ Steven Wright

Journal Juju

Write about returning someplace year after year like the swallows do, whether it's a geographic place or an emotional, creative, or other kind of cyclical place.

Subliminal Message Brought to You by the Kindness and Gathering Potions

Kenny Ausubel said, "Each of us has a spark of life inside us, and our highest endeavor ought to be to set off that spark in one another." What's one small way your spark can ignite the spark of someone else? Visit a retirement home? Compliment someone? Show someone how to do something you know how to do in a way that shows their strengths?

The Ideas of March

Name Today _____

Daily Soul Vitamin
To me, being creative is a very fragile thing, and somehow I've always felt the need to be very protective of that. ~ Holly Hunter

Toast of the Day
Here's to the promise of Spring!

Awe—servances
Happy Birthday to:
William Hurt, 1950, award-winning actor.
Holly Hunter, 1958, award-winning actress.

It's also Proposal Day. A day for singles who are
   seeking marriage.

Non—Serious Play

Aha—phrodisiacs
Break the rules and write a proposal for something other than marriage and back it up with real or imaginary facts. Let your imagination run wild. Propose that we use less packaging. Propose that we grow wings. Propose that there be no war. Make a list of things to propose.

Double Dose of Mirth
I intend to live forever. So far, so good. ~Stephen Wright
I intend to live forever, or die trying. ~Groucho Marx

Journal Juju
William Hurt said, "But I am not going to live forever. And the more I know it, the more amazed I am by being here at all." Knowing our mortality can enhance our awe for being alive. Explore where you are with this in your journal.

SUBLIMINAL MeSSaGes BrouGht to YoU by FOOOF:
Michael Schrage said, "Serious play is not an oxymoron; it is the essence of innovation." List 10 ways you interpret "serious play."
Creativity can be fragile. Be careful when and with whom you share a delicate new idea.

Daily Soul Vitamin

A musician must make music, an artist must paint,
a poet must write, if he is to be ultimately at peace
with himself. ~Abraham H. Maslow

Toast of the Day
Here's to feeling a peak experience in the creative process.

Awe–Servances

Happy Birthday to:

Johann Sebastian Bach, 1685, composer and keyboard virtuoso, who brought the
  Baroque to its maturity.

(Sir Henry) Vivian Stanshall, 1943, musician, painter, singer, broadcaster,
  songwriter, poet, writer, wit, and raconteur, best known for his work with the
  Bonzo Dog Doo-Dah Band.

Aries begins.

Aha–phrodisiacs

Get some crayons or pastels, several pieces of
paper, play Baroque or other classical music, and
scribble a number of works to the music –
filling in any form they may begin to take.
Give each a title and use some of the titles as
inspiration for writing.

Dose of Mirth

If you're going to say anything filthy, please speak clearly.
~ answering machine of Vivian Stanshall

Scribble and Tulip

Journal Juju

Aries is energetic, innovative, original, pioneering, assertive, quick-tempered,
strong drive, leader, ambitious, extroverted, sometimes aggressive, competitive,
enthusiastic, self-reliant and self-assured. Scan the Aries list and write briefly—or
not so briefly—about where you are with one or more of these tendencies even if
you aren't an Aries.

Daily Soul Vitamin

I could not, at any age, be content to take my place in a corner by the fireside and simply look on. ~Eleanor Roosevelt

Toast of the Day
Here's to feeling a part of the flow of life.

Awe-servances

Happy Birthday to:
Marcel Marceau, 1923, mime.
Billy Collins, 1941, US Poet
   Laureate.

International Day of the Seal.

Aha-phrodisiacs

Have a monologue with a mime (or perhaps a mimeologe) Or write a poem or prose piece that uses an alliteration of "m" words.

   Take a seal to lunch. (Doodle yourself having lunch with a seal, sushi maybe?) Have fun with a dialog with a seal as if he were your child (e.g., "Wilbur, would you please take that ball off your nose and eat your sardines?")

Doses of Mirth

The hardest part of being a poet is knowing what to do with the other 23 and 1/2 hours of your day. ~ Billy Collins

Journal Juju

Make a list of all the things (real or imagined) to which you would give a seal of approval.
For example:

1. Tupperware lids that magnetize their bottoms to them when you pick them up.
2. People who send funny emails on those days when you really need them.
3. Peace.

March 23

Name Today _____

Daily Soul Vitamin
There is a muscular energy in sunlight
corresponding to the spiritual energy of wind.
~Annie Dillard

Toast of the Day
Here's to that Special Feeling
Spring Weather can bring.

Happy Birthday to:
Mitch Cullin, 1968, author of six novels, one of which is in verse,
   and a short story collection. His writing is described by the
   New York Times as "brilliant and beautiful... rhythmic and telling."

It's also: World Meteorology Day.

Aha-phrodisiacs
Mitch Cullin's website Title Wave: Why Would Anybody Live Here? My Doorbell,
   look, No Fingerprints, Broken Mouth Blues.

Dose of Mirth
Weather forecast for tonight: dark.
~George Carlin

Journal Juju
Use weather as a metaphor and write what kind of weather is occupying various life
areas: your social life, your work, your creative life, your love life, your mind, ...
make a forecast for your future.
   Mitch Cullin's short story collections is called *The Place in the Valley Deep in the Forest.*
   Use it in a journal entry as another metaphor – e.g. what is your valley deep in the
forest of your life? Is a valley a place of rest, a dip, a clearing for you? Is the forest your
complications, your darkness, or your adventure?

Note to Myself
Enjoy the weather today, whatever it is. It means I'm alive.

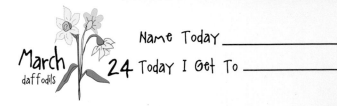

Double Dose Daily Soul Vitamin for Magic

Books are a uniquely portable magic. ~Stephen King

Whatever you think you can do or believe you can do, begin it. Action has magic, grace, and power in it.
~Johann Wolfgang von Goethe

Toast of the Day

Here's to the everyday magic of the way the light looks when it is filtered through the trees.

Awe–servances

Happy Birthday to:
Harry Houdini, 1874, a magician, escapologist, stunt performer.
Curtis Lee Hanson, 1945, Oscar-winning film director.

Aha–phrodisiacs

Curtis Lee Hanson Title Wave: Losin' It, Bad Influence, The Hand that Rocks the Cradle, The River Wild, L.A. Confidential, Wonder Boys, 8 Mile, In Her Shoes, Lucky You

Dose of Mirth

Using words to describe magic is like using a screwdriver to cut roast beef. ~ Tom Robbins

Journal Juju

Prove Tom Robbins wrong. Make a list of events in your life you associate with magic or write how having the power of magic might serve you.
Starter Fluid: "I am the river wild ..."

A Message from A.I.M.

Fuel for confidence: think and feel I can do this.

Name Today _____

25 Today I Get To _____

Daily Soul Vitamin

But, you know, those three words - I need help. If only I'd said them earlier. ~Elton John

Toast of the Day
Hear's to Music that Makes us Move our body.

Awe-servances

Happy Birthday to:
Aretha Franklin,1942, singer icon known as "The Queen Of Soul."
Elton John, 1947, award-winning pop/rock singer and songwriter icon.

Aha-phrodisiacs

Elton John has a song called "Enchantment Passing Through." Make a collage that illustrates this title. Invent an "enchanting" vehicle or the essence of enchantment passing through some place that needs it, or with onlookers responding. Or write about such a situation. Starter Fluid: "A feeling of enchantment ..."

Dose of Mirth

I'm a big woman. I need big hair.
~Aretha Franklin

Journal Juju

"Think" is one of Aretha's best-known songs. Do a rapid fire Repeated Completion on "I think ..." Notice the liberating quality, and if anything comes up that has energy, keep going.

  Successful people know to get help from others. Explore and play with this notion by simply listing some areas in your life where you could benefit from the help of others. Using awareness like this is the first step and can often work its magic by sending subconscious energies into operation to move us closer to making the choices that serve our magnificence.

Brought to You by Awe-wakened Moment Potion

Imagine that everything is unfolding just the way it is supposed to. How can you acknowledge, feel, and embody the fact that many parts of your dream are already happening now?

26

Name Today _____

Today I Get To _____

Daily Soul Vitamin
A prayer for the wild at heart, kept in cages. ~Tennessee Williams

Toast of the Day
Here's to defiance when it leads to creative freedom.

Awe—Servances
Happy Birthday to:

Viktor Frankl, M.D., Ph.D., neurologist, psychiatrist, and Holocaust survivor. Man's Search for Meaning chronicles his experiences as a concentration camp inmate and describes his psychotherapeutic method of finding meaning in all forms of existence, even the most sordid ones, and thus a reason to continue living.

Tennessee Williams, 1911, playwright.

Leonard Nimoy, 1931, actor, writer, director. Famed as Mr. Spock on *Star Trek*.

Make Up Your Own Holiday Day from Ruth and Tom Roy – the holiday inventors (wellcat.com).

National Sleep Awareness Week.

Aha—phrodisiacs
Amanda Bradley said, "Celebrate the happiness that friends are always giving, make every day a holiday and celebrate just living!" Make Up Your Own Holiday: include it's name, the way it should be celebrated, ceremonies or rituals, decorations, costumes and food to be consumed.

Dose of Mirth
A perpetual holiday is a good working definition of hell. ~George Bernard Shaw

Journal Juju
Victor Frankl said, "When we are no longer able to change a situation, we are challenged to change ourselves," and "The one thing you can't take away from me is the way I choose to respond to what you do to me. The last of one's freedoms is to choose ones attitude in any given circumstance." Explore anything these quotes inspire for any situation or attitude in your life.

Quote Brought to You by Kindness Potion
Leonard Nimoy said, "The miracle is this, the more we share, the more we have."

March 27 The Road is Open

Daily Soul Vitamin
Living on Earth may be expensive, but it includes an annual free trip around the Sun.
~Unknown

Awe-servances
Louis Simpson, 1923, a poet who has written 17 volumes of poetry, including *At the End of the Open Road* which won a Pulitzer Prize.

Aha-phrodisiacs
Make a collage entitled *At the End of the Open Road,* or use it as Starter Fluid.

Note to Myself: Pack writing tools.

Name Today _____

Daily Soul Vitamin

You can have anything you want if you want it desperately enough. You must want it with an exuberance that erupts through the skin and joins the energy that created the world. ~ Sheila Graham

Toast of the Day
Here's to the many emotions of good saxophone music.

Awe-servances

Happy Birthday to:

Edmund Muskie, 1914, Democratic politician from Maine.

Russell Banks, 1940, author of *Continental Drift, The Sweet Hereafter,* and *Cloud Splitter.*
   Against the odds of dropping out of school, living with an abusive alcoholic father, and encountering numerous misfortunes, Russell Banks has had a prolific career writing poetry and fiction.

Aha-phrodisiacs

Russell Banks Word Pool: sweet, drift, continental, here, cloud, splitter, after, run-down, factory, town, blue-collar world, writer, butterfly, slowly, plumbing, teenager, life, new, world, trailer park, imprisonment, success, affliction, rule, invisible, stranger, angel roof.

Dose of Mirth

I don't kill flies but I like to mess with their minds. I hold them above globes. They freak out and yell, "Whoa, I'm way too high!"~ Bruce Baum

Journal Juju

Edmund S. Muskie said "Looking at yourself through the media is like looking at one of those rippled mirrors in an amusement park." Imagine looking at yourself through a metaphorical rippled mirror: how would you be distorted? What if it was a rippled mirror that gave you a kid-like look? What if it focused only on your successes? What if it distorted your ambitions by simplifying them? Made you see deep into your soul? Write what you see.

And Now a Word from FOOOf

Lighten up.

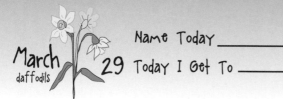

March
daffodils
29

Daily Soul Vitamin

To have a reason to get up in the morning, it is necessary to possess a guiding principle. A belief of some kind. A bumper sticker if you will. ~Judith Guest

Awe—Servances

Happy Birthday to:

Pearl Bailey, 1918 singer and actress.

Judith Guest, 1936, novelist who wrote *Second Heaven, Errands* and, most famously, *Ordinary People.*

Eric Idle, 1943, member of Monty Python. Idle played Sir Robin the Not-So-Brave, who wets his armor at the first sign of danger in *Monty Python and the Holy Grail.*

Aha—phrodisiacs

Pearl Bailey said, "Never, never rest contented with any circle of ideas, but always be certain that a wider one is still possible." Draw a circle, write some ideas in it and then draw a larger circle around it and see if you can write some more ideas about the first ideas.

Word Pool: under, make a circle, hands , sit, still, garage, beside, sleek, watch the woods, about the weather, returning to where, reaches, glove compartment, name, return, corner.

Dose of Mirth

Sticks and stones may break my bones, but words will make me go in a corner and cry by myself for hours. ~Eric Idle

Journal Juju

You are Sir or Madam [your name] the Not-so-Brave. Talk about your day. Write a journal entry from that point of view.

You are Sir or Madam [your name] the Not-So-Ordinary. Write or talk about the errands you run. What does your to-do list look like?

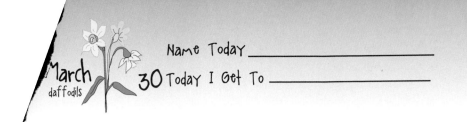

Name Today _____

March
daffodils

30 Today I Get To _____

aily Soul Vitamin

I tell you, the more I think, the more I feel that there is nothing more truly artistic than to love people. ~Vincent van Gogh

Toast of the Day
Here's to losing track of time
While doing something creative.

Awe-servances

Happy Birthday to:
Vincent van Gogh, 1853, artist.
John Fowles, 1926, novelist, whose first novel was *The Collector*.

Aha-phrodisiacs

Find a Van Gogh painting on the Internet or in a book: write a poem from it to the world.

John Fowles wrote, "Time is not a road - it is a room." Step into a room of time and describe what it looks like, what color it is and what you see out the window.

Write about having an unusual collection.

Dose of Mirth

Time's fun when you're having flies.
~Kermit the Frog

Journal Juju

Write your life's associations to the word "collection." Did you ever collect anything? Do you still have that collection? Can you collect your thoughts?

Van Gogh said, "Conscience is a man's compass." Make a collage of a compass conscience with a metaphorical north, south, east, and west or forth, back, ease, and stress.

Starry Starry Still Life

Daily Soul Vitamin

What we call the secret of happiness is no more a secret than our willingness to choose life. ~Leo Buscaglia

Toast of the Day
HERE'S TO THE FEEL OF CLEAN SHEETS.

Happy Birthday to:

René Descartes, 1596, mathematician, scientist, and writer. Dubbed the "Founder of Modern Philosophy", and the "Father of Modern Mathematics," he wrote, "I think, therefore I am."

Octavio Paz Lozano, 1914, Nobel Prize-winning writer, poet, and diploma. He's known for an essay *The Labyrinth of Solitude*.

Leo Buscaglia, 1924, author and professor.

Aha-phodisiacs

In honor of Octavio Paz Lozanao, narrate yourself in first or third person, seriously or with humor, walking through a labyrinth of solitude. Paint or collage the doorway to a garden of solitude.

Large Dose of Mirth

I think, therefore I am. I think. ~ George Carlin

I am because my little dog knows me. ~ Gertrude Stein

I think, therefore Descartes exists. ~ Saul Steinberg

I can therefore I am. ~ Simone Weil

I think, therefore I am single. ~ Liz Winston

Journal Juju

Octavio Paz said, "We have to sleep with open eyes, we must dream with our hands." Write about what your hands may dream of. Begin: "My hands dream of …"

AWe-vanced iNNer Messages
What are you SAYING to yourself? Aim high.

Man often becomes what he believes himself to be. ~Mahatma Gandhi

A.I.M. Advanced Inner Messages (AIM) makes belief possible. Take AIM. Many of us pick up the frequencies of ruthless voices: our own. They belittle us, exaggerate our fears, discourage our efforts, and mock the straw purse with the woven pink tulips that we thought was festive.

Imagine this: hearing a radio broadcast of encouraging messages interrupting your regularly scheduled self-berating on a regular basis. We all have doubts and fears. AIM tunes into encouraging voices that cultivate courage and perseverance—those of us who replace critical inner voices with supportive ones rise to the top in any sphere of existence we choose. This potion, when taken regularly, broadcasts the voices that serve us. As we grow older, what we tell ourselves becomes crucial to our contentment and longevity. *The Awe-manac* will help you receive the signals that that best serve your listening audience: you. Imbibe in a regular regimen of Daily Soul Vitamins and trust that Subliminal messages will keep you programmed for higher living.

Take AIM as directed.

Possible Effects: Confidence, courage, action, self-esteem, contentment, creativity, other people wanting to be like you.

Consult your doctor if self-confidence is sustained longer than four hours because doctors need to see that others can do it too. Side effects may include unexpected success and finished projects. Drink in slowly. Do not operate a TV remote control while on AIM, you might waste a possibility. Caution: Do not tailgate or swerve left before turning right, (just pet peeves of mine).

WELCOME APRIL

April is from the Latin word *aperire*, "to open (bud)." Hence, you may randomly open *The Awe-manac* to any page and see what message speaks to you. Let your imagination conspire with your intuition; ask a question and open the book to see what answer you can pick from the bouquet of possibilities. If it doesn't SEEM to make sense, use your warrior spirit from last month and MAKE IT MAKE SENSE.

Selected Celebrations at April's Door:

Dog Days (*Awe-manac* invented), Poetry Month, Garden Month, Frog Month, Guitar Month, Humor Month, Keep America Beautiful Month, Mathematics Education Month. Weekly Observances: Egg Salad Week (Third Week), TV-Turnoff Week (Third Week). April starts in the sign of Aries and ends in the sign of Taurus.

One of the most satisfying parts of the creative process is breaking rules. Break some yourself. (Offer limited and not applicable where morals and safety are concerned.) Like instead of August being the Dog Days, *The Awe-manac* is making April Dog Days. April can open awe in a deeper way with dog-thinking. The following is an excerpt from a funny email that got forwarded without the author's name. If you are the author, let me know and credit you shall have. Let us ponder the diary of a dog:

> EXCERPTS FROM A DOG'S DAILY DIARY:
> 8:00 am   Dog food! My favorite thing!
> 9:30 am   A car ride! My favorite thing!
> 9:40 am   A walk in the park! My favorite thing!
> 10:30 am   Got rubbed and petted! My favorite thing!
> 12:00 pm   Lunch! My favorite thing!
> 1:00 pm   Played in the yard! My favorite thing!
> 3:00 pm   Wagged my tail! My favorite thing!
> 5:00 pm   Milk bones! My favorite thing!
> 7:00 pm   Got to play ball! My favorite thing!
> 8:00 pm   Wow! Watched TV with the people! My favorite thing!
> 11:00 pm   Sleeping on the bed! My favorite thing!
> ~Anonymous

AWe-Manac Invented Events:

April 7: Eat Cornflakes and Do No Housework Day
April 16: Day to Exalt Good Habits
April 29: Special *Awe-manac* Event: Confidence Day

Suggested Ways to Celebrate

On my walk this morning I thought, "THIS is my favorite temperature." And it dawned on me that I was in dog consciousness. And this was good. It was about 63 degrees. On other days 74 degrees is my favorite temperature; when I'm hiking I like 55 degrees, some days when I'm sitting outside staring blankly at the mimosa tree, I like 81 degrees and when I'm wearing my fuzzy boots, in Taos, I even like 33 degrees. They are ALL my favorite temperatures. Why limit myself to one? Why limit ourselves at all in the realm of awe and appreciation?

Now it's your turn to explore the fluid nature of your mind's ability to grasp dog consciousness. Whatever is happening in the moment, let it be your FAVORITE THING. For example: "I'm reading *The Awe-manac*, MY FAVORITE THING." "I'm working in the garden, MY FAVORITE THING." "Being at work — MY FAVORITE THING! "I'm getting over a lost love, MY FAVORITE THING." (Just act "as if" on that one if it's a stretch). "Leaving work, MY FAVOR . . . " you get the picture. Feel it in your body, your spirit, and your wagging tail. How's that feel? Dog-thinking is liberating, it's an enlightened philosophy, and it does what many people think is more complicated than it needs to be: it helps us love our life, whatever it is, in the moment.

The more you practice dog consciousness, the more it will un-kennel the pit-bull of your preferential belief system and make contentment your best friend. You might say it's dog-magic instead of dogmatic. (Ruff). And I'm a cat person!

If it's hard for you to make whatever you're doing in the moment YOUR FAVORITE THING, do one or more of four things: 1) imagine what it might be like to be able to be in dog consciousness. Imagining is a good first step when "doing" seems hard, 2) Let just 5 percent of dog consciousness infiltrate your discontent dogma, little steps are often easier than big leaps, 3) You have permission to stop doing what you're doing that you're not enjoying, for dog's sake!

Humor, Poetry, and Math Ed Month

Write a funny poem about algebra, multiplication or subtraction. Or division. Literally or figuratively (multiplying ants, dividing sunlight, subtracting an albatross.)

121

Astrological Action Spells:

Aries: Invent hand gestures that represent these words: humble, fiery, secretive or scattered.

Taurus: Take four special walks (one a week) two times slower than usual and see what you notice.

Gemini: Do something creative during TV commercials; if you have TIVO, let a few through but mute them while you do your creative thing.

Cancer: Quit thinking money will bring you happiness; laughter works better.

Leo: Get someone's attention and inspire or encourage them.

Virgo: Write a poem about skepticism but be sure it's not perfect.

Libra: Go to an art gallery or surf the net and look for a painting that has a message for you.

Scorpio: Find something you've written in the past and revise it by cutting out a bunch of words.

Sagittarius: Blow out through your mouth in a way that makes your lips flutter and make a lawnmower sound (preferably in a crowd).

Capricorn: Design your own flower arrangement either with real flowers or with collage pieces.

Aquarius: Write a song about rebellion even if you know nothing about song writing.

Pisces: Write a journal entry using the title "Get Real." Write for 7 minutes.

Tides:

Ebbing: What will you let go?

Flowing: What will you increase (just a little)?

Vessel of strength:

Because these wings are no longer wings to fly

I think that I shall never see....

Grapefruit moon, one star shining...

When they say "Don't I know you?" say no.

the call I made from a corner phone

GARDEN OF POETS

Gardening Information:

Flower: Sweetpea

Monthly Awe-manac Crop: Poets

Planting Tips: Plant seeds soaked in lyricism, angst, and a highly sensitive nature for 30 years. Plant uncritically, and rhythmically harvest with an open mic (limit to 3 minutes).

April 1
Name today

Daily Soul Vitamin
The key question isn't "What fosters creativity?" But why do people not create or innovate? We have got to abandon that sense of amazement in the face of creativity, as if it were a miracle if anybody created anything. ~Abraham Maslow

Toast of the Day
Here's to the nose and the breath of life it gives us
when it's not stuffed up.

Awe-Servances
Happy Birthday to:
Edmond Rostand, 1868, best known as the author of the play *Cyrano de Bergerac*.
Abraham Maslow, 1908, psychologist, noted for his hierarchy of human needs.
Milan Kundera, 1929, wrote a novel, *The Book of Laughter and Forgetting* and *The Unbearable Lightness of Being*.

April Fools' Day started in France in 1582.

Aha-phrodisiacs, My Favorite Thing!
Word Pool: foolish, plate, New York, I confess, plan, the right place, flying, restless, east, lesson, seen, though it seemed, sullen, merciless, describe the nights, alone, turn, ocean, each time , into the dark, last moment , bright, the city, beneath, empty, neck, climb, giddy, how could I see, I'm out here, fling yourself, drop, spirit, nose.

Journal Juju
Play an April fool's joke trick on your inner critic. Make something today that defies seriousness and breaks the rules behind your inner critic's back. Title a journal entry: *The Lightness of My Being* or write, collage or paint about it.

Dose of Mirth
I am thankful for laughter, except when milk comes out of my nose. ~Woody Allen

Today I get to:

Daily Soul Vitamin
Your only obligation in any lifetime is to be true to yourself. ~Richard Bach

Toast of the Day
Here's to the majesty of statues, the enthusiasm of fountains, and the reliability of the sky.

Awe-servances

Happy Birthday to:

Hans Christian Andersen, 1805, fairy tale author.

Frederic Auguste Bartholdi, 1834, sculptor who created the Statue of Liberty.

Aha-phrodisiacs
Hans Christian Andersen's fairy tales are full of humorous details that seem unnecessary to the story. "The Ugly Duckling" begins, "It was so lovely out in the country—it was summer! And the wheat was yellow, the oats were green, hay was stacked up in the green meadows, and the stork walked about on his long, red legs and spoke Egyptian, for he had learned the language from his mother." Write about a story, memory, anecdote, or event in your life but like Andersen add humorous details that seem unnecessary.

Journal Juju
If you were commissioned to build a statue, what would it represent, what would you call it, and who would you give it to? Starter Fluid: My thoughts sculpt my reality . . .

Dose of Mirth
The Statue of Liberty is no longer saying, "Give me your poor, your tired, your huddled masses." She's got a baseball bat and yelling, "You want a piece of me?" ~Robin Williams

 ## Subliminal question from FOOOF
What's one small way I can make today more fun?

Today I get to:

April 3

Name today _____

Daily Soul Vitamin

Great minds have purposes; little minds have wishes. Little minds are subdued by misfortunes; great minds rise above them. ~Washington Irving

Toast of the Day

Here's to wholesome, funny movies from the '40's and '50's.

Awe-Servances

Happy Birthday to:

Doris Day, 1924, singer, actress, and animal welfare advocate.

Washington Irving, 1783, author and historian, best known for his short stories "The Legend of Sleepy Hollow" and "Rip van Winkle."

Aha-phrodisiacs

Washington Irving said, "He is the true enchanter, whose spell operates not upon the senses, but upon the imagination and the heart." Write or create art as if you were under a spell of the imagination and heart. Write about your latest obsession, your future obsession, your favorite room in the house. What would a collage titled *Imagination of the Heart* look like?

Dose of Mirth

The tongue is the only tool that gets sharper with use. ~Washington Irving

Journal Juju

Doris Day sang a song called "Bewitched, Bothered, and Bewildered." Think of three words that start with the same letter as a title for either writing (poetry, an entry in your journal, prose, or stream of consciousness) or art (a collage, a drawing, a painting, or a doodle). For instance, Lost, Loud, and Lascivious: that would make interesting writing or collage (you can use it if you like).

Watchful, Worried, and Weird would make a great journal entry. I think I'll go do that now.

Note to Myself: Whatever will be, will be. _____

Today I get to: _____

Daily Soul Vitamin
You can't use up creativity. The more you use, the more you have. ~Maya Angelou

Awe-servances
Happy Birthday to:
Maya Angelou, 1928, poet, memoirist, actress, and Civil Rights Movement activist.

Tell-A-Lie Day (*Awe-manac* endorsed for fiction purposes only).

Aha-phrodisiacs
Take a not-so-comfortable reality and totally transform it with a beautiful fantasy. Write the before and after. You can do this abstractly with art or in doodling too.

Dose of Mirth
Whoever said nothing is impossible, never tried slamming a revolving door.
~Unknown

Journal Juju
Maya Angelou said, "I believe that every person is born with talent." Write that sentence down and keep going with it in your own direction either with repeating "I believe" with different completions each time or staying on the subject of being born with talent.

Note to Myself
Think outside of the door frame: Write a poem about slamming a revolving door.

Today I get to: Believe
_____

_____

April 5

Name today _____

Daily Soul Vitamin

Faith gives you an inner strength and a sense of balance and perspective in life.
~Gregory Peck

Toast of the Day

Here's to having faith in your intuition and creativity.

Awe-servances

Happy Birthday to:
Bette Davis, 1908, Oscar-winning actress.
Gregory Peck, 1916, Oscar-winning film actor.

It's also National Fun at Work Day—take a playful attitude to work.

Aha-phrodisiacs

Write a list of at least 10 ways you can make your job or your workplace more fun. Draw a doodle of you having fun at work; embellish with your imagination. Draw doodles of imaginative spices that you would keep in your work survival kit.

Journal Juju

Write about what gives you strength, balance, and perspective.

Bette Davis said, "Without wonder and insight, acting is just a trade. With it, it becomes creation." What in your life becomes a creation with wonder and insight?

Dose of Mirth

If it's not fun, you're not doing it right. ~Bob Basso

And now a message made possible by a grant from Anti-aging Potions AIM and FOOOF

Think and feel this: Having fun is often possible. Ask this: What would make this moment more fun?

Today I get to: _____

April 6
Name today

Daily Soul Vitamin
It took me four years to paint like Raphael, but a lifetime to paint like a child. ~Pablo Picasso

Toast of the Day
Here's to an occasional break accompanied by fresh fruit and roasted almonds.

Awe-servances
Happy Birthday to:
Raphael Sanzio (Raffaello), 1483, Italian master painter and architect.
John Waterhouse, 1849, painter.
Merle Haggard, 1937, country songwriter and singer.

It's also Jump Over Things Day.

Aha-phrodisiacs
Search online to find Raphael's painting *Sybils* and pick one of the characters and write from his or her point of view.

Also find Waterhouse's *Ophelia* online. Write a poem or narrative from her point of view or write what happens next in this scene.

Merle Haggard Title Wave for writing, collage, or painting: I'm Looking for My Mind, Swinging Doors, Somewhere Between, Silver Wings, Holding Things Together, In My Next Life.

Dose of Mirth
If opportunity doesn't knock, build a door ~Milton Berle

Journal Juju
Write a poem about jumping over things metaphorically or literally. Doodle yourself jumping over various obstacles in your life. Draw something in your journal that looks like a child drew it.

Note to Myself: Stretch before jumping over things.

April 7
Name today

No Housework Soul Vitamins

Our house is clean enough to be healthy, and dirty enough to be happy. ~Author Unknown

Housework, if it is done right, can kill you. ~John Skow

My idea of housework is to sweep the room with a glance. ~Author Unknown

It's all in the attitude—housework is exercise. Slim your way to a clean home! ~Linda Solegato

On the other hand:

The best time for planning a book is while you're doing the dishes. ~Agatha Christie

Awe-servances

Happy Birthday to:
W.K. Kellogg, 1860, the cornflake man

No Housework Day —No trash. No dishes.
    No making of beds or washing laundry.

Aha-phrodisiacs

Pick a point of view: a kid, an eccentric person, someone who exaggerates, a character from your favorite TV show, a character from your book, and write about finding a prize in a cereal box and what you do with it. Have fun, and since it's No Housework Day, you don't have to keep it clean. Or break the rules and do some housework while thinking of creative ideas.

Journal Juju

Write an ode, poem, rant, or haiku about housework.

Dose of Mirth

My second favorite household chore is ironing. My first being hitting my head on the top bunk bed until I faint. ~Erma Bombeck

ApriL 8
Name today

Daily Soul Vitamin
If we could see the miracle of a single flower clearly, our whole life would change. ~Buddha

Toast of the Day
Here's to toasting small delights.

Awe-servances
Happy Birthday to:

Siddhartha Gautama, a spiritual teacher from Nepal and
the historical founder of Buddhism. He is universally
recognized by Buddhists as the Supreme Buddha of
our age.

Aha-phrodisiac
Buddha said, "Little by little a person becomes evil, as a water pot is
filled by drops of water. . . Little by little a person becomes good, as a water
pot is filled by drops of water." Make a collage of a water pot that is being filled
by good (however you interpret that). Make a photo essay of one flower—
capture its miracle.

Dose of Mirth
When all else fails, there's always a delusion. ~Conan O'Brien

Journal Juju
Buddha is noted as saying, "All that we are is the result of what we have thought.
The mind is everything. What we think, we become." Write a list of thoughts

you would like to think regularly so that they awaken your
higher self. Make a list of thoughts you think regularly that
might not be optimal for your higher purpose (this increases
awareness and activates subconscious interventions).

Tear them up and throw them away.

Daily Soul Vitamins

If I had my life to live over again, I'd be a plumber ~Albert Einstein

If I had my life to live over again, I'd dare to make more mistakes the next time. ~Nadine Stair

I've failed over and over and over again in my life, and that is why I succeed. ~Michael Jordan

Awe-Servances

Happy Birthday to:

W.C. Fields, 1880, comedian and actor.

It's also Name Yourself Day and All Over Again Day.

Aha-phrodisiacs

List a supply of survival tools you would like to keep handy. Include intangible things like courage, quick wit, and perspective, as well as tangible things like stimulants, binoculars, and flashlights. Do not limit the number of things—just have fun with it.

Dose of Mirth

I always keep a supply of stimulant handy in case I see a snake, which I also keep handy. ~W.C. Fields

Journal Juju

Let associations, stories, or emotions spring forth from this journal entry title: All Over Again. Starter Fluid: "If I listen closely in the garden, I can hear my creativity saying . . ."

A Message to You from the A.I.M. Potion

What little 1 to 5 minute step can you take today toward building a creative commitment or habit? The habit can be to practice feeling and thinking differently in a way that better serves you too. What would 15 percent more creative confidence feel like? What would it make you think? What small thing can you do to believe in yourself? Imagine for 20 seconds, really believing you can surpass your limitations.

Daily Soul Vitamin

This is our goal as writers, I think: to help others have this sense of wonder, of seeing things anew, things that catch us off-guard, that break in on our small bordered worlds. When this happens everything feels more spacious. ~ Anne Lamott

Toast of the Day

Here's to things that catch us off-guard, like a delicious breeze through and open window with a wind chimes accompaniment.

Awe—Servances

Happy Birthday to:

William Hazlitt, 1778, writer remembered for his humanistic
   essays and literary criticism.

Anne Lamott, 1954, author.

On this day in 1925, F. Scott Fitzgerald published *The Great Gatsby.*

Aha—phrodisiacs

Scott Fitzgerald said, "You don't write because you want to say something, you write because you have something to say." Write a list of topics that, like Fitzgerald said, are things you feel you have to say. Or just write.

Journal Juju

Anne Lamott said, "I do not at all understand the mystery of grace, only that it meets us where we are but does not leave us where it found us." Repeated completions: I do not understand at all . . . "

Multiple Choice Brought to You by Awe—wakened Moment

Consider doing one of these today:

a: Notice and appreciate the feel of comfortable fabric.

b: Buy fresh flowers and meditate on them as if you've never seen
      flowers before.

c.   Sit in a different chair this week and notice how the view differs.

d.   Eat a piece of fruit and concentrate on the sensory experience of 5 times
      more than you normally would.

e.   All of the above.

April 11
Name today _____

Daily Soul Vitamin
A woman tries to comfort me. She puts her hand under my shirt and writes the names of flowers on my back. ~Mark Strand

Toast of the Day
Here's to poetic minds and the way they expand our world.

Each moment's a place you've never been

Awe-Servances
Happy Birthday to:
Mark Strand, 1934, poet, essayist, and translator.
Leo Rosten, 1908, humorist.

Aha-phrodisiacs
Mark Strand Word Pool: someone was saying, a room with two candles, about shadows, someone watching, began to believe, coffee cup notice, someone dancing, a wall, the night would not end, music was over, saying, stars, how small they were, nothing, ahead, dandelion

Dose of Mirth
One of the great disadvantages of hurry is that it takes such a long time.
~Gilbert K. Chesterton

Journal Juju
Mark Strand said, "Each moment is a place you've never been." Fill in the following sentence 10 times, 10 different ways, but if one of them takes you on a journey, go with it. "Each moment is a place. . ."

Leo Rostan said, "Happiness comes only when we push our brains and hearts to the farthest reaches of which we are capable." Make a list of places that could be defined to you as the farthest reaches of which you are capable.

A Message from Body Temple Potion
You can actually do yoga as you are reading this. As you breathe in, arch the small of your back away from your chair. As you breathe out, flatten it. Imagine that the breath and the movement are connected: the breath orchestrates the movement. Make it an Awe-wakened Moment by noticing what feels good about this yogic practice.

April 12
Name today

Jazz Vitamins
You would not exist if you did not have something to bring to the table of life.
~Herbie Hancock
   The secret is keeping busy, and loving what you do. ~Lionel Hampton

Toast of the Day
Here's to a flowering desert hiking trail in the early morning sun.

Awe-servances
Happy Birthday to:
Lionel Hampton, 1908, jazz percussionist and bandleader.
Herbie Hancock, 1940, award-winning jazz pianist
   and composer.
David Letterman, 1947, award-winning TV personality,
   late-night talk-show host, television producer,
   philanthropist, and Indy racecar owner.

Aha-phrodisiacs
Put on some jazz music and scribble to it with crayons.
Title your scribbles, and use the tiles as Starter Fluid for
poetry. Write to jazz music. Close your eyes and imagine
what film images might be accompanied by jazz music.

Dose of Mirth
*There's no business like show business, but there are
several businesses like accounting.* ~David Letterman

Jazz Bouquet

Journal Juju
Talk about what you would like to put on "the table of life." Collage your table
of life. Write a Table Fable.

Note to Myself: Saying "table" a bunch of times makes
                     the word sound funny and amusing.

Today I get to: _____

April 13
Name today

Daily Soul Vitamin
I pause to record that I feel in extraordinary form.
Delirium perhaps. ~Samuel Beckett,
     from *Malone Dies*

delirum perhaps

Toast of the Day
Here's to the power of taking responsibility.

Awe-Servances
Happy Birthday to:
Samuel Beckett, 1906, dramatist, novelist, and poet
Eudora Welty, 1909, award-winning author and photographer.

On this day in 1796, the first elephant arrived in the US from Bengal, India.
It's also Blame Somebody Else Day.

Aha-phrodisiac
Use this line from Eudora Welty's book *One Writer's Beginning* for Starter Fluid:
"I had the window seat."
     In rebellion of Blame Somebody Else Day, write down something for which
you would like to take responsibility. Delirium perhaps.

Journal Juju
Eudora Welty said, "Never think you've seen the last of anything." Write something you thought you saw the last of in your life, fiction or for real.

Question from Fooof
How can I make the project I'm currently working on more fun! Delirium?
There's a Zen saying: It's okay to wake up laughing. How can I remember to
laugh when I wake up?

Today I get to:

Daily Soul Vitamin

"Keep on beginning and failing. Each time you fail, start all over again, and you will grow stronger until you have accomplished a purpose—not the one you began with perhaps, but one you'll be glad to remember." ~Anne Sullivan

Awe-servances

Happy Birthday to:

Anne Sullivan, 1866, teacher best known as the tutor of Helen Keller.

On this date in 1828, Noah Webster published his American Dictionary of the English Language.

Toast of the Day

Here's to the possibility of combining words.

Aha-phrodisiacs

Steve Martin said, "Talking about music is like dancing about architecture." Dance a cityscape, a museum of art, your house or your backyard. Listen to a painting and then write.

Take a dictionary and pick 10 words arbitrarily. Use them in the order you picked them and add more as you go along to make poetry, prose, or a run-on sentence.

Make up a few words, give them definitions, and doodle pictures of them.

Dose of Mirth

I like a woman with a head on her shoulders. I hate necks. ~Steve Martin

Journal Juju

Keep the dictionary out and open it several times, picking out words you can associate with something to write in your dictionary.

And now a word from Mental Solution

Dictionary—keep it in the bathroom and learn new words on a "regular" basis.

Today I get to:
Daily Soul Vitamin

One can have no smaller or greater mastery than mastery of oneself.
~Leonardo da Vinci

Awe-servances
Happy Birthday to:

Leonardo da Vinci, 1452, inventor, artist, genius—a brilliant man who had a hard time finishing things. Even the pictures of parachutes he doodled in the margin of his notes turned out to be technically perfect designs. It is speculated that he may have used himself as the model when painting the *Mona Lisa.*

Henry James, 1843, author and literary critic.

It's also Rubber Eraser Day

Aha-phrodisiacs
Henry James said, "I hold any writer sufficiently justified who is himself in love with his theme." Write about your themes in art, painting, or life as if you were in love with them.

Dose of Mirth
The Mona Lisa was brought up in court on charges of murder, but it turned out that she'd been framed. ~Unknown

Journal juju
Relating to da Vinci's quote at the top of the page, list and write for at least 5 minutes about one or more ways you have mastered yourself, your life, or your hall closet.

Today I get to:

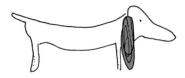

April 16
Name today

A Large Dose of Soul Vitamins for Good Habit Fortification
We are what we repeatedly do. Excellence, then, is not an act, but a habit. ~Aristotle
   Good habits, once established, are just as hard to break as are
bad habits. ~Robert Puller
   Motivation is what gets you started. Habit is what keeps you going. ~Jim Rohn
   Habit is either the best of servants or the worst of masters. ~Nathaniel Emmons

Toast of the Day
Here's to making a habit out of something that honors our higher self: like
meditation, exercise, creative time, loving the moment service.

Awe—servances
Happy Birthday to:
Aristotle, 384 BC, Greek philosopher who had good habits.
Charlie Chaplin, 1889, filmmaker, who wrote, directed, and starred in his movies.
   His habit was to do scenes over and over again until he was satisfied.

Aha—phrodisiacs

Charlie Chaplin said, "Why should poetry have to make sense?" Write a
poem about habits that don't make sense, play in poetic nonsense with
any pain you have in your life in poetic nonsense, or make a habit out
of setting the timer for 5 minutes everyday and during that time writing a short poem or making up a famous quote. (Commit to it).

Dose of Mirth
To truly laugh, you must be able to take your pain, and play with it! ~Charlie Chaplin

Journal Juju
The easiest way to make something a habit is to start out by breaking it down to
just a few minutes a day. Write in your journal while you are waiting for the
coffee to brew, for your computer to come on, during commercials, when one
song which makes writing easy for you plays on a CD.each time or staying on
the subject of being born with talent.

Today I get to:

April 17
Name today

Daily Soul Vitamin
One of the symptoms of an approaching nervous breakdown is the belief that one's work is terribly important. ~Bertrand Russell

Toast of the Day
Here's to lying on the floor and feeling the stress of the body melt into the earth.

Awe-servances
Happy Birthday to:
Thornton Wilder, 1897, playwright and novelist.
   Our Town is one of his most famous plays.

National Stress Awareness Day.

Aha-phrodisiacs, My Favorite Thing!
To honor Thornton, write about your town. Starter Fluid: When no one is looking, our town . . . ; Our town is the most beautiful when . . . ; There is a secret passage way through a manhole cover in our town that leads to . . .

Journal Juju
What if your stress was a character? What kind of voice would it have? What would it look like? What personality characteristics other than stressed would it have?
   What color, sound, type of music, texture, and movement is your stress?
   Do some stress release by making a collage or painting of your stress, then a
      second piece of work showing that stress relieved. Write about what the
      energy that powers your stress could power instead.

Dose of Mirth
The test of an adventure is that when you're in the middle of it, you say to yourself, "Oh, now I've got myself into an awful mess; I wish I were sitting quietly at home." ~Thornton Wilder

Today I get to: _____

Daily Soul Vitamin

If life gives you lemons, make some kind of fruity juice.
~Conan O'Brien

Toast of the day

Here's to the how the body feels after finishing
a long workout.

Believe in the Spin Cycle

Awe-servances

Happy Birthday to:

Conan O'Brien, 1963, award-winning television personality.

In 1934, the first laundromat opened in Fort Worth, Texas

Aha-phrodisiacs

Starter Fluid: "While leaning against the spin cycle at Your Suds Mat, Charlotte
was thinking . . . "

Be a Laundromat Philosopher ~Interpret that however you like.

Word Pool: spin cycle, soft, bulletin board, not sure, window, doubt, rumble,
courage, sing, undone, lint, faraway, work-out, notable, green, search, believe,
blossom, conspire, messy, storefront, green, shadow.

Dose of Mirth

*Scientists announced that they have located the gene for alcoholism. Scientists say
they found it at a party, talking way too loudly. ~Conan O'Brien*

Journal Juju

Write some things about yourself in headline form. Examples: Woman with Messy,
Curly Hair Learns That Little Steps Lead to Conspiring Universes; Author Absent-
Mindedly Puts Car Keys in Refrigerator and is Delayed Several Minutes; Writer Pro-
crastinates Frequently by Cleaning Cat Hair out of Her Keyboard with a Paint Brush.

Question Brought to You by Kindness and Gather Potions

Plato said, "Good actions give strength to ourselves and inspire good actions
in others." What good actions can I engage in this week even for a few minutes
at a time?

Soul Vitamin

"Invent your world; surround yourself with people, color, sounds, and work that nourish you."
~SARK, *Living Juicy*

Awe-servances

Happy Birthday to:

Susan Ariel Rainbow Kennedy, better known as SARK, a speaker, artist, and author of inspirational, motivational self-help books characterized by lively and colorful drawings and watercolors.

Fernando Botero, 1932, neo-figurative Colombian artist who invented his own world of people.

Aha-phrodisiac

Invent a world by using this Word Pool taken from SARK book titles. Begin with "In this new world . . ."

Bodacious, inspiration, daring, succulent, wild life, companion, freedom, morsels, pie, naked mangoes, pleasure, eat, dancing, pits, garden, healing, living, magic, splendidly, finding, nap, succulence, everywhere ,sandwich, imperfect, dancing, creative, make, healing, spirit, real.

Find a Botero painting on the Internet or in a book and write a quick story or caption about it.

Dose of Mirth

Some of the world's greatest feats were accomplished by people not smart enough to know they were impossible. ~Doug Larson

Journal Juju

What people, color, sounds and work can you add more of to your present world?

April 20
Name today

Daily Soul Vitamin
Some men have thousands of reasons why they cannot do what they want to, when all they need is one reason why they can. ~Martha Graham

Toast of the Day
Here's to viewing artwork that speaks to your soul and transports you.

Awe-Servances
Happy Birthday to:

Joan Miro', 1893, Surrealist, painter, and sculptor. He combined abstract shapes with plants, animals and people.

Ian Watson, 1943, author, known for his trilogy: *The Book of the River*, *The Book of the Stars*, and *The Book of Being*

Taurus begins.

Aha-phrodisiac
Starter Fluid for writing or art: It's not easy being abstract . . . .

Find a Miro' painting. Study the colors, composition, and shapes and then pick a subject of your own and depict it using the same Miro' colors and shapes. Or doodle a bunch of geometric shapes and color them in.

Word pool: river, stars, being, trilogy, understand, red, detective, plod, shape, depict, boundary, element, ignore, combine, pick, fascination, recreating, snap, power, transport, act, being, vivid imagination

Dose of Mirth
Sometimes I wonder if men and women really suit each other. Perhaps they should live next door and just visit now and then. ~Katharine Hepburn, Actress and a Taurus

Journal Juju
Taurus is determined, efficient, stubborn, cautious, introverted, conservative, conventional, materialistic, security conscious, stable, industrious, dependable, and one generally having significant financial ability. Pick three or four of these qualities and report your status on them even if you are not born under the Taurus sun.

April 21
Name today

Daily Soul Vitamin
The clearest way into the Universe is through a forest wilderness. ~John Muir

Toast of the Day
Here's to the smell of and the sunlight streaming into a forest.

Awe-servations
Happy Birthday to
John Muir, 1838, one of the first modern preservationists.
Alistair MacLean, 1922, novelist.

1952—Administrative Professionals' Day was started.

Aha-phrodisiacs
Alistair MacLean wrote a book called *Breakheart Pass*. Write a poem, make a collage or paint a picture using that title.

    Do something creative for an Administrative professional—buy some fun pencils and pens that are included in a bouquet of wildflowers.

Journal Juju
John Muir wrote, "I only went out for a walk and finally concluded to stay out till sundown, for going out, I found, was really going in." Sit out in nature and write in your journal. Make note of how nature takes you inside yourself. Imagine that one part of the nature that you are writing within has a message for you. Look for it, listen for it. If you cannot find it, imagine what it might be. Write, doodle, or muse about it.

Dose of Mirth
You can fire your secretary, divorce your spouse, abandon your children. But they remain your co-authors forever. ~Ellen Goodman

Note of Awe
Alistair Maclean said, "I wrote each book in 35 days flat—just to get the darned thing finished." I'm just in awe.

Soul Vitamin
Making the simple complicated is commonplace; making the complicated simple, awesomely simple, that's creativity. ~Charles Mingus

Awe-servances
Happy Birthday to:

Immanuel Kant, 1724. He wrote hugely influential treatises and tried to define the limits of the human mind, and argued that we cannot know anything outside of the realms of mathematics and science.

Charles Mingus, jazz bassist, composer, bandleader, and occasional pianist.

Earth Day—first celebrated in 1970.

Aha-phrodisiacs
Make every day Earth Day. Recycle your scrap paper into art and your emotions into writing. Be kind to the earth, be kind to your body.

Treat the earth well. It was not given to you by your parents. It was loaned to you by your children. ~Kenyan Proverb.

Kant published a work called *Observations On the Feeling of the Beautiful and the Sublime*. Make your own entry into this work . . . just a paragraph or poem.

Dose of Mirth
The difference between perseverance and obstinacy is that one often comes from a strong will, and the other from a strong won't. ~Henry Ward Beecher

Journal Juju
Immanuel Kant said, "Act as if the maxim of your action were to become through your will a general natural law."

Write about "will." Repeated completions: I will . . ., but I won't . . . .

Today I get to: _____

April 23
Name today

Daily Soul Vitamin
It is neither good nor bad, but thinking makes it so. ~William Shakespeare

Awe-servances
Happy Birthday to:

William Shakespeare 1564, an English poet and playwright widely regarded as the greatest writer of the English language, and as the world's preeminent dramatist.

Shirley Temple, 1920, Oscar-winning former child actress, diplomat.

It's also Picnic Day, Book Day, Lover's Day, and Blue Day.

Aha-phrodisiacs
Take a blue blanket and a book on a picnic with a lover today. Bring cucumber and cream cheese sandwiches, blueberries, blue corn chips, some blues music, and a pillow. Blow bubbles and read to each other.

Dose of Mirth
I stopped believing in Santa Claus when I was six. Mother took me to see him in a department store and he asked for my autograph. ~Shirley Temple Black

Journal Juju
Write a poem using the word "picnic" to begin each line.

Anti-aging Application
Age cannot whither her, nor custom stale her infinite variety.
~Shakespeare

Uniqueness keeps us young. As we get older we can toss "custom" for creativity.

April 24
Name today

Daily Soul Vitamin

We all need to look into the dark side of our nature—
that's where the energy is, the passion. People are afraid of
that because it holds pieces of us we're busy denying.
~Sue Grafton

Toast of the Day

Here's to compassionately accepting little bits of ourselves
that we have been denying.

Awe—Servances

Happy Birthday to:
Robert Bailey Thomas, 1766, founder of *The Farmers Almanac*.
Shirley MacLaine, 1934 actress, author.
Barbra Streisand, 1942, singer, actress, icon.
Sue Grafton, 1940, novelist.

Aha—phrodisiacs

Robert Bailey Thomas, founder of *The Farmers Almanac* was born in 1766. I know,
we already said that, but *The Farmer's Almanac* inspired *The Awe-manac* so we are
repeating because we awe-preciate it.

    What would you do about the weather if you could do something?

Dose of Mirth

On this day in 1897 American newspaper editor Charles Dudley Warner said,
'Everybody talks about the weather, but nobody does anything about it.'

Journal Juju

Barbra Streisand said, "You have got to discover you, what you do, and trust it."
Shirley MacLaine said, "I think of life itself now as a wonderful play that I've written for myself, and so my purpose is to have the utmost fun playing my part."

    So discover you, write a part in the play of your life and have fun. What
would the write-up in the program say about your play? Talk about
how you got discovered, the synopsis of the play, and don't forget
the part about fun. Make it up if you have to.

April 25
Name today

Soul Vitamin
Just don't give up on trying to do what you really want to do. Where there is love and inspiration, I don't think you can go wrong. ~Ella Fitzgerald

Awe-Servances
Happy Birthday to:
Ella Fitzgerald, 1918, the First Lady of Song, is considered one of
the most influential jazz vocalists of the 20th Century. She
loved to sing and dance as a child; and when she was 16,
she entered a dance contest but once she got on stage
she lost her nerve. So instead of dancing, she sang.
Flannery O'Connor, 1925, author.

In 1684, a patent was granted for the thimble.

Aha-phrodisiac
Flannery O'Connor said, "The writer should never be
ashamed of staring. There is nothing that does not require his attention." Write
about staring.

Jazz Bouquet too

    In honor of the thimble, write some verse or poetry that uses a lot of words
that start with "th". (e.g. Three thieves named Theodore were thoughtlessly
thunking down Thistle Drive) You can make up words like "thunking" too.

Dose of Mirth
There's many a bestseller that could have been prevented by a good teacher.
~Flannery O'Connor

Journal Juju
*In honor of Ella Fitzgerald who sang "April in Paris," here's an April quote: "Spring has
a way of erasing doubt. Violets, come April, no longer worry that their careers may be
over. The grass and the spinster alike toss aside their armor of frost."* ~Tom Robbins
    What doubts would you like to have erased? What would you write in their
place once they ARE erased?

Soul Vitamin

Take full account of the excellencies which you possess, and in gratitude remember how you would hanker after them, if you had them not. ~Marcus Aurelius

Toast of the Day

Here's to the amazing tricks that technology enables us to do.

Awe-servances

Happy Birthday to:

Marcus Aurelius, A.D. 121, Roman emperor.

Carol Burnett, 1933, actress and comedienne.

Charles Richter, 1900. The Richter Scale, which
    measures earthquake magnitude, is named for him.

Aha-phrodisiacs

Marcus Aurelius said, "Be content with what you are, and wish not change; nor dread your last day, nor long for it." Writing a list of things about your self with which in this moment you are content fuels creative confidence.

Journal Juju

Carol Burnett said, "When you have a dream, you've got to grab it and never let go." Write about a dream that can talk back to you. What does it whisper to you? What does it shout to you? What does it want you to do? What does it do when you grab at it? What does it murmur when it doesn't think anyone is listening? Make a list of all the creative endeavors you would like to embark upon. Then rate them on your Richter scale of eager-energy from 1 to 10. One being the littlest amount of energy you feel for the idea and 10 for exuberant energy.

Dose of Mirth

How many people thought of the Post-It note before it was invented but just didn't have anything to jot it down on? –Unknown

Note to self

I'm going to be 5 percent more content with who I am today and add 5 percent a month.

Daily Soul Vitamin

First, I do not sit down at my desk to put into verse something that is already clear in my mind. If it were clear in my mind, I should have no incentive or need to write about it. We do not write in order to be understood; we write in order to understand. ~Cecil Day-Lewis

Toast of the Day

Here's to the mystery of dreams.

Awe-Servances

Happy Birthday to:

Cecil Day-Lewis, 1904, an Irish poet, the British Poet Laureate from 1967 to 1972, and, under the pseudonym of Nicholas Blake, a mystery writer.

National Hairball Awareness Day—a day to recognize hairballs in cats.

National Dream Hotline—Faculty and staff of the College and School of Metaphysics Centers throughout the Midwest offer 30 years of research into the significance and meaning of dreams by manning the phones from Friday to Sunday.

Tell a Story Day

In 1984, over 70 inches of snow fell in Red Lake, Montana

Aha-phrodisiac

Write what a National Dream Hotline conversation might sound like. If you could order a dream on a hotline, how would that work? Collage a telephone that is a dream hotline.

> Starter Fluid: "Over 70 of inches of snow fell that day . . . "
> Write a dialog between a dust bunny and a hairball.

Journal Juju

Like Cecil Day-Lewis, write about something that is not clear in your mind. Write what you think about it, sense about it, and know about it. Have it write to you. Write about it without stopping. Write about it as if you were explaining it to someone else.

> Write your dreams down.. write snippets of what you can remember about people, objects, and how you feel about your dreams.

Daily Soul Vitamin

A poem begins with a lump in the throat. ~Robert Frost

Toast of the Day

Here's to a poem recited or read so well it reaches the soul.

Awe–servances

Happy Birthday to:

Jay Leno, 1950, comedian, current host of *The Tonight Show*.

It's also National Sense of Smell Day and Great Poetry Reading Day.

1985, the world's largest sand castle was completed near St. Petersburg, Fl. It was
4 stories high and contained hidden treasure for kids who, with permission,
came in and demolished it one week later.

Aha–phrodisiacs

Start a story, poem or performance art piece with some smell (cookies baking, a
sweaty locker room, gas leaking).

Treat yourself to a favorite smell. *The Awe-manac* staff loves rose-pome-
granate and cloves. Smells can transport. Make a list of your favorite smells. Buy
yourself an essential oil. Cedar is nice. Write about smell memories.

Dose of Mirth

*Scientists are complaining that the new Dinosaur movie shows dinosaurs with lemurs,
who didn't evolve for another million years. They're afraid the movie will give kids a
mistaken impression. What about the fact that the dinosaurs are singing and dancing?*
~Jay Leno

Journal Juju

Read something you have written out loud and see if
there is new clarity when you do that.

April 29
Name today

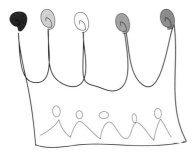

Special Awe-manac Event
Confidence Day
Today is an infusion of confidence-releasing soul vitamins, a mind wrap of inspiring spirit nutrients, and an oxygenating shot of belief. Believe it.

Creativity Tool
Confidence is vital to the creative process. We are attracted to those people who deeply believe in themselves sometimes even more than we are attracted to talent. People buy the belief they feel from one another—we are magnetized and inspired by that energy because our higher self knows it is key to reaching our higher purpose. Many talented people do not reach their potential because of lack of confidence, whereas many people who have less talent flourish because of their audacious beliefs.

Confidence Release Soul Vitamins, Mind Wraps and Belief Potions
Thousands of geniuses live and die undiscovered—either by themselves or by others.
    ~Mark Twain
Nothing splendid has ever been achieved except by those who dared believe that something inside of them was superior to circumstance. ~Bruce Barton
A great deal of talent is lost to the world for want of a little courage. Every day sends to their graves obscure men whose timidity prevented them from making a first effort. ~Sydney Smith
Aerodynamically the bumblebee shouldn't be able to fly, but the bumblebee doesn't know that so it goes on flying anyway. ~Mary Kay Ash
Without a humble but reasonable confidence in your own powers you cannot be successful or happy. ~Norman Vincent Peale
If the creator had a purpose in equipping us with a neck, he surely meant us to stick it out. ~Arthur Koestler

Daily Soul Vitamin

There is a muscular energy in sunlight corresponding to the spiritual energy of wind. ~Annie Dillard

Toast of the Day

Here's to getting a hairstyle you really like and here's to good hair days.

Awe-servances

Happy Birthday to:

Alice B. Toklas 1877, life partner of writer Gertrude Stein.

Annie Dillard, 1945, author, best known for her narrative nonfiction. She has
   also published poetry, essays, literary criticism, autobiography, and fiction.

It's also National Honesty Day and Hairstylist Appreciation Day

Aha-phrodisiacs

Allow yourself to write in non-stop stream of consciousness, writing thoughts before you understand what they mean. Read a work of a favorite author first to warm up your literary muscles but do not have any concern for writing well, just write.

   Gertrude Stein said, "To write is to write is to write is to write is to write is to write is to write is to write." Possible subjects: start with Kurt Vonnegut's quote , "To whom it may concern: It is springtime. It is late afternoon."; write about honesty, hairstylists, hair history, lunching on the grass.

   Write a poem, limerick, or ode to your hairstylist.

Dose of Mirth

This has been a most wonderful evening. Gertrude has said things tonight it will take her 10 years to understand. ~Alice B. Toklas

Journal Juju

What is one thing with which you could be more honest with yourself? What do you feel you have been honest with yourself about?

   If you could host a salon, who would you invite? Make up a cast of characters and give a sample of the conversation that might be exchanged.

In the right light, at the right time, everything is extraordinary.
~Aaron Rose

Awaken in the right light at the right time fairly frequently! Become aware of the wonder of common but extraordinary moments. Stop experiencing life in a numb, half conscious state distracted by thoughts of your retirement plan, what you said last fall to your relative, or why you ate dessert when you told yourself you wouldn't. Be present and win. Wake up!!!!!!

With a daily dose of these aware-ness-heightening ingredients and small delight time-release radar-makers, not only do you fully awaken to moments of delight, but over time you also feel more appreciative to them in a full body-mind-soul present way versus a "Oh yeah—that" kind of missing-the-point distracted sleep-state.

Awe-wakened Moment wipes out the build-up of indifference that leads to taking life's best moments for granted.

The moment one gives close attention to anything, even a blade of grass, it becomes a mysterious, awesome, indescribably magnificent world in itself.
~Henry Miller

If we could see the miracle of a single flower clearly, our whole life would change. ~Buddha

POSSIBLE EFFECTS: Elevates small delights to the place they deserve, as the ingredients of a fulfilling life. Helps us absorb and appreciate this reality and begin to notice that small wonders are EVERYWHERE.

Note: Do not consult your doctor if wild delight is sustained longer than four hours (keep it to yourself). Side effects may include elation (make sure you have supportive shoes), and open mouths (watch for bugs).

Entry Way to MAY

The most widely accepted explanation on how May got its name is that it was named for Maia, the Roman goddess of spring and growth. Her name seems to be related to a Latin word that means increase or growth. It's hard to resist breaking the rules . . . "Abbreviate" is *The Awe-manac* word for *decrease or simplify*, thus this is a shorter intro to May. May is the shortest name of all the months, so it makes sense to us, (that would be me, but not my editor).

Just Some of the Events at May's Doorway

Flower Month, American Bike Month, Mental Health Month, Correct Posture Month, National Asparagus Month, National Egg Month, National Photo Month, National Salad Month, Good Car-Keeping Month, National Physical Fitness & Sports Month, Older Americans Month, Better Sleep Month, National Barbeque Month, Date Your Mate Month, May Is Better Hearing Month, National Hamburger Month, National Strawberry Month, Personal History Awareness Month, Revise Your Work Schedule Month. Mother's Day is the second Sunday. May begins in the sign of Taurus and ends in the sign of Gemini.

Awe-Manac Invented Days

Month of Dance
May 8: The Awe-manac's Day of Socks
May 11: Day of Dance
May 24: Change Day
May 31: Walt Whitman Day

Hail, bounteous May, that doth inspire
Mirth, and youth, and warm desire;
Woods and groves are of thy dressing,
Hill and dale doth boast thy blessing.
~John Milton

Suggested Ways to Celebrate

In May you may want to be an earth goddess who bikes with flowers in your basket or you may want to listen to a strawberry. You may want to make up a dance called the Tossed Salad or you may simply want to meditate on your mental health and dance with wild abandon for physical fitness. If none of these things appeal to you, you may want to discover yourself this month (see Mark Twain quote below). Begin by writing a list of your favorite movies and TV shows and exploring their common themes . . . quirky, romantic, rebellious, intelligent, original, dramatic, satirical . . . these may be adjectives you want to take credit for, believe in, and fly with about 5 percent more this month.

Astrological Simplicity Spells

Aries: Make time to put some music on and simply dance in your living room

Taurus: Buy some Lilies of the Valley or just smell them while you think in simple poetry.

Gemini: Go to a restaurant and order something you wouldn't normally order just for simple adventure.

Cancer: Pamper yourself this month with a simple manicure or a facial.

Leo: Take a simply creative approach to making salads . . . add something different.

Virgo: Simply offer to take someone's car to a carwash for them.

Libra: Take a day to do some bike riding even if you have to rent one—watch for simple epiphanies.

Scorpio: Get rid of some clothing you don't wear, watch what simplicity replaces it.

Sagittarius: Write in your journal about where in your life you feel most simple right now.

Capricorn: Lie on the ground, look up to through the trees. Listen to your intuition.

Aquarius: Notice the blessing of simplicity.

Pisces: Go out into nature and look or listen for its message to you, then say simply, "thank you."

Thousands of geniuses live and die undiscovered—either by themselves or by others.
~Mark Twain

HEY, YOU CAN'T STOP ME

Tides:

Ebbing: What are you letting go of this month (just a little bit)?

Flowing: Where are you thriving this month (just a little bit more)?

Vessel of strength: What saying or quote will navigate you and keep you afloat through the month? (See Awe-wakened Inner Messages for ideas.)

Gardening Information:

FLOWER: The Hawthorn and the Lily of the Valley

MONTHLY AWE-MANAC CROP: Dancers (just three to keep it simple).

PLANTING TIPS: Fouettè jetè some seeds across a classical plot and pirouette them deep into the cultured mass with your toes pointed. Check daily, arabesque and bow adagio. Blooms leap when least expected.

May 1
Name today

Daily Soul Vitamin
Today is May Day, a day on which you should wash your face with morning dew to keep yourself looking young and beautiful. You should also gather wildflowers and green branches, make some floral garlands, and set up a Maypole to dance around. ~Garrison Keillor

Toast of the Day
Here's to creativity's ability to make an uncomfortable emotion useful.

Awe-Servances
Happy Birthday to:
Dante Alighieri, 1265, poet.
Judy Collins,1939, folk and standards singer and songwriter.

Mother Goose Day was founded on this day in 1987 by Gloria T. Delamar.

Aha-phrodisiacs
Dante said, "'A mighty flame followeth a tiny spark." What one small spark can you ignite this month through a small, small, small step toward your creativity? What one small thought can you practice to ignite your creative confidence?
    Make a nursery rhyme or song out of a Dante quote: "Follow your own star" or "Beauty awakens the soul to act."

Journal Juju
Judy Collins said, "When inspiration does not come, I go for a walk, go to the movie, talk to a friend, let go... The muse is bound to return again, especially if I turn my back!" Make a list of things you can do to nurture yourself if the muse is not readily available to you.

Dose of Mirth
Humpty Dumpty sat on a wall,
Humpty Dumpty had a great fall,
And his winter wasn't bad either. ~Unknown

Note to Myself
Let go of intense effort every now and then.Glide.

May 2

Name today _____

MAY IS AMERICAN
BIKE MONTH

Daily Soul Vitamin

Anxiety is the essential condition of intellectual and artistic creation.
~Charles Frankel

Toast of the Day

Here's to creativity's ability to make an uncomfortable emotion useful.

Awe-servances

Happy Birthday to:
Bing Crosby, 1903, singer and actor icon.

National Anxiety Disorders Screening Day.

Aha-phrodisiacs

Approach these Bing Crosby titles in writing or art with an anxious point of view and see if it lends any new insight in writing or art: "At Your Command," "I Surrender Dear," and "Wrap Your Troubles In Dreams."

Journal Juju

Make a list of anxieties you have about the creative process and at the end of the list, list any insights you have about those anxieties.

Title a work, *Anxiety Screening* and make a mixed media picture of anxious scribbles and put some screen material over it.

Dose of Mirth

If you have a bunch of odds and ends and get rid of all but one of them, what do you call it? ~Unknown

Today I get to: _____

May 3

Daily Soul Vitamin

Help us to be ever faithful gardeners of the spirit, who know that without darkness nothing comes to birth, and without light nothing flowers. ~May Sarton

Toast of the Day

Here's to the sense of sight and the sense of hearing and the world they permit us to see and hear.

Awe-servances

Happy Birthday to:

May Sarton, 1912, poet, novelist, and memoirist . She wrote about her daily habits like gardening, washing the dishes, taking care of pets, and looking at the ocean. She referred to her journals as "the sacramentalization of ordinary life." I think she made that word up but I like it.

Frankie Valli, 1937, singer.

Aha-phrodisiacs

To honor Frankie Valli's birthday make a collage, a doodle, or a painting entitled *Can't Take My Eyes Off of You.*

Journal Juju

May Sarton said, "Loneliness is the poverty of self; solitude is the richness of self."

Write about where you are with loneliness versus solitude. Do you have enough solitude in your life? Get out your calendar and schedule some as if it were as important as a doctor's appointment or a pedicure. Repeated Completion: "I find solitude . . . "

Dose of Mirth

Make up a word that describes the essence of your journal like May Sarton did. One of the essences of my journals is "darkdistractibulisticness intermingling with ideabilities and renegadoodles."

Today I get to: _____

Daily Soul Vitamin

For beautiful eyes, look for the good in others; for beautiful lips, speak only words of kindness; and for poise, walk with the knowledge that you are never alone.
~Audrey Hepburn

Toast of the Day

Here's to icons of grace and kindness.

Awe-servances

Happy Birthday to:
Audrey Hepburn, 1929, award-winning actress, ballerina, fashion model, and humanitarian.
Randy Travis, 1959, influential country singer.
It's also National Weather Observer's Day, International Tuba Day, and Movie Day.

Tuba Storm

Aha-phrodisiacs

Audrey Hepburn said, "If I'm honest I have to tell you I still read fairy tales and I like them best of all." A fairy tale is a fictional story that usually features folkloric characters (such as fairies, goblins, elves, trolls, witches, giants, and talking animals) and enchantments, often involving a far-fetched sequence of events. Recount a recent event or memory in your life but add some folkloric characters and a few far-fetched features.

Dose of Mirth

Weather Joke: Whatever happened to that cow that was lifted into the air by the tornado. Udder disaster!

Journal Juju

Randy Travis said, "I pursued a career in music because I love it so much and I enjoy what it does to those who hear it." Make a list of things you love to do and circle ones you have not done in awhile.

Today I get to:

May 5
Name today

Daily Soul Vitamin
Life has its own hidden forces which you can only discover by living. ~Søren Kierkegaard

Toast of the Day
Here's to remembering the feeling of first learning to ride a bike.

Awe—Servanres
Happy Birthday to:
Søren Kierkegaard, 1813, philosopher and theologian.
Karl Marx, 1818, founder and father of modern communism.
Michael Palin, 1943, comedian, actor and member of Monty Python.
Cartoonist Day

Aha-phrodisiacs
Michael Palin said, "I always wanted to be an explorer, but—it seemed I was doomed to be nothing more than a very silly person." Use the following title for writing, a cartoon, or collage: *Because I'm Just Not Taking Myself Too Seriously This Lifetime.*

Or make a collage, doodle, cartoon painting or poem called *The Hidden Forces of Life.*

Make a cartoon of something that happened in your life.

Dose of Mirth
How many Marxists does it take to change a light bulb?
None. The light bulb contains the seeds of its own revolution.
~Glenn Miller

Journal Juju
Michael Palin said, "One of the most important days of my life was when I learned to ride a bicycle." Write about your experience learning to ride a bike, biking in general, or one of the most important days of your life relating to learning.

Soren's Subliminal Message
Don't forget to love yourself. ~Søren Kierkegaard

May 6
Name today

Daily Soul Vitamin
The only failure is not to try. ~George Clooney

Toast of the Day
Here's to the abundance of art one finds in nature.

Awe-servances
Happy Birthday to:

Sigmund Freud, 1856, founder of psychoanalysis.

Orson Welles, 1915, Oscar-winning screenwriter, director, producer, and actor

George Clooney, 1961, award- winning actor, director, producer, and screenwriter.

On this day in 1851, Dr. John Gorrie patented a "refrigerator machine"

In 1992 Mary Evans Young, the director of the British anti-diet campaign Diet
Breakers, established May 6 as No Diet Day.

Aha-phrodisiacs
Orson Welles said, "Create your own visual style… let it be unique for yourself
and yet identifiable for others." Make a list of things you like about the visual
style of others, write a list of adjectives of what you want your visual style or
literary voice to sound like.

Take a break from your diet and have an adventure in your refrigerator.

Journal Juju
Write what your refrigerator would say about you. Name your refrigerator—
name it something like The Nurturing Box of Succulent Sustenance or Herman
or something like that.

Dose of Mirth
Ask not what you can do for your country. Ask what's for lunch.
~Orson Welles

Note to self: Put some baking soda in the fridge.

May 7
Name today _____

Daily Soul Vitamin
The great mind knows the power of gentleness.
~Robert Browning

Toast of the Day
Here's to a moment of relief.

Awe—servances
Happy Birthday to:
Johannes Brahms, 1833, German composer
Robert Browning, 1812, poet, husband of poet
Elizabeth Barrett Browning.
Peter Tchaikovsky, 1840, Russian composer.

Aha—phrodisiacs
Browning Starter Fluid: "Room after room, I hunt the house through . . ."
Tchaikovsky said, "Truly there would be reason to go mad were it not for music."
Play some music that soothes your soul and color, scribble, or paint to it. Or do
this repeated completion: "I go mad when . . ."

Dose of Mirth
If there is anyone here whom I have not insulted, I beg his pardon. ~Johannes Brahms

Journal Juju
Robert Browning said, "Grow old with me! The best is yet to be." Keep going with
this in prose, poetry, collage, humming, or hopscotch.

Subliminal Message Brought to You by Kindness/Gathering Potions
Ask yourself: What's one small way I can be kind to myself today? Design an
intention to connect with someone who makes you feel good about yourself.
Pay attention to people who have this quality as you interact with them daily.
Connect in a kind way with one person today.

May 10
Name today

Daily Soul Vitamin
The higher up you go, the more mistakes you are allowed. Right at the top, if you make enough of them, it's considered to be your style. ~Fred Astaire

Toast of the Day
Here's to clear gut feelings that spare us emotions and save us time.

Have a Cup of Kindness

Awe—servances
Happy Birthday to
Sir Thomas Lipton, 1850, the tea magnate.
Fred Astaire, 1899, film and Broadway stage dancer, choreographer, singer and actor.

It's also Human Kindness Day, Clean Up Your Room Day, and Trust Your Intuition Day.

Aha—phrodisiacs
The Dalai Lama said, "If you want others to be happy, practice compassion. If you want to be happy, practice compassion." Ask this question frequently: What can I do in the next minute to be more kind or compassionate to myself? As you practice kindness with yourself, it will spread to others.

Just clean a room for the duration of a favorite song. Five minutes at a time is better than an hour never.

Dose of Mirth
Everyday I beat my own previous record for number of consecutive days I've stayed alive. ~Unknown

Journal Juju
What mistakes have you made that could be considered a style? Write about a mistake you made but frame it as an intention rather than a mistake.

And Now a Word from Gather Potion
Think of a few people who have made you feel appreciated and special. Think of five people you enjoy spending time with.

May 11

Name today

Soul Vitamin

The body is a sacred garment. ~Martha Graham

I am convinced that life in a physical body is meant to be an ecstatic experience. ~Shakti Gawain

Toast of the Day

Here's to the joy that dancing can bring.

Awe-servances

Happy Birthday to:

Irving Berlin, 1888, American composer and lyricist.

Martha Graham, 1894, one of the giants of modern dance.

Salvador Dali, 1904, leading painter in the Surrealist movement.

Aha-phrodisiacs

Martha Graham said, "Nobody cares if you can't dance well. Just get up and dance. Great dancers are not great because of their technique, they are great because of their passion."

Experiment with a variety of different kinds of music and then draw shapes and colors of the feeling and write, starting with "To fly . . . "

Get drugged through dance. Dance surrealistically like a Dali painting. Or write about a dancer who does.

Dose of Mirth

I don't do drugs; I am drugs. ~Salvador Dali

Journal Juju

Start a journal entry with either "I am drugs . . . " or "My drug is creativity . . . "and keep going, quickly, with little thought and no concern for grammar, logic, or non-surrealism. Make a non-judgmental assessment about how you have been treating your body.

Brought to you by Body Temple Potion

Movement is a medicine for creating change in a person's physical, emotional, and mental states. ~Carol Welch

Daily Soul vitamin
Life is to be lived. If you have to support yourself, you had bloody well better find some way that is going to be interesting. And you don't do that by sitting around wondering about yourself. ~Katharine Hepburn

Toast of the Day
Here's to the parts of our jobs that we love.

Awe-servances
Happy Birthday to:

Edward Lear, 1812, artist, illustrator and writer known for his literary nonsense, in poetry and prose, and especially his limericks.

Katharine Hepburn, 1907, Oscar-winning film, television and stage actress.

George Carlin, 1937, stand-up comedian, actor, and author.

Steve Winwood, 1948, musician.

It's also Nonsense Day.

Aha-phrodisiacs
Write a poem or limerick about nonsense, Frisbees, or fierce Hepburn independence.

George Carlin said, "There are nights when the wolves are silent, and only the moon howls." I just wanted to put this quote somewhere, there's nothing you need to do with it.

Dose of Mirth
Frisbeetarianism is the belief that when you die, your soul goes up on the roof and gets stuck. ~George Carlin

Journal Juju
Katharine Hepburn said, "Without discipline, there's no life at all." Write with compassion (that means no judgment), where you are with discipline. Consider forming a new neural pathway of discipline by incorporating a routine for just 1 to 5 minutes a day, repeated over time.

Write or make art about your soul being stuck up on a roof.

Today I get to:

Daily Soul Vitamin
You can't base your life on other people's expectations.
~Stevie Wonder

Toast of the Day
Here's to a slice of crusty hot apple pie, the apple of
your eye, and some milk.

Awe-Servances
Happy Birthday to:
Mary Wells, 1943, Motown's first big star, whose famous song was "My Guy."
Stevie Wonder, 1950, award winning singer, songwriter, and record producer.

National Apple Pie Day.

Aha-phrodisiacs
Wells Starter Fluid or Repeat Completions: "My guy . . ."
    Eat some apple pie while listening to Motown music.
    Wonder Repeated Completions or Starter Fluid: "I just called to say . . ."

Dose of Mirth
The only thing to prevent what's past is to put a stop to it before it happens.
~Sir Boyle Roche

Journal Juju
We are not sure of the context, but Mary Wells was quoted as saying, "I'm here
today to urge you to keep the faith. I can't cheer you on with all my voice, but
I can encourage, and I pray to motivate you with all my heart and soul and
whispers." Imagine that it was you that Mary was encouraging. What is she
encouraging you to do and trust? Write about it and write about how her heart,
soul, and whispers motivate you or imagine that they do.
    Possibility Pie: In your journal, draw a circle and label it as a possibility in
your life ~make it some thought or action that will serve your creativity or joy,
(e.g., thinking more confidently, being more disciplined). Now section off the
pie into small slices and know that you don't have to eat the whole pie at once.
Just bite off a little more each day. Have a coff of cuppee with it.

May 14
Name today

Daily Soul Vitamin
Understand life's mysteries as mysteries to be lived.
~Robert Zemeckis

Toast of the Day
Here's to a buttermilk biscuit with real
butter and strawberry jam.

Awe-servances
Happy Birthday to:

George Walton Lucas, Jr., 1944, financially successful independent director and
   producer, famous for his epic *Star Wars* saga and *Indiana Jones* films.
Robert Zemeckis, 1952, award-winning movie director, producer and writer.

It's also Crazy Day, Help Clean Up Your Street Day, and National Buttermilk
   Biscuit Day.

Aha-phrodisiacs
Run (or hobble) outside and pick up one or five pieces of trash and throw them
away. Extra credit (pick up ten or fifteen pieces). Bonus: make a found object
sculpture with some things . . . found.

Dose of Mirth
Twist your tongue three times saying this, "A box of biscuits, a box of mixed
biscuits, a box of mixed biscuits and a biscuit mixer."

Journal Juju
George Lucas said, "Train yourself to let go of the things you fear to lose." What
are the things you fear to lose? Pick one or two of them and write about letting go
of just 5 percent (or more) of their power over you. What would that feel like?
How would you think or act differently toward them? How would you compensate? What benefit would it have for you? What would you lose?

   Since today is the birthday of two renowned movie directors, write about what
happens next in the screenplay of your life: Who is the hero in the story? What is
the desire? What is the conflict? How will the hero triumph?
Is there a sequel?

May 15

Name today

*The world is but a canvas
to our imagination.*
~Henry David Thoreau

Daily Soul Vitamin

*As one gets older one sees many more paths that could be taken. Artists sense
within their own work that kind of swelling of possibilities, which may seem
a freedom or a confusion.* ~Jasper Johns

Toast of the Day

Here's to classic movies that we never grow tired of.

Awe-servances

Happy Birthday to:

Frank Baum,1856, author, actor, and independent filmmaker best
known as the creator, along with illustrator W. W. Denslow, of
one of the most popular books ever written in American
children's literature, *The Wizard of Oz.*

Jasper Johns, 1930, painter and printmaker.

Aha-phrodisiacs

Jasper Johns said, "Do something, do something to that, and then do something to that." Is there a piece of art or writing with which you can explore
this concept?,

Starter Fluid: "If I only had a brain . . . "

Refer to the "swelling of possibilities" in the Jasper Johns' quote at the
top, but see it as a freedom rather than as a confusion. Creativity creates
new mental, emotional, spiritual, artistic and fulfilling pathways. Remind
yourself what in the past motivated your creative action. Your participation
will be the only way you discover how expanded your existence can be.

Dose of Mirth

Don't be silly, Toto. Scarecrows don't talk. ~Dorothy

Journal Juju

Riffing off of the quote, ". . . We're not in Kansas anymore," decide on some
place you no longer are literally or metaphorically in your life and title a journal entry: *I'm not in _____ anymore.* Then decide on a place you no longer
want to be—like in debt, a bad relationship, a stressful job—and write a journal
entry about how you got out of that place. Feel free to bring a tin-man along.

Daily Soul Vitamin
When people don't believe in you, you have to believe in yourself.
~Pierce Brosnan

Toast of the Day
Here's to the magnificence of the ocean.

Awe-servances
Happy Birthday to:
Adrienne Rich, 1929, poet, teacher, and writer.
Pierce Brosnan, 1953, actor, producer, James Bond.

It's also Never Turn Your Back on the Ocean Day and Biographers Day.

Aha-phrodisiacs
Write about the ocean. Repeated Completions: "The ocean is . . .",
"When I turn my back on the ocean . . . ."

Starter Fluid: "Once when I was looking out at the ocean . . ."
or "Once upon an ocean."

Write a short biography of a character that turned his or her
back on the ocean.

Believe in yourself 5 percent more today . . . feel it in your
body or imagine what it would feel like.

Dose of Mirth
Sponges grow in the ocean. That just kills me. I wonder how much
deeper the ocean would be if that didn't happen. ~Stephen Wright

Journal Juju
Adrienne Rich said, "It's exhilarating to be alive in a time of awakening consciousness; it can also be confusing, disorienting, and painful." Write a list of ways that
becoming more conscious might be exhilarating, confusing, and painful.

Today I get to:

Note to Myself: Believe in yourself.

May 17
Name today _____

Daily Soul Vitamin
*If I had my life to live over, I would start barefoot
earlier in the spring and stay that way later in
the fall. I would go to more dances. I would ride
more merry-go-rounds. I would pick more
daisies.* ~Nadine Stair

Toast of the Day
Here's to the season of being barefoot approaching.

Awe-servances
Happy Birthday to:
Erik Satie, 1866, French composer, pianist, and writer.

Awe-manac Invented: Wear Something Freeing Day.

Aha-phrodisiacs
Go buy something that you don't have; everyone needs something that feels
freeing interpret "freeing" however you like.

Journal Juju
Erik Satie said, "When I was young, I was told: 'You'll see, when you're fifty.'
I am fifty and I haven't seen a thing." Make a list of some things you were told
when you were young and what your thoughts are about them now. Repeated
completions to choose from: "Secretly I..." "I will be sure to..." "Before too long..."

Brought to you by Arpeggio Spirit Potion
Listen to some music that evokes a movie scene in your mind. Be your
own director and discover a new freeing world with a soundtrack inside
your head, available to you whenever you want.

Today I get to:

Daily Soul Vitamin

Thought is subversive and revolutionary, destructive and terrible, thought is merciless to privilege, established institutions, and comfortable habit. Thought looks into the pit of hell and is not afraid. Thought is great and swift and free, the light of the world, and the chief glory of man. ~Bertrand Russell

Toast of the Day

Here's to the sight of a falling star.

Awe-servances

Happy Birthday to:

Bertrand Russell, 1872, philosopher, logician, mathematician, and prolific writer.
Perry Como, 1912, crooner, television performer, and recording artist.

It's also Visit Your Relatives Day and on this date in 1980 there was a major eruption of Mount St. Helens volcano in Washington state.

Aha-phrodisiacs

Perry Como Title Wave: Hoop-Dee-Doo, A Bushel and a Peck, Catch a Falling Star, Round and Round, Magic Moments, Say You're Mine Again, Ko Ko Mo, Hot Diggity Dog Ziggity, Boom, Juke Box Baby, More, It's Impossible, For the Good Times.

Write about a commemoration called Visit Your Volcano Day—metaphorically or for real.

Dose of Mirth

If you cannot get rid of the family skeleton, you may as well make it dance. ~George Bernard Shaw

Journal Juju

Bertrand Russell said, "No one gossips about other people's secret virtues." Gossip about your own virtues in your journal. Write a gossip column titled *My Secret Virtues.* Notice that Bertrand Russell did a Repeated Completion with "Thought is…" Try your own out for size.

Daily Soul Vitamin
We need creativity in order to break free from the temporary structures that have been set up by a particular sequence of experience. ~Edward de Bono

Toast of the Day
Here's to May's initial prelude to summer nights.

Awe-Servances
Happy Birthday to:
Malcolm X, 1925, minister and spokesman for the Nation of Islam, civil rights activist.
Edward de Bono, 1933, psychologist and physician. De Bono writes prolifically on subjects of lateral thinking, a concept he is believed to have pioneered.
Nora Ephron, 1941, award-winning film director, producer, screenwriter, novelist, and blogger.

Dose of Mirth
Every time I close the door on reality it comes in through the windows.
~Jennifer Unlimited

Journal Juju
Nora Ephron said, "I try to write parts for women that are as complicated and interesting as women actually are." Write a list of ways you are interesting and complicated; men can do this too. Pick one and write a detailed anecdote that illustrates that trait.

Malcolm X said, "If you don't stand for something you will fall for anything." What do you stand for? What do you sit for? What have you fallen for? What are you here for? When will I stop asking these questions? Are you still reading?

Today I get to:

May 20
Name today _____

Daily Soul Vitamin
Until you're ready to look foolish, you'll never have the possibility of being great. ~Cher

Toast of the Day
Here's to your jeans feeling looser when you put them on.

Awe-servances
Happy Birthday to:
Cher, 1946, award-winning actress, singer, songwriter, and entertainer.

Flower Day: Buy or pick some fresh
    flowers; do a blind contour
    drawing of one or all of them.

On this day in 1874 Levi Strauss
    markets blue jeans with copper rivets, priced at $13.50 for a dozen.

Dose of Mirth
Souls wouldn't wear suits and ties, they'd wear blue jeans and sit cross-legged with a glass of red wine. ~Carrie Latet

Aha-phrodisiacs
Cher Title Wave: Moonstruck, If I Could Turn Back Time, And The Beat Goes On, Strong Enough, All or Nothing.

Carrie Latet shared the attire of souls quote (above). Where would souls congregate? What would they talk about? What would their hobbies be? How would they dance? Write or make art about it.

Journal Juju
Write about your relationship to jeans.

Subliminal Message Brought to You by FOOOf
Ask yourself: What's one small playful thing I can do to amuse my partner/colleague/neighbor today? (A funny card in the medicine cabinet, a wind-up toy on the desk, a cut-out cartoon on a computer monitor, a quote on a note in a pocket, a cocktail umbrella in a sandwich, a cupcake in a cubicle?)

May 21

Daily Soul Vitamin

Nothing makes me so happy as to observe nature and to paint what I see. When I go out into the countryside and see the sun and the green and everything flowering, I say to myself, "Yes indeed all that belongs to me!" ~Henri Rousseau

Toast of the Day

Here's to the feeling of belonging to nature.

Awe—servances

Happy Birthday to:

Henri Rousseau, 1844, painter. Though ridiculed during his life he came to be
   recognized as a self-taught genius whose works are of high artistic quality.
Plato, 428/427 BC, mathematician, writer of philosophical dialogues.

Gemini begins.

Aha—phrodisiacs

Search online for Henri Rousseau, and find his painting titled *The Snake Charmer*, click on it to enlarge it and write from the Snake Charmer's point of view or give the picture a caption.

   Billy Collins wrote a poem called *Shoveling Snow with Buddha*. Pick a famous person, character, or really anyone and write about doing a task with that person. If you like, roughly follow this structure. First paragraph: Describe your character's relation to the task and anything that seems ironic or odd about that. Second: Describe the two of you doing the task together. Third: Add something you say to your character and your character's response. Last: Describe completing the task and what happens next.

Journal Juju

Gemini is flexible, versatile, restless, a jack-of-all-trades, lively, alert, quick-witted, literary, communicative, a good conversationalist, changeable, sociable, logical. Pick three or four of those traits and write about how you stand with them even if you are born under another sign.

Today I get to: _____

Daily Soul Vitamin

Mediocrity knows nothing higher than itself, but talent instantly recognizes genius. ~Sir Arthur Conan Doyle

Toast of the Day

Here's to the medicinal effects that viewing a work of art can lend.

Awe-servances

Happy Birthday to:

Mary Cassatt, 1844, Impressionist artist.

Sir Arthur Conan Doyle, 1859, creator of Sherlock Holmes.

Aha-phrodisiacs

Mary Cassatt's paintings, *Boating Party* and *Tea*, both found on her page at Wikipedia.org, each lend themselves to writing. Pick one or both, enlarge them, and write about them from the point of view of the characters, or as a dialog between characters. Add a detective character.

Dose of Mirth

Never trust a man who, when left alone in a room with a tea cozy, doesn't try it on. ~Billy Connolly

Journal Juju

Mary Cassatt said, "I have touched with a sense of art some people—they felt the love and the life. Can you offer me anything to compare to that joy for an artist?" Write a list of ways you would like to touch people with your life. Identify a very small step you could take this week.

Write the completions of the following sentences with the immediate associations, senses or images that come to mind. Go quickly.

When I'm on the beach . . . , In a bookstore . . . , When I'm at home . . . , When I'm in my closet . . . , When I pound a drum . . . , When I dance . . . , When I stare into oblivion . . . , When the telephone rings . . . , When someone serves me my favorite food . . . , When I awake in the morning . . . .

Questions from the Gather Potion

Who are some friends who have helped you through a difficult time? Is it time to reconnect or time to pass it forward?

May 23
Name today _____

Daily Soul Vitamin
The especial genius of women I believe to be electrical in movement, intuitive in function, spiritual in tendency. ~Margaret Fuller

Toast of the Day
Here's to experiencing the prehistoric in the simple turtle.

Awe—servances
Happy Birthday to:
Margaret Fuller, 1810, writer, reformer, journalist.
Rosemary Clooney, 1928, singer and actress.
Jewel Kilcher, 1974, singer, songwriter, actress, poet, and philanthropist.

It's also World Turtle Day.

Aha—phrodisiacs
Write something in your life from a turtle's point of view.

Dose of Mirth
Anytime you see a turtle up on top of a fence post, you know he had some help. ~Alex Haley

Journal Juju
Rosemary Clooney said, "… you can't do everything alone." Successful people know when to ask for help. Explore asking for help in your journal. Where could you use help? Who could you ask?

James Bryant Conant said, "The turtle makes progress only when he sticks his neck out." Stick your neck out just a little sometime this week. Maybe do it to ask for help.

Today I get to:

CHANGE DAY

There is nothing so stable as change. ~Bob Dylan

Journal Juju

Price Pritchett said, "Change always comes bearing gifts." List some changes in your life and beside them write the obvious gifts as well as the not so obvious ones. Extra credit: go into detail about one of them. Speculate how your life might change in the future.

Dose of Mirth

Change is inevitable—except from a vending machine. ~Robert C. Gallagher

May 24

Name today _____

Aha-phrodisiacs

William Trevor said, "The capacity you're thinking of is imagination; without it there can be no understanding, indeed no fiction." Write down a change you are going through and use your imagination to write a fictional account of how you get through it; make sure there's some conflict before the hero triumphs.

Bob Dylan wrote a song called "Everything Is Broken." Use this as a title for a collage, doodle, or painting. Or use it as Starter Fluid for poetry or prose.

Take something you've written and change it. Suggestions: Take something from the middle and put it at the beginning. Take out lots of words and make it poetry. Change a character. Make it fiction. Make it real. Make it come ALIVE.

Awe-servances

Happy Birthday to:
William Trevor, 1928, short story writer, novelist and playwright.
Bob Dylan, 1941, award-winning singer-songwriter, author, musician, and poet.

Toast of the Day

Here's to creativity's ability to make an uncomfortable emotion useful.

I get to Today: _____

May 25
Name today

Daily Soul Vitamin
Silly is you in a natural state, and serious is something you have to do until you can get silly again. ~Mike Myers

Toast of the Day
Here's to detecting and enjoying the inner beauty of an older person or yourself.

Awe-servances
Happy Birthday to:
Ralph Waldo Emerson, 1803, essayist, poet
Raymond Carver, 1938, short-story writer
Mike Myers, 1963, award-winning comic actor, screenwriter, and film producer.

It's also Towel Day, which is celebrated every May 25 as a tribute to the late author Douglas Adams. First held in 2001, fans carry a towel with them throughout the day. The use of a towel is homage to the frequent references to towels in the five books of *The Hitchhiker's Guide to the Galaxy*.

Aha-phrodisiacs
In honor of Mike Myers and Douglas Adams, write something silly. Take a recent event or a memory and just get silly with it. In it, give someone an accent, a sidekick or a superpower. Notice how being "silly" can loosen up your mind for new ideas. Do some silly art work to silly music with serious crayons.

Use this Raymond Carver title as Starter Fluid: *Will You Please Be Quiet, Please?*

Journal Juju
Write about the role of and your thoughts about towels in your life. Any towel quirks? (I had short hair as a child, so I wore a towel on my head and pretended I had long hair).

Write a list of 5 silly things about some event that has recently transpired for you. Don't judge whether it's funny, just be silly in a carefree, imperfect way.

 ### And now a word from Kindness Potion
Buy a new fuzzy towel for yourself. Just one that is especially fluffy and nurturing.

Daily Soul Vitamin

I've been around a long time, and life still has a whole lot of surprises for me. ~Hank Williams Jr.

Toast of the Day

Here's to surprising ourselves with a little spontaneous wildness every now and then.

Awe–servances

Happy Birthday to:

Peggy Lee, 1920, singer.

Miles Davis, 1926, jazz musician, trumpeter, bandleader, and composer.

Hank Williams, Jr., 1949, country and southern rock artist.

Aha–phrodisiacs

Peggy Lee Title Wave: In My Solitude, Rockin' Chair, Just Like a Gypsy, Please Don't Talk About Me When I'm Gone, Back in Your Own Backyard, Swingin' on a Star.

Miles Davis said, "Don't play what's there, play what's not there." Entitle a poem, collage, painting or doodle *What's Not There* and see what happens.

Dose of Mirth

I am returning this otherwise good typing paper to you because someone has printed gibberish all over it and put your name at the top. ~Anonymous English professor

Journal Juju

Hank Williams sang a song called, "Howlin' at the Moon." Make a collage of yourself howling at the moon in preparation for Isadora Duncan's birthday tomorrow where you will let a little "wild" out.

Start with this sentence and keep going: "I've got to get moving…"

Today I get to: _____

Note to Myself

Prepare clothes, shoes, music, and champagne for getting a little wild tomorrow.

Daily Soul Vitamin

Those who dwell among the beauties and mysteries of the earth are never alone or weary of life. ~Rachel Carson

Toast of the Day

Here's to standing at the edge of the sea feeling the knowledge of the earthly eternal.

Awe-servances

Happy Birthday to:

Isadora Duncan, 1877, dancer, considered by many to be the mother of modern dance.

Rachel Carson, 1907, marine biologist whose landmark book, *Silent Spring*, is often credited with having launched the global environmental movement.

Aha-phrodisiacs

Simply read this Rachel Carson quote, close your eyes, breathe, like the waves of the ocean ebbing and flowing, and see a scene of the eternal. See what writing or art it may inspire: "To stand at the edge of the sea, to sense the ebb and flow of the tides, to feel the breath of a mist moving over a great salt marsh, to watch the flight of shore birds that have swept up and down the surf lines of the continents for untold thousands of years, to see the running of the old eels and the young shad to the sea, is to have knowledge of things that are as nearly eternal as any earthly life can be."

Dose of Mirth

There are short-cuts to happiness, and dancing is one of them. ~Vicki Baum

Journal Juju

Isadora Duncan said, "You were once wild here. Don't let them tame you." WERE you once a little wilder? Art and writing are places to return to that wildness—remember your wildness or invent some that's new on the page, the board, or the canvas. Do a repeated completion with "I get wild when . . ." and then take just your response and string them together adding anything that emerges spontaneously.

Message Brought to You by Body Temple Potion and Arpeggio Spirit

Dance for Cardio-bliss to some favorite music.

Daily Soul Vitamin

I think it is impossible to explain faith. It is like trying to explain air, which one cannot do by dividing it into its component parts and labeling them scientifically. It must be breathed to be understood. ~Patrick White

Toast of the Day

Here's to an occasional juicy hamburger with all your favorite fixin's.

Awe-servances

Happy Birthday To:

Thomas Moore, 1779, poet, singer, songwriter, and entertainer, now best remem-
   bered for the lyrics of *The Minstrel Boy* and the *The Last Rose of Summer.*
Patrick White, 1912, Nobel Prize-winning author.
It's also National Hamburger Day

Aha-phrodisiacs

Patrick White wrote a novel called *Three Uneasy Pieces.* Make a work of art or a collage with the same title. Or divide a piece of sketching paper into three sections and with expressive media like paint, pastels, or crayon; express with art three things about which you are uneasy. Make another picture the same way, but with three things you are comfortable with.

   List 28 titles of possible art works or writing—just list the titles now, do not worry about doing the work yet. Listing titles can jumpstart incubation in your subconscious.

Dose of Mirth

Sacred cows make the best hamburger. ~Mark Twain

Journal Juju

Breathe in a breath of faith, let it fill your body and spirit and then continue with this sentence: "Filled with faith I…"

May 29
Name today _____

Double Dose Daily Soul Vitamin
Conformity is the jailer of freedom and the enemy of growth. ~John F. Kennedy
Don't let anyone tell you that you have to be a certain way. Be unique.

Be what you feel. ~Melissa Etheridge

Toast of the Day
Here's to finding your own unique approach,
identity or style.

Awe-Servances
Happy Birthday to:
Gilbert Keith Chesterton, 1874, writer.
Bob Hope, 1903, entertainer, comedian.
John F. Kennedy, 1917, the 35th president of the United States.
Melissa Etheridge, 1961, award winning rock musician.

Dose of Mirth
*I grew up with six brothers. That's how I learned to dance—waiting for the
bathroom.* ~Bob Hope

Aha-phrodisiacs
Melissa Etheridge Title Wave: Refugee, Like the Way I Do, Bring Me Some Water,
You Can Sleep While I Drive, No Souvenirs, Ain't It Heavy, Come to My Win-
dow, If I Wanted To.

Put some music on and do a waiting-for-the-bathroom dance . . . just to
make yourself laugh.

Journal Juju
G. K. Chesterton said, "The way to love anything is to realize that it might be lost."

Make a list of three things you could potentially lose (relationships, abilities,
things) and see if you can muster up appreciation for them before they are gone.

Today I get to: _____

Name today _____

Daily Soul Vitamin

Lack of activity destroys the good condition of every human being, while movement and methodical physical exercise save it and preserve it. ~Plato

Toast of the Day

Here's to the feeling right after a strenuous workout.

Awe-Servances

Happy Birthday to:

Mel Blanc, 1908, a prolific voice actor, most famous for being the voice for Bugs Bunny, Daffy Duck, Porky Pig, and Barney Rubble, among hundreds of others.

National Senior Health and Fitness Day.

Aha-phrodisiacs

Use one or more of the quotes from Mel Blanc characters in a dialog with another character unrelated to the Warner Bros. cartoons.

Starter Fluid: "Late at night . . . "

Doses of Cartoon Mirth from Mel Blanc

Great hornytoads! A trespasser! Gettin' footyprints all over my desert!

I knew I shoulda taken that left toin at Albakoikee.

I say, I say, that boy's about as sharp as a pound of wet liver.

I wonder if that silly duck will remember that he can fly? . . . Nope, I guess not.

Watch out for that first step, mac! It's a lulu!

What's up, doc?

You're despicable!

Journal Juju

For health- and fitness-related journaling, write about what it might mean to "find the breath within the breath" in yoga, meditation, or just in general.

If you were a cartoon character, what might you say regularly?

Today I get to: _____

Daily Soul Vitamin
Imagination is the true magic carpet. ~Norman Vincent Peale

Toast of the Day
Here's to the feeling right after a strenuous workout.

Awe—servances
The Awe-manac staff voted today Whitman-Eastwood-Peale Day since three
  awe-inspiring men (Walt Whitman, Clint Eastwood, Norman Vincent Peale)
  were born today.

Aha—phrodisiacs
Read the quotes and write, paint, doodle, or make a film to any inspiration they
bring up for you.

Walt Whitman, 1819, poet, essayist, journalist, and humanist.
  I exist as I am, that is enough.

Norman Vincent Peale, 1898, preacher and author of *The Power of Positive Thinking*.
  *Any fact facing us is not as important as our attitude toward it, for that determines
our success or failure.*
  Empty pockets never held anyone back. Only empty heads and empty hearts can do that.

Clint Eastwood, 1930, iconic actor, director, producer, writer, composer, living legend.
  *My father used to say to me, 'Show 'em what you can do, and don't worry about what
you're gonna get. Say you'll work for free and make yourself invaluable.'*
  Whatever success I've had is due to a lot of instinct and a little luck.

Dose of Mirth
They say marriages are made in Heaven. But so is thunder and lightning. ~Clint Eastwood

Note to Myself
Clint Eastwood is a great role model for someone staying creatively
active way over the age of 70.

Mind Solutions
What's in Your Mind?

Where there is an open mind, there will always be a frontier. ~ Charles F. Kettering

Go on, Get Your Mind Out. Explore a New Frontier without Leaving the Dip in Your Hammock! Grab Your Mind by the Brilliance!

Legally cross your mental borders a little almost every day by harnessing a potion that activates curiosity, stretches wide the limits of possibility, and expands your mental abilities so that those who know you will say things like "Dang, I had no idea you were so gifted". Discover untapped accessories of the mind and watch your existence unfold with new reasons to get up in the morning.

Thought takes man out of servitude, into freedom. ~Henry Wadsworth Longfellow

The purpose of learning is growth, and our minds, unlike our bodies, can continue growing as we continue to live. ~Mortimer Adler

The energy of the mind is the essence of life. ~Aristotle

POSSIBLE EFFECTS: Mental sharpness past the age of 99. Impressing even yourself with mental achievements.

Side effects vary. Consult your doctor if mind expansion is sustained longer than four hours - people will start expecting more from you. Side effects may include discovering parts of your mind you were unfamiliar with before taking this potion. Surprise. You may discover new interests, intersections, inner worlds and intergalactic phenomenon- make sure you have paper to write on. Caution: Do not stop yourself from operating anything while on Mind Solutions - you will find new uses for all sorts of gadgets including blenders, mother boards and marshmallows.

WELCOME to JUNE

"Happy. Just in my swim shorts, barefooted, wild-haired . . . that's the way to live." ~Jack Kerouac

June was named for the Roman goddess Juno, who was also known as Hera, queen of the gods. Coincidentally, my name is Jill but I am also known as Monkey Feet, queen of the people who can pick up clothes with their toes. Juno, (aka. Hera) could throw lightning bolts like her husband, Jupiter. I, (aka. M.F.), can throw socks (with my feet) like a dog named Rosie, (although her aim is a little more accurate and she uses her mouth). The word June is also from *juvenis*, Latin for *youth* or in my case, *juvenile*.

SOME Events at JUNE's Door

It's Zoo & Aquarium Month, National Pest Control Month, Adopt-A-Shelter Cat Month, Cancer from the Sun Awareness Month, Black Music Month, Ragweed Control Month, Children's Awareness Month, National Accordion Awareness Month, National Bless-A-Child Month, National Burglary Prevention Month, National Candy Month, National Fabric Care Month, National Frozen Yogurt Month, National Iced Tea Month, National Rivers Month, National Rose Month, National Seafood Month, and Rebuild Your Life Month. Father's Day is the third Sunday. June begins in Gemini and ends in Cancer.

AWe-Manac INVented Events:

June 12: Awe-manac Dreamwork Day
June 13: Arpeggio Spirit Day
June 19: Butterfly Day

Suggested Ways to Celebrate

In June, your Muses will throw summer lightning to jumpstart your creative light sockets. The Aha-phrodisiacs this month were designed to restore, rejuvenate, and recharge your passions.

1. Okay, it's your turn to combine the above events and commemorations. Fun keeps us in *juvenis* so have fun combining the occasions and commemorations of this month to a-muse yourself. I'll begin: It's Play Your Accordion in a River with a Rose in Your Mouth Month.

2. Rebuild Your Life. If you need some Life Improvements, this could be an approach that provides some insight. Look at your life as if you were rebuilding a house. What would you like to keep? Make these your raw materials. What would you like to release? What would you like to add on? Would you have a sun roof, and if you did, what kind of light would it let in?

3. Bless a child, bless a cat, bless a rose, have a jelly bean. Bless a pest, foil a theft, sun-block your chest, have a fish taco.

Astrological Spells From Quotable Mortals

Aries: *Sit quietly, and when the scenery shifts, slip between it.* ~John Cage

Taurus: *Reminisce about tomorrow.* ~Edwin Newman

Gemini: *No matter how fast you run, your shadow more than keeps up. Sometimes it's in front.* ~Rumi

Cancer: *As soon as you have made a thought, laugh at it.* ~Lao Tzu

Leo: *All of us invent ourselves. Some of us just have more imagination than others.* ~Cher

Virgo: *Vision is the art of seeing things invisible.* ~Jonathan Swift

Libra: *You've got to stand for something, or you'll fall for anything.* ~Country Western Song

Scorpio: *Don't call yourself a secret unless you mean to keep it.* ~Leonard Cohen

Sagittarius: *Create degrees of silence.* ~Don de Lillo

Capricorn: *Invent a past for the present.* ~Daniel Stern

Aquarius: *If you have an imagination that goes far afield, you can live far afield.* ~Patricia High Smith

Pisces: *The more poetic, the more real.* ~Novalis

Tides:

Ebbing: _____

Flowing: _____

Vessel of strength: _____

Gardening Information

FLOWER: Rose

MONTHLY AWE-MANAC CROP: Controlled pests and Aquarium Creatures

PLANTING INFORMATION: Lay 5 to 10 crispy rice cereal and marshmallow squares
    out on a red and white checkerboard table cloth by a sea that is home to
    tropical fishes. Add fantasy, mirth, and water daily.

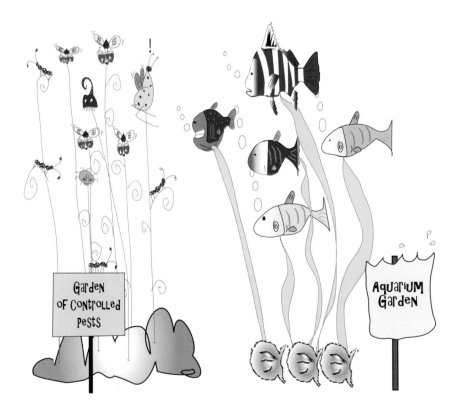

Daily Soul Vitamin
"If I'd observed all the rules, I'd never have got anywhere." ~Marilyn Monroe

Toast of the Day
Here's to the feeling of getting up early enough to enjoy the morning light.

Awe-servances
Happy Birthday to:

Marilyn Monroe, 1926, award-winning actress, singer, model, and pop icon

It's also Don't Give Up the Ship Day, Simple Speak Day, Early Bird Day, and Dare Day

Aha-phrodisiacs
Break the rules and use the four daily observances in some combined creative fashion: Simple Ship Day? Early Speak Day? And then collage, doodle, or write about it.

Choose a topic: early birds, clichès, daring, the beginning of summer, sunrise, poison ivy, tapioca, growing young. Explore it with any way you interpret "simple speak":

Journal Juju
Oscar Wilde said "He lives the poetry that he cannot write. The others write the poetry that they dare not realise." Write about how your existence is poetry and how your writing might limit or expand your experience of life.

Dose of Mirth
"Rise early. It is the early bird that catches the worm.
Don't be fooled by this absurd saw; I once knew a man who tried it.
He got up at sunrise and a horse bit him." ~Mark Twain

Today I Get to: _____

JUNE 2

Name today _____

Daily Soul Vitamin
Confusion is the welcome mat at the door of creativity. ~Michael J. Gelb

Toast of the Day
Here's to clever welcome mats.

Awe-servances
Happy Birthday to:

Marquis de Sade, 1740, French aristocrat, writer of philosophy-laden and often
    violent pornography. "Sadism" was created from his name.

Marvin Hamlisch, 1944, composer.

Festival of Utter Confusion.

Aha-phrodisiacs
Take Marvin Hamlisch's Broadway musical title, *Imaginary Friends*, and
use it as Starter Fluid for poetry, a letter, a description of a gathering,
whatever. Extra credit: Add the ingredient of utter confusion.
    Describe what you think a Festival of Utter Confusion would be like
or plan a fictional celebration for it.

Journal Juju
Starter Fluid: "You're enough..."
    Marquis de Sade said, "Happiness is ideal, it is the work of the imagination."
Use your imagination, pick a state of mind you like and write in your journal
under the influence of this state of mind. Suggestions: giddy, peaceful, uninhibited, expansive, abbreviated.
    Use this journal title: *Inner Sky.*

Dose of Mirth
I'm not confused, I'm just well mixed. ~Robert Frost

Today I get to

Awe-vanced Inner Message Potion
Think: "I'm doing better than I thought."

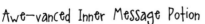

Daily Soul Vitamin

Follow your inner moonlight; don't hide the madness. ~Allen Ginsberg

Toast of the Day

Here's to cooperating with inner moonlight.

Awe-servances

Happy Birthday to:

Raoul Dufy,1877, French Fauvist painter.

Allen Ginsberg, 1926, poet of the Beat Generation.

Reba Spencer, 1962, actress, writer, comedienne.

On this date in 1875: the first telephone transmission by voice occurred, thanks to Alexander Graham Bell.

Aha-phrodisiacs

If your voice was the first transmitted, just what would you say?

Ginsberg Starter Fluid: "Understand that this is a dream…"

Reba Spencer made up this word when she was a kid: "rootintootinblabber-gate." Make a definition of this word and use it in a short piece or make up your own word and do the same.

Dose of Mirth

Blastnostricate: To have a liquid pass through one's nose.

~Christopher Plyem, Awe-manac staff member

Journal Juju

Raoul Dufy said, "My eyes were made to erase all that is ugly." Write or paint what you would see if your eyes erased all that is ugly. Now do the opposite.

He also said, "The subject itself is of no account; what matters is the way it is presented." This is creative thinking and can be applied to life: Make a list of 3 or more circumstances in your life and then list different ways you could view each one.

And now a Message from The Gather Potion

We are pack animals. The current pool of consciousness is alive with the desire to make connections. Find your tribe members. Put some effort into maintaining connections that support you. Feel the anti-aging properties of supporting and giving to others.

JUNE 4
Name today

Daily Soul Vitamin
Wisdom begins in wonder.
Be as you wish to seem. ~Socrates

Toast of the Day
Here's to filling our souls with gratitude.

Awe-servances
Happy Birthday to:
Socrates, circa 470 BC, Greek philosopher credited for laying the foundation for
    Western philosophy.
Aesop, legendary Greek source of over 600 fables.
Angelina Jolie, 1975, award winning film actress and a Goodwill Ambassador for
    the UN Refugee Agency.

Swing Day.

Aha-phrodisiacs
Clara Barton said, "The door that nobody else will go in at, seems always to swing
open widely for me." Use the word "swing" as Starter Fluid for art, dance, or writing. Choose any form of the word and see where it leads you.

Dose of Mirth
The world is a playground, and life is pushing my swing. ~Natalie Kocsis

Journal Juju
Angelina Jolie said, "We come to love not by finding the perfect person, but by
learning to see an imperfect person perfectly." Write about seeing yourself more
perfectly. Do the same for someone else.

    Aesop said, "Gratitude is the sign of noble souls." Take a moment to do a
gratitude inventory to feed your soul.

Daily Soul Vitamin
Creativity is piercing the mundane to find the marvelous.
~Bill Moyers

Toast of the Day
Here's to the world: "… a strange and wonderful place."
~Laurie Anderson

Awe-servances
Happy Birthday to:
David Wagoner, 1926, author of many books of poetry.
Bill Moyers, 1934, journalist and public commentator.
Laurie Anderson, 1947, experimental performance artist and musician.

Aha-phrodisiacs
Use one or both of David Wagoner's poem titles as Starter Fluid for art, doodling, dancing, or writing. *Baby, Come On Inside*, and *The Hanging Garden*.
　　Keep going with the Laurie Anderson Dose of Mirth.

Dose of Mirth
Paradise is exactly like where you are right now… only much, much better.
~Laurie Anderson

Journal Juju
Bill Moyers said, "When I learn something new—and it happens every day—I feel a little more at home in this universe, a little more comfortable in the nest." Write in your journal about learning. Search on a topic you know little about on the Internet or be a detective discovering something new ~write it in your journal.

A Message from Awe-wakened Moment
Melt into the moment and breathe into all that feels good about it.

JUNE 6
Name today

Daily Soul Vitamin
Time cools, time clarifies; no mood can be maintained quite unaltered through the course of hours. ~Thomas Mann

Toast of the Day
Here's to time that heals and clarifies.

Awe—servances
Happy Birthday to:
Paul Thomas Mann, 1875, novelist, social critic, philanthropist,
    Nobel Prize laureate.

Today in 1933 the first drive-in movie opened in Camden, NJ.

Aha—phrodisiacs
Word pool: flicker, drive-in movie theater, bent, laughingly, surprise, pretty, twenty-five, indistinct, affection, daffodil, silence, scratches, bewildering, word-less, plenty, liquor, buttoned, mascara, fall, unfolded, tow, cushion, open, flowers, stoop, shiver.
    Make a collage, painting, or a poem titled *Entertaining Flaws*.

Dose of Mirth
If I find a film dull, I find it infinitely more entertaining to watch the scratches. ~Norman McLaren

Journal Juju
Thomas Mann said, "One must die to life in order to be utterly a creator." Write about this quote pro or con and/or what it means to you. Or write something else.
    Like Norman McLaren, take a moment and look at the flaws in whatever environment you are writing—name them, or invent an imaginative reason why they are there.
    Time to do a Credit Report (write a list of those things you have accomplished or are glad you did this week).

JUNE 7
Name today

Daily Soul Vitamin
I shut my eyes in order to see. ~Paul Gauguin

Toast of the Day
Here's to a bowl of chocolate ice cream melted just the way you like it and eaten with eyes closed to fully enjoy it.

Awe-servances
Happy Birthday to:

Still Life with Wrong Colors

Paul Gauguin, 1848, painter. He worked as a stockbroker, until middle age when he became a painter and moved to Tahiti.

It's also Festival of All Possible Worlds and National Chocolate Ice Cream Day.

Aha-phrodisiacs
Gauguin said, "It is the eye of ignorance that assigns a fixed and unchangeable color to every object; beware of this stumbling block." Paint a picture using unpredictable colors. Plan the celebration for the Festival of All Possible Worlds; if you had unlimited use of your imagination and resources, what food would you serve? Where would you hold it? Who would attend? What activities or parades would occur?

Dose of Mirth
Research tells us fourteen out of any ten individuals likes chocolate.
~Sandra Boynton

Journal Juju
Muse in your journal what "The best of all possible worlds" would look like for you. Shut your eyes and listen to your soul, and then write colors, sounds, smells, textures, other features.

Eat some chocolate ice cream with undivided attention and then write or dance about it.

Today I get to: _____

JUNE 8
Name today

Daily Soul Vitamin
An idea is salvation by imagination. ~Frank Lloyd Wright

Toast of the Day
Here's to the feeling of enthusiasm.

Awe-Servances
Happy Birthday to:
Robert Schumann, 1810, composer and pianist.
Frank Lloyd Wright, 1867, famous architect.
Andrew Thomas Weil, 1942, author and integrative medicine physician.

It's also Watch Day.

Stamp of
Enthusiasm

Aha-phrodisiacs
"No architect has so blatantly ignored the rules of architecture, so well," said
Robert Campbell, architectural journalist, speaking of Frank Lloyd Wright.
Ignore the rules; make a list of ways to break rules in whatever creative endeavor
you are in. (Note: thinking is a creative endeavor.)

Dose of Mirth
*Turn the world over on its side and everything loose will land
in Los Angeles.* ~Frank Lloyd Wright

Journal Juju
Robert Schumann said, "Nothing right can be accomplished in art without
enthusiasm. To send light into the darkness of men's hearts, such is the duty of
the artist." Write about what you would do with a sudden gift of 10 percent
more enthusiasm bestowed upon you.

Ponder This for a Weil
Andrew Weil: "Pay attention to your body. The point is everybody is different.
You have to figure out what works for you."

"Watch" what works for your body. Write some observations about: nutrition,
exercise, relaxation, energy, intuition, sleep, and emotions, and their impact
on the body.

Daily Soul Vitamin

Night fell clean and cold in Dublin, and wind moaned beyond my room as if a million pipes played the air. ~Patricia Cornwell

Toast of the Day

Here's to staring into the eyes of a pet that is staring back at you affectionately.

Awe—servances

Happy Birthday to:

Donald Duck, 1934, cartoon and comic-book character from Walt Disney.

Patricia Cornwell, 1956, author. She is widely known for writing a popular series of crime novels featuring the fictional heroine Dr. Kay Scarpetta, a medical examiner.

Michael J. Fox, 1961, award-winning actor.

Johnny Depp, 1963, award-winning actor.

Aha—phrodisiacs

Michael J. Fox said, "One's dignity may be assaulted, vandalized and cruelly mocked, but cannot be taken away unless it is surrendered." We just thought you should know that.

Dose of Mirth

I pretty much try to stay in a constant state of confusion just because of the expression it leaves on my face. ~Johnny Depp

Journal Juju

Donald Duck has the catchphrase: "Nothing to it!" Write down some of your fears about life or creativity and then reply with his catchphrase.

What state would you like to stay in, in order to take advantage of the expression it leaves on your face?

Today I get to: _____

Daily Soul Vitamin
Always be a first-rate version of yourself, instead of a second-rate version of somebody else. ~Judy Garland

Toast of the Day
Here's to the ruby slippers in whatever form they appear to you.

Still Life and Ruby Slippers

Awe-servances
Happy Birthday to:

Judy Garland, 1922, film actress, considered one of the greatest singing stars of Hollywood's Golden Era of musical film, best known for her role as Dorothy in *The Wizard of Oz*.

Maurice Sendak, 1928, author and illustrator: *Where the Wild Things Are, Outside Over There, In the Night Kitchen*

On this date in 1952, the first drive-through restaurant opened.

Aha-phrodisiacs
Use Maurice Sendak's In the Night Kitchen as Starter Fluid for art, writing, or improvisational comedy.

Begin poetry or prose with something about a drive-through restaurant. Make a list of businesses that might lend themselves to being amusing drive-throughs.

Dose of Mirth
My favorite birthday meal was when a friend took me to the Kentucky Fried Chicken drive-through. We ate it all in the car, the extra crispy, the biscuits and the gravy. Then we hit the Dairy Queen. Going down, it was the best meal I've ever had. ~Sandra Bullock

Journal Juju
Write about your relationship or experience with drive-through restaurants. Use details.

Where are the wild things in your life? Where are the calm things?

Repeat Advertising
Are you being kind to yourself? What's one small way you can do that today?

JUNE 11

Name today

Daily Soul Vitamin

From birth, man carries the weight of gravity on his shoulders. He is bolted to earth. But man has only to sink beneath the surface and he is free. ~Jacques Cousteau

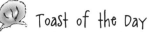 ### Toast of the Day

Here's to the ethereal feeling of floating in the sea, and here's to the sea itself.

Awe-servances

Happy Birthday to:

Jacques Cousteau, 1910, French undersea explorer, world famous oceanographer.

On this day in 1978, Christa Tybus of London set a hula-hoop record by hula-hooping for 24 1/2 hours.

Aha-phrodisiacs

Ralph Waldo Emerson said, "Live in the sunshine, swim the sea, drink the wild air . . . "

Take a drink of the wild air and imagine a spell it can put you under to draw, collage, or doodle. Or just swim in the sea and feel your link to millions of years of swimming beings.

Journal Juju

Cousteau said, "A lot of people attack the sea, I make love to it." Write about your relationship to the sea: a metaphorical, subconscious, or real sea.

And now a word from Body Temple Potion

To breathe like an ocean wave can relax the mind, the body, and the spirit. Preferrably on your back, but however you are, raise the abdomen, the midsection, and then the chest with the inhale. On the exhale, first press in the abdomen, then the midsection, and then the chest. Imagine this breathing practice as an ocean wave.

Today I get to: _____

Double Dose Daily Soul Vitamin

Dreams are road signs along the nighttime highway of sleep. ~Astrid Alauda
Dreams are answers to questions we haven't yet figured out how to ask. ~The X-Files

Toast of the Day

Here's to the freedom we experience in our private world of dreams.

Awe-servances

Happy Birthday to:
Chick Corea, 1941, musician.

Awe-manac Invented: Dreamwork Day.

Aha-phrodisiacs

Chick Corea Title Wave: Got a Match? No Mystery, Light as a Feather, Interplay.
Extra credit: Use these words to write about dreams.

Before you go to bed, ask yourself one or more of these questions without expecting an answer: What one small thing will I remember about my dreams? How will my dreams manifest this evening? Who will I encounter in my dreams tonight? What insight will my dreams give me?

The subconscious loves questions and helps orchestrate our dreams.

Dose of Mirth

Dreaming permits each and every one of us to be quietly and safely insane every night of our lives. ~William Dement

Journal Juju

Writing about dreams can unearth ideas for creativity. Even if you can only remember bits and pieces write little phrases under these headings: events, situations, people, feelings, symbols ~you will begin to remember more and more. Repeated completions: "Dreams are . . . "

Soul Vitamins for Musical Fortification

Music washes away from the soul the dust of everyday life. ~Berthold Auerbach

Without music life would be a mistake. ~Friedrich Nietzsche

Music was my refuge. I could crawl into the space between the notes and curl my back to loneliness. ~Maya Angelou

Toast of the Day

Here's to the many blessings of music.

Awe-servances

Happy Birthday to:

Natalie MacMaster 1972, award-winning fiddle player from Canada, a favorite musician of *The Awe-manac* Staff.

Aha-phrodisiacs

Make time today to listen to, dance to, write to or make music . . . real or metaphorical. Listen to the music of your soul and see what picture it inspires you to doodle.

What are the titles to a few of your favorite songs? Take those titles and make them into a Title Wave.

Journal Juju

Write about your relationship to music. Journal while listening to various types of music and see if it changes your approach, mood, or words. William Butler Yeats said, "Do not wait to strike till the iron is hot; but make it hot by striking." What are you waiting for? A theme song? Write about it. What would be the title of your theme song if you had it?

Dose Of Mirth

Too many pieces of music finish too long after the end.
~Igor Stravinsky

Today I get to: listen to lots of music

Daily Soul Vitamin
Most people are much more unusual and complicated and eccentric and playful and creative than they have time to express. ~Oliver Herring

Toast of the Day
Here's to the part of our family history that created what we love about ourselves.

Awe-Servances
Flag Day.
Family History Day.

Aha-phrodisiacs
Aimlessly wander with your writing in the following way: Start with a first sentence. Use the last word of the first sentence to start the next sentence. For example: *It was one of those days when the sun stood still. Still life paintings have very little movement but they seem to be fine with that. That the world is suddenly in summer solstice again means it keeps turning despite my requests for it to slow down.*

Word pool: decipher, life, shoe, imprint, circle, fate, preposterous, rumble, this leads to, nervous, flicker, exclusive, celebrate, partake, wealth, used to explain, deep satisfaction, flag, forward, another, morning, playful, unusual, time to express.

Dose of Mirth
"Control your fate or somebody else will." ~Heinrich von Pierer

Journal Juju
Make a flag that represents you. Just do it quickly without thinking or worrying about perfection. Or spend a whole weekend on it and get it close enough. Extra credit: Add glitter, rickrack, and other embellishments.

Jacques Delille said, "Fate chooses our relatives, we choose our friends." Write the family history you wish you had. If it is the same as reality, celebrate your fate.

Note to Myself
Check on fate and make sure someone else isn't controlling it—then glide.

JUNE 15

Name today

Daily Soul Vitamins

True courage is like a kite; a contrary wind raises it higher. ~John Petit-Senn
Imagination is the highest kite one can fly. ~Lauren Bacall

Toast of the Day

Here's to the invisible force of a gentle wind.

Awe—Servances

On this day in 1752, Ben Franklin, while flying a kite with a key attached, proved that lightening and electricity are related. Thus it has been made Fly a Kite Day.

Aha—phrodisiacs

Make a list of small displays of courage according to your own definition.

Write poetry or verse with mostly "w" words like wind, waiting, wig. Doodle a picture of a flying "W" as if it were a kite.

Journal Juju

Draw a courage picture using a kite as a symbol of going against the wind. In the wind write what you feel you are working against; in the kite put a quote of courage (perhaps one of the soul vitamins above). Write how the wind may help in creating your flight.

Repeated completions: "I feel courage when . . ." (answers not in the back of the book).

Today I Get To: _____

Daily Soul Vitamin

There is a well of infinity hidden within each Soul. There you will find an incredible energy source, beyond your broadest understanding. It is Light and Healing. The Force of Nature. The essence of Love. ~Royce Addington

Toast of the Day

Here's to love in all its different forms

Aw-Servances

Happy Birthday to:
Erich Segal, 1937, Author of *Love Story*.
Joyce Carol Oates,1938, prolific author.
Royce Addington, 1955, writer.

On this day in 1893, Cracker Jacks were invented by R.W. Rueckheim.

Journal Juju

Repeated completions: "The essence of love is . . . "
Starter Fluid: "The thing about love and me is . . . "

Dose of Mirth

True love comes quietly, without banners or flashing lights. If you hear bells, get your ears checked. ~Erich Segal

Aha-phrodisiacs

Use this Joyce Carol Oates book title for Repeated Completions for poetry, prose or art: *I Am No One You Know* . . .

Take another Oates title, *Them*, and use it as Starter Fluid.

Write a fictional account of an unusual prize you found in your Cracker Jack box. Write an ode to Cracker Jack prizes. Write about finding love in or with a Cracker Jack box.

Today I Get to:

JUNE 17
Name today

Daily Soul Vitamin
There is a certain type of writer that likes to take everything out from under the table —stuff that no one wants to look at—and say "Let's look at this." For better or worse, that happens to be what fascinates me. ~David Mura

Toast of the Day
Here's to surpassing expectations.

Awe-servances
Happy Birthday to:

Dean Martin, 1917, actor/comedian.

David Mura, 1952, poet author of collections of
poetry, including *After We Lost Our Way*.

On this day in 1893, Crackerjacks, a concoction
of peanuts, popcorn, and molasses, was
introduced at the World's Colombian
Exposition in Chicago.

Aha-phrodisiacs
Using the David Mura's Soul Vitamin as guidance, write about something you've never wanted to write about before.

Use one or more of the following sounds to start poetry or prose or have the sound show up at some point during the piece: door slamming, car screeching to a halt, a bell in the distance, the distant sound of a train, someone else's voice in your head, footsteps in the hall way.

Dose of Mirth
If you drink don't drive. Don't even putt. ~Dean Martin

 ### Journal Juju
Use this David Mura title as an inspiration, a journal entry titled, *After I Found My Way*.

If your life was a box of Crackerjacks, what would the prize be inside?

JUNE 18

Name today _____

Daily Soul Vitamin

Only those who attempt the absurd will achieve the impossible.
I think it's in my basement... let me go upstairs
and check. ~M. C. Escher

Toast of the Day

Here's to staring at an ingenious Escher creation.

Salvatore Dali Still Life Wannabe

Awe-Servances

Happy Birthday to:

M. C. Escher, 1899, graphic artist known for his often mathematically inspired
   art that features impossible constructions, explorations of infinity, architecture, and tessellations.

Isabella Rossellini, 1952, actress, filmmaker, author, philanthropist, and model.

National Splurge Day—indulge!

Aha-phrodisiacs

Write about a character who is normally very conservative but who takes a
day to splurge. Go to Escher's Wikipedia page and scroll to his work entitled
Relativity—write about what it's like to walk on that staircase and where it leads.
Or pick any Escher work and write about it.

 ## Dose of Mirth

Are you really sure that a floor can't also be a ceiling? ~M. C. Escher

Journal Juju

Isabella Rossellini said, "If we are completely honest with ourselves, everyone has
a dark side to their personalities." Be completely honest in your journal and
make a list first of what you consider your dark traits, then personify them by
letting them talk from their point of views uncensored.

   Make a list, even if you do not intend on doing them, of all the ways you
could splurge.

   Title a journal entry *The View From Infinity*.

Today I get to: _____

Daily Soul Vitamins

Just like the butterfly, I too will awaken in my own time. ~Deborah Chaskin

Beautiful and graceful, varied and enchanting, small but approachable, butterflies lead you to the sunny side of life. And everyone deserves a little sunshine. ~Jeffrey Glassberg

We are like butterflies who flutter for a day and think it is forever. ~Carl Sagan

Toast of the Day

Here's to the colorful creatures that look like flying flowers.

Awe-servances

It's Butterfly Day.
Happy Birthday to: Suzie Stambaugh, 1947, Artist.

Aha-phrodisiacs

Chuang Tzu Starter Fluid: "I do not know whether I was then a man dreaming I was a butterfly, or whether I am now a butterfly dreaming I am a man." Ask questions as if you are a butterfly dreaming you are a person. Make butterfly art. Do an Internet search on butterflies just to acquaint yourself with the varieties, and expose yourself to another example of life's art. Explore it in any way you want to interpret the term "simple speak".

Dose of Mirth

Butterflies are self propelled flowers. ~R.H. Heinlein

Journal Juju

When will you get your wings—what thoughts, images, music and action will take you from your cocoon and give you flight? Do a credit report for yourself today: write a list of things you're glad you did today or this week.

Suzie Stambaugh, spokeswoman for Awe-vanced Inner Message sez, "We DO endure, don't we, despite the non-linear nature of our humanness and of life."

June 20
Name today

Daily Soul Vitamin

How many a man has thrown up his hands at a time when a little more effort, a little more patience would have achieved success? ~Elbert Hubbard

Toast of the Day

Here's to awesome feats s performed by jugglers.

Awo Sorvancos

Happy Birthday to:
Lionel Richie, 1949, singer

Yesterday was Still Need to Do Day and Elbert Green
    Hubbard's birthday (1856, writer, publisher, artist,
    and philosopher). We still needed to do them, so
    here they are.
World Juggling Day.

Still Life Juggling People

Aha-phrodisiacs

Lionel Richie Title Pool or Starter Fluid for art or writing: Running With the Night, Dancing on the Ceiling, Still.

Dose of Mirth

You can't juggle pâté. ~Dale Launer

Journal Juju

Draw three balls on paper as if they were being juggled. Write in each one something you still need to do and feel you are juggling in your life, then underneath write three questions about each ball without expecting immediate answers. Then draw a fourth ball and label it with something you don't need that you can toss in a field of wild pigs and laughing hyenas.

    Write about your level of procrastination and how it might be serving you.

Subliminal Question Brought to You by FOOOF

What's one small way you can make your work more fun today or tomorrow or three weeks from Friday? Bring a beach ball to work? Buy a fun pen? Bring your lunch in a Mary Poppins lunch box?

JUNE 21
Name today

Summer Solstice

Daily Soul Vitamin
*The best work is not what is most difficult for you;
it is what you do best.* ~Jean-Paul Sartre

Toast of the Day
Here's to cultivating patience.

Awe-servances
Happy Birthday to:
Jean-Paul Sartre, 1905, existentialist
    philosopher, dramatist, screenwriter,
    novelist, critic.

It's also the day Cancer begins, Summer Solstice, Baby Boomers Recognition Day,
    and Aimless Wandering Day.

Aha-phrodisiacs
Cancer is introverted, reserved, sensitive, moody, retentive, sympathetic, prudent, domestic, maternal, protective, quiet, calm, and imaginative. From Cancer sign traits, create three characters having a discussion: for instance, an imaginative fireman talking to a maternal tattoo artist, and a protective bouncer.
    Make a list of nostalgic summer smells and then pick one and write a memory about it in 3rd person.
    Repeated Completions or Starter Fluid: "It's a sure sign of summer . . . "

Dose of Mirth
It's a sure sign of summer if the chair gets up when you do. ~Walter Winchell

Journal Juju
Inspired by Sartre's quote, review a list of things you feel you do best and what's been working for you in the past week. Review your strengths and decide one small way you could be employing one or more of them.
    If you are a Baby Boomer, write about a favorite TV show you watched when you were growing up.

Today I get to: _____

JUNE 22
Name today

Duet of Daily Soul Vitamins

Integrate what you believe in every single area of your life. Take your heart to work and ask the most and best of everybody else, too. ~Meryl Streep

Tell the truth. Sing with passion. Work with laughter. Love with heart. 'Cause that's all that matters in the end. ~Kris Kristofferson

Toast of the Day

Here's to celebrities who tell us encouraging things to do.

Awe-Servances

Happy Birthday to:
Kris Kristofferson, 1936, singer and songwriter.
Meryl Streep, 1949, multi-award-winning theater, TV, and film actress.

Aha-phrodisiacs

Word Pool: laughter, catch, culture, with passion, in every single, blue, June, rather, extreme, inside out, live-wire, wonderment, steal, showcase, recipe, smooth, peek.

Come up with a list of ingredients for something other than a cooking or baking recipe. the news, a day off, a day at work, a perfect day, summer morning, poetry, etc..

Starter fluid: "I would write something brilliant right now but . . . "

Journal Juju

What are one or two things that you believe but you can't integrate into other areas of your life?

Meryl Streep quote: "Joni Mitchell once said, 'Happiness is the best face-lift.' And I believe that. I will say this about plastic surgery: It is not a wonderful development for our culture." Forget about how you look and write about your passion for the creative process. Focus on your next steps. Creativity keeps us young from the inside out.

Daily Soul Vitamin

The more I want to get something done, the less I call it work. ~Richard Bach

Toast of the Day

Here's to a group of people gathered around a summer night's bonfire.

Awe—servances

Happy Birthday to:
Richard Bach, 1936, author of *Jonathan Livingston Seagull* and *Illusions*.
Meredith Deal, 1954, baby boomer, civic participator, communications expert.

Let It Go Day. Release whatever is bothering you.
Midsummer Eve celebrated with bonfires and merrymaking.

Aha-phrodisiacs

Lao Tzu said, "When I let go of what I am, I become what I might be." Erich Fromm said "Creativity requires the courage to let go of certainties." Let go and write nonstop for five minutes, recklessly, furiously, deeply, without much thought and no judgment. Optional Starter Fluid: "So I let go of the rope…"

Dose of Mirth

Keep your favorite things nearby to remind you of your good taste! ~Meredith Deal

Journal Juju

Write some things that are bothering you on some scrap paper and burn them in a bonfire and make merry. (Use a match over a sink if no bonfire is in your vicinity.)

Make a list of your favorite things and see which ones you can post, hang or display nearby.

Repeat Advertisement

What is one small way I can I make what I'm doing at work or at home more fun?

JUNE 24
Name today

Daily Soul Vitamin
Gratitude is the fairest blossom which springs from the soul. ~Henry Ward Beecher

Toast of the Day
Here's to sight, smell, sound, touch, taste—
the sensational experiences of being alive.

Awe-Servances
Happy Birthday to:
Henry Ward Beecher, 1813, theologically liberal
clergyman, social reformer, and speaker.

Aha-phrodisiacs
Pick a sense or two: taste, touch, sight or sound, and if you're so inclined your
sixth sense, ESP, and write about it. Pick a memorable event from your life and
recount it only using a sense or senses.

Celebrate the senses today with exuberance; share the celebration with a friend.

Dose of Mirth
*Humor is perhaps a sense of intellectual perspective: an awareness that some things
are really important, others not; and that the two kinds are most oddly jumbled in
everyday affairs.* ~Christopher Morley

Journal Juju
Henry Ward Beecher said, "Every artist dips
his brush in his own soul, and paints his
own nature into his pictures."

Let your soul blossom with a list of
that which you are grateful. If you do this
often and want a fresh approach, make cate-
gories: Gratitude in the areas of health, people, opportunities, safety, rights, food, skills,
beauty, prosperity, freedom, etc.

JUNE 25
Name today

Daily Soul Vitamin
All great work is preparing yourself for the accident to happen.
~Sydney Lumet

Toast of the Day
Here's to accidents that result in unexpected creative destinations.

Awe-servances
Happy Birthday to:
George Orwell, 1903, author of *Animal Farm* and *1984*.
Sidney Lumet, 1924, film director.

1630, the fork was introduced to American dining by MA Governor John Winthrop.
1947, the tennis shoe was first designed.

Aha-phrodisiacs
Creativity Tip: do some work that prepares you for the creative accident to happen; look up some facts, daydream with a focus on your idea, expose yourself to something different or inspiring, defy the rut today, make a list of ideas.

Dose of Mirth
On this day in 1977, lightening struck Roy Sullivan for the seventh time in his life while he was fishing. Let's pause for a moment to be awe-struck!

Journal Juju
George Orwell said, "Enlightened people seldom or never possess a sense of responsibility," He also said, "For a creative writer, possession of the truth is less important than emotional sincerity." Write with emotional sincerity about your level of responsibility in a role you have and how you feel about it.

Repeat Advertising from Awe-wakened Moment
Imagine believing that everything is unfolding just the way it is supposed to. How can you acknowledge, feel and embody the fact that many parts of your dream are already happening now?

June 26
Name today

Daily Soul Vitamin
I don't wait for moods. You accomplish nothing if you do that. Your mind must know it has got to get down to work. ~Pearl S. Buck

Toast of the Day
Here's to the feeling of gliding downhill on a bike.

Awe-Servances
Happy Birthday to:
Pearl Buck, 1892, Nobel Prize-winning author and humanitarian.
Chris Isaak, 1956, singer, songwriter, and actor.

On this day in 1498, the toothbrush was invented in China. In 1819, the bicycle was patented by William Clarkson, Jr. of NY.
Festival of Ranting & Vaporing.

Dose of Mirth
I rant, therefore I am. ~Dennis Miller

Aha-phrodisiacs
From the Auto-Flame Rant-O-Matic Page: "Guidelines for effective ranting: 1. The smaller the nit, the better the picking. 2. Spelling/grammar/knowledge mean nothing. It's the force of your convictions that count. 3. Don't be afraid to say things that would get you either beat up, kicked out, or completely ignored in any normal social situation." Pick a nit and go off on a rant and see what that is like. Then turn around and passionately defend something and see what THAT's like. Buy yourself a new, fun toothbrush. Start a rant about toothbrushes or bikes.

Journal Juju
See if any of these Chris Issak song titles reflect a part of your experience that you can record in your journal: "Wicked Game, " "You Owe Me Some Kind of Love, " "Heart Shaped World, " "Heart Full of Soul," "Dancin', "Nothing's Changed," "Voodoo," "Lie to Me."

Daily Soul Vitamin

Many persons have a wrong idea of what constitutes true happiness. It is not attained through self-gratification but through fidelity to a worthy purpose. ~Helen Keller

Toast of the Day
Here's to ladybugs.

Awe-servances
Happy Birthday to:
Helen Keller, 1880, author and lecturer.
Bob Keeshan, 1927, better known as Captain Kangaroo.

Decide to be Married Day.

Wanna Get Married?

Aha-phrodisiacs
Write an ode to deciding to be married.

    To honor Captain Kangaroo, write as if you are talking to a group of kids about one of these subjects: your latest creative endeavor, walking on the ceiling, hiding in a tree, drawing with your non-dominant hand, messes.

    Make up a quote as if you were a kid.

Dose of Mirth
You should never wear a red shirt with black polka dots because your friends will call you a ladybug. ~Stefanie, age 8

Journal Juju
Bob Keeshan said, "One of the big secrets of finding time is not to watch television." Start your journal entry with the title: *TV and Me* or *My Fidelity to a Worthy Cause.* Go.

    Helen Keller said, "Although the world is full of suffering, it is full also of the overcoming of it." Write about what has worked best for you in overcoming suffering or write about a worthy purpose to which you would like to be married.

June 28
Name today

Daily Soul Vitamin
While we have the gift of life, it seems to me the only tragedy is to allow part of us to die—whether it is our spirit, our creativity, or our glorious uniqueness. ~Gilda Radner

Toast of the Day
Here's to movies that make us laugh out loud.

Awe-servances
Happy Birthday to:
Jean-Jacques Rousseau, 1778, philosopher of the Enlightenment.
Mel Brooks, 1926, award-winning actor, writer, director, and producer
    of comedy parodies.
Gilda Radner, 1946, comedian and *Saturday Night Live* actress.

Aha-phrodisiacs
Gilda Radner said, "I can always be distracted by love, but eventually I get horny for my creativity."

Dose of Mirth
"If you're quiet, you're not living. You've got to be noisy and colorful and lively." ~Mel Brooks

Journal Juju
Title a journal entry, *My Glorious Uniqueness*. In it wax uniquely, remember unique aspects of yourself that need to be revisited, revel in the current ones. Jean-Jacques Rousseau said "The world of reality has limits; the world of imagination is boundless." Add an imaginative element to defy the previous limits of reality~your job, your relationship, your creative passion. What force, power, new character, new emotion, or different dimension can be fun to explore within one of these realms?

June 29
Name today

Daily Soul Vitamin

It is in the compelling zest of high adventure and of victory, and in creative action, that man finds his supreme joys. ~Antoine de Saint-Exupery

Toast of the Day

To laughing so hard you cry.

Awe-servances

Antoine de Saint-Exupéry, 1900, writer, aviator, author of *The Little Prince*.

1964, the first remote control for a TV was invented.
It is also Flower and Camera Day.

Aha-phrodisiacs

Antoine de Saint-Exupéry said, "It is such a secret place, the land of tears." Make a painting, collage, or doodle of *The Land of Tears* and then have it write a poem to you.

Celebrate Flower and Camera Day by getting creative with the camera. Anyone can take a picture of a flower; find a unique twist. Play with pictures in Photoshop. Choose an attitude from the Viewfinders and set out to photograph with that perspective.

Dose of Mirth

"Laughter and tears are both responses to frustration and exhaustion. I myself prefer to laugh, since there is less cleaning up to do afterward." ~Kurt Vonnegut

Journal Juju

Eileen Mayhew said, "Let your tears come. Let them water your soul." Title a journal entry *Tears* and write what associations you make. Choose one of the associations and explore it in detail.

If you could change emotions like you change channels, what three emotions would you spend the most time in, and what kind of commercials would they have?

Daily Soul Vitamin

There are few things in life more heartwarming than to be welcomed by a cat.
~Tay Hohoff

Toast of the Day

Here's to the festive occasion of having an ice cream soda in the summertime.

Awe-servances

Happy Birthday to:
Lena Horne, 1917, singer.

National Ice Cream Soda Day.
It's the last day of Adopt-a-Cat Month.

Aha-phrodisiacs

Did you adopt a cat? Write from the point of view of a cat who is adopted.
Doodle a happy cat.
  Invent a character that has something to do with ice cream sodas.

Dose of Mirth

"Cats can work out mathematically the exact place to sit that will cause most inconvenience." ~Pam Brown

Journal Juju

Lena Horne said, "Don't be afraid to feel as angry or as loving as you can, because when you feel nothing, it's just death." Let your feeling amplify in your journal today. Today's journal title: *As ___ As I Can Be* (fill in the blank with an emotion that needs to come out.) Rinse and repeat.

Today I get to:

Well it's the halfway point of another
Awe-mazing Year.

Take a moment and reflect on the first half
with light fascination.

What were your highlights?

What things
are you glad you did?

What worked for you?

What small moments brought you delight?

What made you laugh?

Who did you connect with?

Where did you leave your glasses?

Ask these questions for the rest of the year:

In what small way can I
pay attention to small delights?

How can I be a little kinder to myself?

Can I give myself permission
to have more fun and less pressure?

How can I remember to sing in the shower?

Passion fuels the embers of positive self-esteem and creativity births another reality. You watch in awe of your own power as others make a circle of Life around you.
~AlixSandra Parness

Birth another reality under the spell of *The Awe-manac's* own special blend of Aha-phrodisiacs -a powerful potion that intensifies your creative desires though a daily dose of musings guaranteed to tap the source of youth and inventive thinking-defeating age and experiencing ever-new joy. Creativity is discovered as its own reward.

During those rare moments of creativeness, when an ordinary person has something in common with the making of the universe, he feels a sense of transcendence, of moving beyond his daily life. What could be a greater reward? ~Joseph Zinker

Making time for creativity can be a break from the confusion of the surface to the stillness of the center. ~Krishanna

Creativity does not depend on inherited talent or on environment or upbringing;; it is the function of the ego of every human being.
~Silvano Arieti

Possible Effects: Feeling more creative with less effort, running away without leaving home, reinventing yourself, joy, enjoying youthfulness, improving relationships, multiplying possibilities, adopting soaring attitudes, and inventing new stuff.
    Consult your doctor if brilliance is sustained longer than four hours—(frizzy Einstein-like hair may ensue). Side effects may include a chronic facial expression of amusement including an invincible nymph-like smile and drooling glee. Caution: Do not operate a checkbook while on Aha-phrodisiacs —inventing balances and income sources is hazardous to your credit rating.

ENTRY WAY TO JULY

July was named to honor Roman dictator Julius Caesar. With the help of Sosigenes, he developed the Julian calendar, the precursor to the Gregorian calendar we use today. July is the birth month of *The Awe-manac* staff so we made this fact an excuse to take July liberties and invent a commemoration that is easy to draw. We unanimously voted to make July Cultivate your Wings Month, because wings represent so many uplifting things and things that lift up—which can keep us young. Plus having faith that you will grow wings when you are jumping into the unknown comes in handy during the creative process.

Some of the Observances at July's Door

National Ice Cream Month, Anti-Boredom Month, National Baked Bean Month, National Bison Month, National Foreign Language Month, National July Belongs to Blueberries Month, National Recreation and Parks Month, National Tennis Month, National Cultivate Character Month (dare to be original).

And Awe-Manac Invented:

Cultivate Your Wings Month
July 6: Kindness Day
July 12: Claim Your Inner Elixir Day

Our arms start from the back because they were once wings.
~Martha Graham

If you were born without wings, do nothing to prevent their growing.
~Chanel

Suggested Ways to Celebrate

Whether you are a fiction writer or collage artist, creating characters builds character in more than one way. For National Cultivate Character Month, make a list of different aspects of your personality. Then for each one give a name, a motivation or desire, and wings—ways to obtain those desires. Invent a character that you can hang out with . . . I've always wanted a nanny (preferably one that sings) to do my laundry and fix meals (as an adult), I have also wanted a next-door neighbor who is a crazy inventor/musician with a satirical sense of humor to perhaps share sweet iced peppermint tea with me on my front porch. I've also wanted a front porch and the ability to eat sugar without turning into a slug. The beauty of creativity is that we can create and be anyone that our imagination can muster up. Plus there are less dishes to do afterwards.

Pancakes with strawberries, blueberries, and whipped cream is just ever-so-red-white-and-blue, so feel free to make this concoction for your favorite friends (in an open fire pit on the beach is even more July-y).

Astrological Spells

Aries: Buy a wind-up toy for yourself and bring it to dinner with a friend.

Taurus: Find a comfortable chair somewhere and daydream, 10 minutes, about being a free range person

Gemini: Plan a hike this month and make a poem up about anything blue that you see on your hike. Bring a picnic (include blueberries but leave sticky marshmallow treats at home).

Cancer: Buy or smell some Larkspur and see what tune it makes you hum.

Leo: Nap in a hammock and imagine that the sky (or the roof) is a movie screen. Play the first seen of any movie your imagination cooks up, give it a review that begins "A triumph . . . " Buy a hammock if you don't have one.

Virgo: Be 5 percent kinder to yourself this month. Decide what kind of voice your heart would have if it could sing.

Libra: Visit your imaginary room with the window that opens to the elsewheres of possibilities while getting a massage (tell the masseuse "I need quiet so please no talking").

Scorpio: In your journal, doodle where secrets are kept and then add an escape hatch.

Sagittarius: Make a map of your heart's desired journey and indicate pit stops and side tours.

Capricorn: Make a blueprint of how to be 5 percent more playful this month: first make a list of ideas then illustrate them with really primitive doodles.

Aquarius: Turn one of your works of art upside-down, or begin at the end of a
writing, or think of the big picture optimistically for a change.

Pisces: Write a word or poem that gives you protection from people or things
that might dampen your spirit- emboss on a T-shirt and wear it under
your clothes.

Tides:

Ebbing: What are you letting go of this month (just a little bit)?

Flowing: Where are you expanding this month (just a little bit)?

Vessel of strength: What saying or quote will navigate you and keep you afloat
through the month? (See Awe-wakened Inner Messages.)

Gardening Information

Flower: Larkspur

Monthly *Awe-manac* Crop: Ice cream

Planting Tips: Plant some suppressed
hankerings for creamy, cool, flavored
delights. Place some cold stones around
the perimeter, let the soil *bask in
robin's* droppings, Ben and Jerry
chunky mulch over the top, and
scoop when chilled.

Ice Cream
Crop

JULY 1

Name today _____

Soul Vitamin

Art is the only way to run away without leaving home. ~Twyla Tharp

Toast of the Day

Here's to being transported by art or the wind.

Awe-servances

Happy Birthday to:
Twyla Tharp, 1941, award-winning dancer and choreographer.

It is also Joke Day and National Cultivate Character Month.
On this day in 1200, sunglasses were invented in China to conceal eyes of
    judges sitting in court.
In 1874 the Philadelphia Zoological Society opened the first U.S. zoo.

Aha-phrodisiacs

Make a collage of animals with sunglasses.

Cultivate a character who dances at a zoo while wearing sunglasses; give
him or her a name and a reason to dance and begin writing: "While elephants
watched . . . " See where it takes you if you do not think too much.

Journal Juju

List five ways that you can add originality to your life. Find a number of pictures in
magazines, or print images from the Internet. Cut them out and pick a few. Write
captions, stories or how they are answers to questions in your life.

Dose Of Mirth

Woman driving down street with three penguins in the back
seat. Cop: "What are you doing with those penguins?
Take them to the zoo!" Next day, same scenario, but with
penguins in sunglasses. Cop: "I thought I told you
to take those penguins to the zoo." Woman: "I did.
Today we're going to the beach."

Today I get to: Let go of the struggle.

JULY 2

Name today _____

Daily Soul Vitamin

A book must be an ice-axe to break the seas frozen inside our soul. ~Franz Kafka

Toast of the Day

Here's to pausing to reread a sentence more than once because it is written so wonderfully.

Awe-Servances

Happy Birthday to:

Franz Kafka, 1883, influential fiction writer.

It's also I Forgot Day, a day to make up for all the birthdays, etc. you have forgotten. On this day in 1843, an alligator fell from the sky during a Charleston, SC thunderstorm.

Aha-phrodisiacs

Write about an alligator shower or make a collage, doodle, or painting of one.

Send someone you forgot a book, a card, or an alligator doodle.

Kafka's work creates worlds that are at once real and dreamlike with individuals burdened with guilt, isolation, and anxiety who make a futile search for personal freedom.

"Kafkaesque" suggests something that is marked by a senseless, disorienting, often menacing complexity. This is not an easy assignment, but the hard ones often push us into unfamiliar territories that offer fresh ideas. Try a rough, rough first draft that integrates forgetfulness, alligators, and Kafka's style.

Journal Juju

Repeated Completions: "I forgot . . . "

See if you can assemble these words as something you might write in your journal. Word Pool: moonrise, underneath, staying, tip, enough, ramble, noise, through, wide, deep, walk, square, capacity, goose, sky, particular, sea, influence, shower, menacing.

Dose of Mirth

I have a seashell collection. I keep it on the beach. ~Stephen Wright

Today I Get To: _____

JULY 3
Name today _____

Daily Soul Vitamin
You use a glass mirror to see your face; you use works of art to see your soul. ~George Bernard Shaw

Toast of the Day
Here's to the comfort that the air conditioner gives us.

Awe-servances
Happy Birthday to:
Dave Barry, Jr., 1947, bestselling, award-winning author and humorist.

The Dog Days of Summer begin: hottest days of the
    year in the Northern Hemisphere.
It's also Air Conditioning Appreciation Days, Compli-
    ment Your Mirror Day, Stay Out of the Sun Day.

Aha-phrodisiacs
Write an ode to the air conditioner.
    Stay in the a/c today, clean your mirror and draw a sun picture with this
quote from Buddha: "Three things cannot be long hidden: the sun, the moon,
and the truth."

Journal Juju
Make a collage, doodle or write a poem titled *My Soul.*
    Give yourself a credit report today. Write about your relationship to watching
TV and end with a conclusion (without beating yourself up if you watch a lot).

Dose of Mirth
*If somebody thinks they're a hedgehog, presumably you just give 'em a mirror and a
few pictures of hedgehogs and tell them to sort it out for themselves.* ~Douglas Adams

Aha-phrodisiac Application
The nuclear generator of brain sludge is television. ~Dave Barry

Mental Solution Question
What energizes you the most about your writing or art?

JULY 4
Name today _____

happy fourth of july!

Daily Soul Vitamin
Solitude is independence. ~Hermann Hesse
*The beauty of independence, departure, actions that
   rely on themselves.* ~Walt Whitman

Toast of the Day
Here's to feeling free and never taking it for granted.

Awe—servances
Happy Birthday to:
Nathaniel Hawthorne, 1804, novelist known for *The Scarlet Letter*.
Ann Landers and her twin Dear Abby, 1918, the advice columnists.

On this day in 1862 Lewis Carroll created *Alice in Wonderland* for Alice P. Liddell.
It's also Independence Day! In 1776 US gained independence from Great Britain.

Aha—phrodisiacs
Make a list of quirks you have or any quirks you find interesting. Like Lewis
Carroll, combine them or use them alone and invent fanciful characters who
have exaggerated versions of those quirks. Make it a rough, rough draft. Or write
about Freedom.

Journal Juju
If you had a scarlet letter to wear on your chest, what would that letter be?
What would it stand for? Might it be something you don't like
about yourself? Something you're known for? Something people
don't really know about you?

Dose of Mirth
No wonder you're late. Why, this watch is exactly two days slow.
~Mad Hatter from *Alice in Wonderland*.

And now a word from A.I.M.
What is one small way you can stay true to yourself during your creative
process? Ask a list of questions about a creative endeavor, then quickly answer
as if you've completed it.

JULY 5

Name today _____

Daily Soul Vitamin

Doing nothing is better than being busy doing nothing. ~Lao Tzu

Toast of the Day

Here's to the occasional bliss of doing nothing and not feeling guilty about it.

Awe-servances

Happy Birthday to.
Bill Watterson, 1958, author of the comic strip *Calvin and Hobbes*

Workaholics Day: Give yourself a break from work and pamper yourself.

Aha-phrodisiacs

To relax, put on some music and color. See coloring page in the back.
Have a bubble bath, take a dip in a hot tub, or float in a pool and look up at the sky.
Have your creative idea, character, concept write to you what it wants to do next.

Journal Juju

Title your journal entry *In the Space Between the Worlds* and see what comes out.

Question from Aha-phrodisiac Potion

What writing, art, or music that you've started or completed can you revisit?

Today I Get To:

_____

_____

KiNdNeSS Day

"Be kind whenever possible. It is always possible." ~Dalai Lama

Toast of the Day

Here's to making your habit compassion and patience—and getting really good at them.

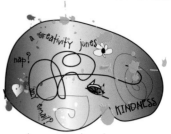

Paint What Passes Through Your Head

Awe-Servances

Happy Birthday to:

Tenzin Gyatso,1935, fourteenth and current Dalai Lama, author of many Buddhist teachings.

Frida Kahlo, 1907, Mexican painter combining Realism, Symbolism and Surrealism.

Aha-phrodisiacs

Frida Kahlo said, "I paint my own reality. The only thing I know is that I paint because I need to, and I paint whatever passes through my head without any other consideration." Take some time and free yourself with permission to imperfectly paint whatever is in your head.

Journal Juju

The Dalai Lama said, "Spend some time alone every day." Journal writing is a good time to do that.

Repeated completion: "My reality is . . . "

Frida Kahlo said, "Feet, what do I need you for when I have wings to fly?" Write where you go when you fly. Draw, collage or doodle a picture of yourself or anything with wings.

Dose of Mirth

If you were arrested for kindness, would there be enough evidence to convict you? ~Unknown

A Message from Kindness Potion

What's one small way you can incorporate gratitude into your creative process? How about service? How about kindness to yourself?

Today I Get To: be kind

JULY 7

Daily Soul Vitamin
Sometimes I sits and thinks and sometimes I just sits.
~Satchel Paige

Toast of the Day
Here's to allowing ourselves to create a life based on intuition not the opinions of others.

Awe-Servances
Happy Birthday to:

Pierre Cardin, 1922, designer.
Satchel Paige, July 7, 1906, baseball player and pitcher.

It's also International Cherry Pit Spitting Contest.
The Running of the Bulls starts in Spain and runs until July 14.

Aha-phrodisiacs
Write a haiku to go along with *The Running of the Bulls* or *The Spitting of the Pits*. Design a new outfit for a bull, a cherry, or a country. Make it into a collage.

Journal Juju
Satchel Paige asked, "How old would you be if you didn't know how old you are?" How would you answer? Write about what was important about that age for you.

Dose of Mirth
Don't cross this field unless you can do it in 9.9 seconds. The bull can do it in 10.
~Sign on bison range at the Fermi National Accelerator Laboratory

Subliminal Message Brought to You by the Kindness and Gather Potions
What is one small thought you can think in this very moment that is a gesture of kindness to yourself? Think another thought of kindness for another person.

Anti-aging Application
Anti-aging Tip: Be as young as you feel spiritually; our spirits do not age, just our bodies. Live from your spirit, not your body, and not from any societal influence—be an artist of being alive by creating your own world and not listening to rules that limit your existence. Caution: there are a lot of them.

Daily Soul Vitamin

There is no need to go to India or anywhere else to find peace. You will find that deep place of silence right in your room, your garden or even your bathtub.
~Elisabeth Kubler-Ross

Toast of the Day

Here's to a garden where tomatoes, daisies, and peace can
be cultivated.

Awe—servances

Happy Birthday to:
Elisabeth Kübler-Ross, M.D. 1926, psychiatrist and author of *On Death and Dying*.

Aha—phrodisiacs

Make a collage of people's pictures into a stained glass window with this Kübler-Ross quote beneath it. "People are like stained glass windows, the true beauty can be seen only when there is light from within. The darker the night, the brighter the windows."

   Repeated Completion: "People are . . . ."

Journal Juju

Write quotes in your journal that inspire life:
   I shall not die of a cold. I shall die of having lived. ~Willa Cather;
   Life is better than death, I believe, if only because it is less boring, and because it has fresh peaches in it. ~Alice Walker;
      The idea is to die young as late as possible. ~Ashley Montagu
         Make up your own.

Dose of Mirth

They say such nice things about people at their funerals that it makes me sad to realize that I'm going to miss mine by just a few days. ~Garrison Keillor

Note to Myself: say nice things to people
            before they die.

JULY 9

Name today _____

Daily Soul Vitamin

If you're funny, if there's something that makes you laugh,
then every day's going to be okay. ~Tom Hanks

Toast of the Day

Here's to a picnic with a magnificent view, a placid breeze, and walnut brownies.

Awe-servances

Happy Birthday to:

Tom Hanks, 1956, award-winning film actor, director, voice-over artist, and
    movie producer

It's National Picnic Month.

Aha-phrodisiacs

Tom Hanks said, "If it wasn't hard, everyone would do it. It's the hard that makes
it great."

   What are some things you want to do that are hard? Make a list and pick one
to do for 5 to 10 minutes. Write, do art, make a call, work out. Do it early and
make the rest of the day easier.

Journal Juju

   Robert Fulghum said, "The examined life is no picnic." Prove him
wrong. Examine your life as if it were a picnic. What's sweet? What's bittersweet?
What's in the middle of your positive-negative-positive sandwich? What ants are
invading? What's the weather like? The view?

Dose of Mirth

Of all the wonders of nature, a tree in summer is perhaps the most remarkable; with the
possible exception of a moose singing, "Embraceable You" in spats. ~Woody Allen

Repeat Advertising from to you by the A.I.M. Potion

What little 1 to 5 minute step can you take today toward building a creative
commitment or habit? What would 15 percent more creative confidence feel
like? What small thing can you do to make you believe in yourself? Imagine for
20 seconds, really believing you can surpass your limitations.

Daily Soul Vitamin
Aerodynamically, the bumble bee shouldn't be able to fly, but the bumble bee doesn't know it so it goes on flying anyway. ~Mary Kay Ash

Toast of the Day
Here's to bees and their pollinating miracles.

Awe-Servances
Happy Birthday to:

Camille Pissarro, 1830, French Impressionist painter.

Marcel Proust, 1871, French intellectual, novelist, essayist and
critic, author of *In Search of Lost Time*

Plus it's Don't Step on a Bee Day.

Aha-phrodisiacs
Google or somehow locate Pissaro's painting,
The Garden at Pontoise, and write a poem about it.

Or paint or doodle a picture or write some prose and
then add one or more bees.

Write about opening a drawer and finding some lost time.

bees

Journal Juju
Marcel Proust said, "The real voyage of discovery consists not in seeking new
landscapes but in having new eyes" and "We don't receive wisdom; we must
discover it for ourselves after a journey that no one can take for us or spare us."
Use the Viewfinders in the back of the book to see your daily landscape differently. Pick a recent event or situation and write about it shortly with three
different Viewfinders.

Dose of Mirth
Every saint has a bee in his halo. —Elbert Hubbard

Note to Myself: Just bee today.

July 11

Name today _____

Daily Soul Vitamin
Dare to reach out your hand into the darkness, to pull another hand into the light. ~Norman B. Rice

Toast of the Day
Here's to unzipping the veil of beauty with words.

Awe-servances
Happy Birthday to:
E. B. White, 1899, essayist, author, humorist, poet and literary stylist.
Harold Bloom, 1930, professor and prominent literary and cultural critic.
Suzanne Vega, 1959, songwriter and singer known for her highly literate lyrics and eclectic folk-inspired music.

Aha-phrodisiacs
E. B. White said, "A poet dares be just so clear and no clearer . . . He unzips the veil from beauty, but does not remove it." Reveal beauty with words which are illusive enough to be art but tangible enough to relate to.

Doses of Mirth
A good farmer is nothing more nor less than a handy man with a sense of humus. ~E. B. White

Journal Juju
Harold Bloom wrote a book called *The Anxiety of Influence: A Theory of Poetry*. Write a journal entry titled *The Influence of Anxiety on My Today* and talk about your relationship to worry. Extra credit: Make it poetry, art or accompany it with an anxious scribble. Optional: Replace anxiety with calm.

Today I Get To:
_____

JULY 12 CLAIM YOUR POWER DAY:

There is nothing in a caterpillar that tells you it's going to be a butterfly.
~Buckminster Fuller

Daily Soul Vitamin

I know of no more encouraging fact than the unquestionable ability of man to elevate his life by a conscious endeavor. ~Henry David Thoreau

Toast of the Day

Here's to understanding that power comes from an inner world of strength and peace undisturbed by any other or anything on the outside.

Claiming your power is an inside job.
—Brought to you by Inner Awe-lixir

Awe-servances

Happy Birthday to:

Henry David Thoreau, 1817, author, naturalist, and philosopher.
Buckminster Fuller, 1895, visionary, designer, architect, poet, author, and inventor.
Pablo Neruda, 1904, Chilean writer and poet.

Journal Juju

Thoreau said, "To affect the quality of the day, that is the highest of the arts." Write a list of ways you might use your power to affect the quality of your day. Pick one and execute it imperfectly for 5 minutes acting as if you have 4 times more power.

Write in your journal when you are having good days where you feel your power and can put it into words with quotes and vision. Make those pages accessible so you can reread them on those days you need them.

Today I Get To: use more power for my higher purpose

A Message from Awe-wakened Moment

Buckminister Fuller used to get up at 5:30 in the morning to go out and see the sunrise. As it came up, he would throw his arms in the air and say: "Thank you, thank you, thank you!"

JULY 13
Name today _____

Daily Soul Vitamin
Make it so. ~Captain Picard, *Star Trek: The Next Generation*

Toast of the Day
Here's to the confidence that imagination can empower.

Awe-Servances
Happy Birthday to:
Patrick Stewart, 1940 film, television and stage actor, portrayed Captain Picard.
Harrison Ford, 1942, blockbuster movie star.

In 1939 Frank Sinatra recorded his 1st record "From the Bottom of My Heart" and
    "Melancholy Mood" with the Harry James Orchestra.
It's also Skeptics' Day, a national celebration of skepticism. And in1977 NYC was
    plunged in 25 hours of darkness after lightening struck upstate power lines.
    (25 hours of darkness? Where was the sun?)

Aha-phrodisiacs
Harrison Ford said about acting: "I don't use any particular method. I'm from
the let's-pretend school of acting." Pretend that you are a poet, songwriter,
bestselling fiction writer, actor, or expert non-fiction writer and write a rough,
rough first draft for 15 minutes of a work called *25 Hours of Darkness*. If you
already know you are one or more of those, make your pretending about being
more courageous.

Dose of Mirth
*You know you are getting old when all the names in your black book have
MD after them.* ~Harrison Ford

Journal Juju
When asked why he went into acting, Harrison Ford replied,
"Failure in all other fields." Write about how your failure in
one thing may have led to discovery in another.

CLOSE ENOUGH !!!!

And now Two Words from Awe-vanced Inner Messages
When you are feeling in a perfectionistic dither, say these two words
to yourself: "Close enough!"

JULY 14

Name today _____

Daily Soul Vitamin
If a day goes by that don't change some of your old notions for new ones, that is just about like trying to milk a dead cow. ~Woody Guthrie

Toast of the Day
Here's to imagining we can hear all the children in the world who are laughing in this very moment.

Awe—servances
Happy Birthday to:
Woodie Guthrie, 1912, prolific folk musician.

On this day in 1850, 1st demonstration of ice by refrigeration took place and in 1990 Fast Eddy McDonald of Prince Edward Island did 8,437 loops in 1 hour with his yo-yo (a moment of awe please).
And it's Cow Appreciation Day in Woodstock, VT.

Aha—phrodisiacs
Word pool: doorway, roam, under, centerpiece, key, traverse, parties, cellar, cross-eyed, lunch, manhole cover, cow, telegram, launch, seat, modesty, creep, occupy, middle, sideways glance, pocket, innuendo, ice, yo-yo, wanting to understand

Dose of Mirth
Parties who want milk should not seat themselves on a stool in the middle of the field in hopes that the cow will back up to them. ~Elbert Hubbard

Journal Juju
Grant Wood said, "All the really good ideas I ever had came to me while I was milking a cow." List some of the places that you come up with good ideas (driving? showering? walking?)

Get ready to walk your houseplants on July 27.

Daily Soul Vitamin

Painting is the grandchild of nature. It is related to God. ~Rembrandt

Toast of the Day

Here's to the invention of the banana split.

Awe-servances

Happy Birthday to:

Rembrandt, 1606, one of the greatest painters and printmakers in art history.

It's National Ice Cream Day.

Aha-phrodisiacs

Search online for Rembrant's painting *Susanna and the Elders*, and write from the point of view of the woman in the painting.

Feel or imagine the following feelings or concepts in your body, mind and spirit and then see what you are inspired to write, doodle, draw, dance, or paint: nature, patience, audaciousness, skilled confidence, minimalism, ala ice cream, floral crazy, nervous, an inclination to favor the edge of the page, wild abandon, controlled.

Dose of Mirth

My advice to you is not to inquire why or whither, but just enjoy your ice cream while it's on your plate—that's my philosophy. ~Thornton Wilder

Journal Juju

See today's Soul Vitamin. The staff of *The Awe-manac* think most creative processes are connected to something very spiritual. To persevere creatively we must tackle our inner demons and stay true to our higher purpose. Write about your spiritual connection to your creative passions. If your creativity could speak to you, what would it say?

JULY 16
Name today _____

Daily Soul Vitamin
Trouble springs from idleness.
~Benjamin Franklin

Toast of the Day
Here's to staying out of trouble.

Awe—servances
1994, the first fragment of the comet Shoemaker-Levy crashed into the planet
    Jupiter, beginning a series of collisions, each unleashing more energy than
    the combined effect of an explosion of all the world's nuclear arsenal.
It's also National Get Out of the Doghouse Day.

Aha—phrodisiacs
Word Pool: collision, series, unleash, effect, arsenal, planet, crash, beginning,
explosion, comet, first, combine, each, energy, world, fragment, dance, doghouse,
out, announce, arsenal, trouble.

    Write about a time you got in trouble but exaggerate and embellish the
story to near-fiction (or near science fiction if you prefer). Optional: use third-
person point of view.

Journal Juju
Unleashing My Energy: See what intuitive sparks flash when you use this as a
journal entry title.

    Make a 15 minute collage in your journal with images that energize you.
Repeated Completions: The trouble with . . .

Dose of Mirth
*If you don't learn to laugh at troubles, you won't have anything to laugh at
when you grow old.* ~Ed Howe

Awe—vanced Inner Messages has this to say
Just think to yourself, "I can do this."

Daily Soul Vitamin

The hours of folly are measured by the clock, but of wisdom no clock can measure.
~William Blake

Toast of the Day

Here's to lengthening a moment by being fully present.

Awe-servances

Happy Birthday to:

Phyllis Diller, 1917, comedian.

Phoebe Snow, 1952, singer.

And it's the Feast of the Clockless Nowever: cited on the
     Internet but not explained. Nevertheless, we like the name.

Aha-phrodisiacs

Define, write a poem, or make a collage about Feast of the Clockless Nowever.
Phoebe Snow Title Pool: Majesty of Life, Ride the Elevator, Something So Right,
Never Letting Go, We're Children , Middle of the Night, Garden of Joy Blues

Dose of Mirth

I'm eighteen years behind in my ironing. ~Phyllis Diller

Journal Juju

Pick a certain time of your life past or present
and write some wisdom it would like to
impart to you. Write about the eternal flow
of the "now" eliminating the past and the
future.

Subliminal Message brought to you by Body Temple Potion

Are you listening to the wisdom of your
body? Are you taking stress breaks? Tapping
the shoulders can release endorphins, the
body's anti-aging; feel-good chemicals.

Daily Soul Vitamin
The real source of wealth and capital in this new era is not material things.. it is the human mind, the human spirit, the human imagination, and our faith in the future.
~Steve Forbes

Toast of the Day
Here's to listening to your favorite instrument as it plays a song you like with skill and passion.

Awe-servances
Happy Birthday to:

Nelson Mandela, 1918, former president of South Africa,

John Glenn, Jr., 1921, astronaut, and politician.

Hunter S. Thompson, 1937, journalist and author. He is credited as the creator of Gonzo journalism, a style of reporting in which the reporter involves themselves in the action to such a degree that they become the central figure of the story itself.

Steve Forbes, 1947, publisher of business magazine *Forbes*, son of Malcolm Forbes.

In 64 A.D. Rome burned while Nero fiddled.

FOUR SUNSETS

Aha-phrodisiacs
I don't know what you could say about a day in which you have seen four beautiful sunsets. ~John Glenn (a moment of awe indeed and possibly a collage or painting of four different sunsets with four different titles.)

Use Gonzo journalism to write about Rome burning (or any other real or fictional news story) making yourself a central figure in the story.

Dose of Mirth
Call on God, but row away from the rocks. ~Hunter S. Thompson

Journal Juju
Nelson Mandela said, "I learned that courage was not the absence of fear, but the triumph over it. The brave man is not he who does not feel afraid, but he who conquers that fear." Write a list of your fears and dialog with one or more of them on the page compassionately but as if you are in charge.

Daily Soul Vitamin
A woman who has no way of expressing herself and of realizing herself as a full human being has nothing else to turn to but the owning of material things.
~Enriqueta Longauex-Vasquez

Toast of the Day
Here's to having a sense of humor.

Awe—Servances
Happy Birthday to:
Edgar Degas, 1834, impressionist painter.

On this day in 1994 Susan Montgomery blew the world's largest bubble gum bubble. It had a diameter of 23 inches.

Aha—phrodisiacs
Find Degas' painting titled *The Dance Class* online. Write a poem or caption. Write about ballet dancers having bubble gum on the bottom of their feet.

Starter Fluid: "I noticed my feet started to lift off the ground as the bubble got bigger . . . " Make an impressionistic painting, scribble, or doodle of bubble gum out of control.

Dose of Mirth
I go from stool to stool in singles bars hoping to get lucky, but there's never any gum under any of them. ~Stephen Wright

Journal Juju
Petronius said, "Outward beauty is not enough; to be attractive a woman must use words, wit, playfulness, sweet-talk, and laughter to transcend the gifts of Nature." Write, paint, or doodle a journal entry employing some of those traits (if you're a man use respect, acceptance, understanding and gift-giving).

Another Message from the Makers of Awe—wakened Moment
Narrate some of the things you do during the day. It can make you be more present.

Note to Myself: (Write your own note to yourself here)
_____

JULY 20
Name today _____

Daily Soul Vitamin
Boredom is the feeling that everything is a waste of time; serenity, that nothing is.
~Thomas S. Szasz

Toast of the Day
Here's to having your curiosity satisfied.

Awe-servances
Happy Birthday to:
Thomas Berger, 1924, novelist, best
known for the movie made from
his novel *Little Big Man*.

It's Anti-Boredom Month.

aerial view

of someone looking up through the trees

Aha-phrodisiacs
Make a list of 10 ways to defeat boredom, then pick one of them and make it into
an advertisement. (Example: sit under a tree and look up into the sky). Go to the
bookstore and flip through some magazines that you do not usually peek into.
　　　Write a poem called "Big Little Sky" or "Little Big Sky," or just "Little Big."

Dose of Mirth
*The word aerobics comes from two Greek words: aero, meaning "ability to,"
and bics, meaning "withstand tremendous boredom.* ~Dave Barry

Journal Juju
Ellen Parr said, "The cure for boredom is curiosity. There is no cure for
curiosity." List 10 things about which you are curious, pick two and
find some answers.

Subliminal Message Brought to You by the FOOOF Potion
The "inner brat" is powerful, especially for the determination you need to stay
with a passion, a dream, a creative pursuit, a new way you want to be. When some
thought discourages you or brings up doubt, mobilize your "inner brat" by
thinking, saying out loud or yelling in a really bratty voice "So what, I'll do it
anyway." Stomping at the same time is recommended.

Daily Soul Vitamin
You're only given a little spark of madness. You mustn't lose it. ~Robin Williams

Toast of the Day
Here's to listening to one of those songs that changes your mood to a better one.

Awe—servances
Happy Birthday to:
Ernest Hemingway, 1899, Nobel Prize-winning novelist,
    short-story writer, and journalist.
Robin Williams, 1951, award-winning actor and comedian.

Aha-phrodisiacs
Ernest Hemingway said, "All my life I've looked at words as though I were seeing them for the first time." Look at words or phrases in this word pool as if you were seeing them the first time: seeing, spark, lose, petal, million, lifestyle, choose, stage, prominent, role, wonder, make-believe, may, doubt, fire, quick, float, cartoon, require, dragon wings, first, blustery day. Look up a word in the dictionary that you really do see for the first time. Add a "little spark of madness."

Dose of Mirth
A woman would never make a nuclear bomb. They would never make a weapon that kills, no, no. They'd make a weapon that makes you feel bad for a while. ~Robin Williams

Journal Juju
Hemingway also said, "I never had to choose a subject, my subject rather chose me." Write a list of subjects, emotions, patterns, and/or ideas and see which top three seem to choose you.

JULY 22

Name today _____

Daily Soul Vitamin
If you take any activity, any art, any discipline, any skill—take it and push it as far as it will go, push it beyond where it has ever been before, push it to the wildest edge of edges, then you force it into the realm of magic. ~Tom Robbins

Awe-Servances
Happy Birthday to:

Edward Hopper, 1882, painter and printmaker best remembered for his eerily realistic depictions of solitude in contemporary American life.

Tom Robbins, 1936, author of wild stories with strong social undercurrents, a satirical bent, and obscure details.

It's Rat-catchers Day, observed on the anniversary of the Piper of Hamelin. According to legend, either in 1284 or 1376 (records were eaten by rats), the German town of Hamelin was plagued with rats. Townspeople hired a pied piper to pipe the rats out of town and into the Weser River. When the town refused to pay him, the piper then piped the children out of the town and into a hole in the hill, never to be seen again.

Aha-phrodisiacs
Write about using a pied piper to rid your town, job or neighborhood of something you don't want. Write about where the children went and the band they started. Starter fluid: That day I heard music more mysterious than the sky being blue, so I followed . . .

Journal Juju
Edward Hopper said, "If you could say it in words there would be no reason to paint." Title a painting or a doodle: *This is Hard to Say* and see what kind of art comes out.

Dose of Mirth
I'm not a vegetarian because I love animals. I am a vegetarian because I hate plants. ~A. Whitney Brown

Fooof here
Are you making work fun? Pretend you are an uncover agent for the competition. Take notes.

Daily Soul Vitamin
When genuine passion moves you, say what you've got to say, and say it hot.
~D.H. Lawrence

Toast of the Day
Here's to escaping into a well-written crime novel.

Awe-Servances
Happy Birthday to:
Raymond Chandler, 1888, crime novel author.

Today is National Hot Enough for Ya Day?
Leo the Lion begins. Leo is ambitious, a lover of limelight, optimistic, honorable, dignified, confident, sunny, flamboyant, charismatic, dramatic, a leader and an organizer.

Aha-phrodisiacs
Using Leo characteristics, sunny and flamboyant, write about the word "hot" in poetry or prose.

Dose of Mirth
From 30 feet away she looked like a lot of class. From 10 feet away she looked like something made up to be seen from 30 feet away. ~Raymond Chandler

Journal Juju
Use the private eye talk of Chandler's character, Philip Marlow, to make a journal entry. Start with: *It was one of those days when . . .*
 Write about what's hot and what's cold in your life right now.
 Rewrite a previous journal entry with more confidence.

Note to Myself: Breathe. Life is good. _____

Today I Get To: _____

Daily Soul Vitamin

The most difficult thing is the decision to act, the rest is merely tenacity. The fears are paper tigers. You can do anything you decide to do. You can act to change and control your life; and the procedure, the process is its own reward. ~Amelia Earhart

Toast of the Day

Here's to life's conveniences.

Awe-Servances

Happy Birthday to:
Amelia Earhart, 1898, first woman to cross the Atlantic by plane solo.

Instant coffee was developed on this day in 1938 and it's Hitchhiking Month.

Aha-phrodisiacs

Use your imagination and pick a word that hitchhikes and is picked up by another word. The first column is the hitchhiking words and the second word is the ride. See where it takes you when you pair one column up with the other.

Making	cookies
Ironing	flowers
Hiding	good intentions
Throwing	stones
Giving	songs

Dose of Mirth

"Never interrupt someone doing what you said couldn't be done." AMELIA EARHART

Journal Juju

Amelia Earhart said, "The most effective way to do it, is to do it." Write how you could associate this quote to something in your life. Ruth Buzzi said "Life has all sorts of hills and valleys, and sometimes you don't end up doing what you had your heart set out on, but sometimes that's even better!" Write how this quote relates to your life.

JULY 25

Name today _____

Daily Soul Vitamin
Truth, like gold, is to be obtained not by its growth, but by washing away from it all that is not gold. ~Leo Tolstoy

Toast of the Day
Here's to an exquisitely made salad, delicious and healthy.

Awe-servances
On this day in 1850 gold was discovered on the Rogue River in Oregon and the first electric light bulb was lit. It's also National Salad Week.

Happy Birthday

Aha-phrodisiacs
Make a light bulb collage or draw one and decorate it as if it were a great idea. For ideas on varying your salad creations, search for award-winning salad recipes or browse in a recipe book or gourmet magazine in a bookstore. (Note to myself: make a chopped salad tonight).

Dose of Mirth
Q: How many admin assistants does it take to change a light bulb?
A: None. I can't do anything unless you complete a light bulb design change
     request form. ~Unknown

Journal Juju
Claude M. Bristol said, "One secures the gold of the spirit when he finds himself." Journaling helps us find ourselves. Write about some things you may have forgotten about yourself that you would like to rediscover,—what did you like doing 20 years ago that you could return to? Put a few images in your journal that indicate how you want to reinvent yourself based on the riches of who you are.

A Message from makers of the Gather Potion and Awe-vanced Inner Messages
Spirituality has no age (compassion, grounded wisdom, character and grace are all more possible with age). Adopt someone as your younger sister or brother, even if they are older than you. Defy age-limiting thought by shifting into the agelessness of creative thought and the liberation of your sense of humor.

JULY 26

Name today _____

Daily Soul Vitamin

The creation of something new is not accomplished by the intellect but by the play instinct acting from inner necessity. The creative mind plays with the objects it loves. ~Carl Jung

Toast of the Day

Here's to never forgetting to be playful, it's a fringe benefit of being alive.

Awe-servances

Happy Birthday to:

George Bernard Shaw, 1856, Irish playwright.

Carl Jung, 1875, Swiss psychiatrist and founder of analytical psychology.

Kevin Spacey, 1959, award-winning actor and director.

Staff of *The Awe-manac*, 1956.

Aha-phrodisiacs

George Bernard Shaw said, "I often quote myself. It adds spice to my conversation." Invent three sayings you would like to be quoted as saying. Extra credit: Make art or a collage to go with one or more of those quotes.

Journal Juju

Kevin Spacey said, "If you feel you have something to give, if you feel that your particular talent is worth developing, is worth caring for, then there's nothing you can't achieve."

Dedicate every breath in your body to achieve your dream. Start by writing one small question in your journal that can turn you in this direction: What one small way can I demonstrate my dedication to that which I believe? How can I make it fun?

Today I Get To: _____

Daily Soul Vitamin

Plants not only add beauty to a room, but also make it a friendly, inviting place to live or work. Plants symbolize friendship and appear to have a calming, spiritual effect on most people. Plants and their root microbes are nature's biological cleaning machines. ~Bill Wolverton

Toast of the Day

Here's to houseplants, their beauty, friendliness and air cleaning ability.

Awe-Servances

Happy Birthday to:

Norman Lear, 1922, script writer and producer (*All in the Family* and *Maude*).

Bugs Bunny made his debut in 1940.

Take Your Houseplants for a Walk Day: Walking your plants around the neighborhood enables them to know their environment, thereby providing them with a sense of knowing, bringing on wellness. —From Thomas and Ruth Roy, Holiday Inventors.

Aha-phrodisiacs

Write about taking your houseplants for a walk, in poetry, prose, or haiku. How would the different varieties respond? Have one of your houseplants write to you. Take your houseplant for a walk.

Dose of Mirth

There once was a man from Montauk, Who would take his plants for a walk,
At the end of their roots, They wore little boots, And hats at the top of each stalk.
~Ira Paull

Journal Juju

Mind map: Do a diagram with one word in the middle and lines to word association bubbles to that middle word and then take those words and make lines with word association bubbles to them. Then when it looks kind of like a spider plant (a common houseplant), see how you can weave all those words together.

Daily Soul Vitamin

The world is charged with the grandeur of God. ~Gerard Manley Hopkins

Toast of the Day

Here's to stopping long enough to appreciate the grandeur.

Awe-servances

Happy Birthday to:

Gerard Manley Hopkins, 1844, English Victorian poet

Marcel Duchamp,1887, modern artist.

Jim Davis, 1945, *Garfield* cartoonist.

Beatrix Potter, 1866, English children's book author and illustrator.

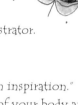

Aha-phrodisiacs

Gerard Manly Hopkins reflects, "I want the one rapture of an inspiration." Writing down inspirations can bring more. Noting the feel of your body and the charge of an idea makes the moment come alive with an inspiration's presence.

Dose of Mirth

Bring me an order of everything, with a side order of everything else. ~Garfield

Journal Juju

Beatrix Potter said, "Thank goodness I was never sent to school; it would have rubbed off some of the originality." And, "I cannot rest, I must draw, however poor the result, and when I have a bad time come over me it is a stronger desire than ever." Make a journal entry about how school affected your creativity. Make another one about how the creative process can be a refuge in the midst of difficulty.

Note to Myself: If everyone likes me or what I'm doing, I haven't gone far enough.

Daily Soul Vitamin
I write down thoughts as they occur to me.
You never know when you're going to need a good idea.
~Peter Jennings

Toast of the Day
Here's to the breath you take when you get
a good idea.

Awe-servances
Happy Birthday to:

Peter Jennings, 1938, journalist and news anchor.
A high school dropout, he transformed
himself into one of America's most
prominent journalists.

July is National Ice Cream Month: Have you
celebrated yet?

St. Martha's Day (patron saint of innkeepers,
cooks, housekeepers, laundresses, waitresses)

Ice Cream Bouquet

Aha-phrodisiacs
Write an ode to one of your favorite flavors of ice cream.

Write a dialog between a waitress and a regular customer. Develop a character
who is an innkeeper. What's his or her motivation, conflict, personality quirks,
favorite saying? Then write a scene with that character.

Dose of Mirth
Yogi ordered a pizza and the waitress asked how many pieces do you it cut into? Yogi
responded, "4, I don't think I could eat 8." ~Yogi Berra

Journal Juju
Peter Jennings said, "Have a sense of humor about life—you will
need it. And be courteous." Create a quote of advice you would
give about life, you're just as important as the people being
quoted in this book.

JULY 30

Name today _____

Double Dose Daily Soul Vitamins

When everything seems to be going against you,
remember the airplane takes off against the wind,
not with it. ~Henry Ford

   What I learned is that we are always stronger
than we know. ~Arnold Schwarzenegger's
inaugural speech, 2003

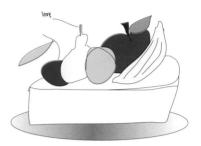

Toast of the Day

Here's to the texture and taste of cheesecake.

Awe—servances

Happy Birthday to:

Henry Ford, 1863, the founder of the Ford Motor Company and father of modern
   assembly lines.

Arnold Schwarzenegger, 1947, bodybuilder, actor and politician.

National Cheesecake Day.

Aha—phrodisiacs

Have some cheesecake and then afterward lift weights, real or metaphorical.
Repeated completions: "I'll be back . . . ."

   Starter Fluid: "Arthur started the day without thinking . . . "

Dose of Mirth

   . . . the automobile is only a novelty, a fad. ~Michigan Savings Bank
President about investing in Ford Motor Company

Journal Juju

Henry Ford said, "Thinking is the hardest work there is, which is
probably the reason why so few engage in it." Write in your journal today without thinking, or with very little thought. Starter
Fluid: "I'm not thinking . . . "

   List times in your life when you were stronger than you
thought you were. Extra credit: pick one and expound on it.

Daily Soul Vitamin

You sort of start thinking anything's possible if you've got enough nerve.
~J. K. Rowling

Toast of the Day

Here's to the imagination of others when it inspires our own.

Awe-servances

Happy Birthday to:

J. K. Rowling, 1965, English fiction writer, the author of the Harry Potter
fantasy series.

Official Friendship Day. Visit *The Awe-manac's* Friendship Day on September 2
and celebrate it twice; friends are worth it.

Aha-phrodisiacs

Write about a creature who keeps his brain in one of these locations: his junk
drawer, his shirt pocket, in the frig, in her garden, in a locker at the Y.

Write about an imaginary friend; embellish him or her with special powers
and abilities. How does your friend help you, how
do you help her or him?

Dose of Mirth

*Never trust anything that can think for itself if you
can't see where it keeps its brain.* ~J.K. Rowling

Journal Juju

J. K. Rowling: "There are some things you can't
share without ending up liking each other." Write
about what you have shared with another person
that has brought you closer. Repeat completions:
"If I had enough nerve I would . . ."

The Inner AWe-liXer
Finding Your Inner-view

It's what's on the inside that counts

Take the time to come home to yourself every day. ~Robin Casarjean

The outer conditions of a person's life will always be found to reflect their inner beliefs. ~James Allen

With the realization of one's own potential and self confidence in one's own ability, one can build a better world. ~Dalai Lama

There is no place like inner space . . . a place of acceptance, relaxation, peace and calm: home. Wherever you go there it is. The Inner Awe-lixir is filled with all of your favorite inner states of being: the middle of marvels, at-one, letting go, and of course, inner peace. These beings grow when the meditative spirit is cultivated, when we opt to release the struggle, when we flow with the peaceful vine of the flowing breath.

Remember, the entrance door to the sanctuary is inside you. ~Rumi

It is not easy to find happiness in ourselves, and it is not possible to find it elsewhere. ~Agnes Repplier

POSSiBLe eFFects: results in discovering a calm presence, grace, strength of spirit, the possible-self, expansiveness, assured contentment, a fountain of inner beauty visible on the outside, brilliant corridors of imagination; grounded in visceral clarity; restoring through stillness, meditation and spiritual connection.

Side EFFects: Consult your doctor if bliss is sustained longer than four hours—out of body floating could lead to knocking valuable clocks off the wall and scaring the cat. Side effects may vary: Furrowed brows, frowns and pasty grumpiness may disappear. Do not stand in the express line while on The Inner Awe-lixir. I'm not exactly sure why.

Welcome to August

Learn to value yourself, which means: to fight for your happiness. ~Ayn Rand

August was named to honor the first Roman emperor Augustus Caesar. What would a month's name be if it were named after you? I believe my month would be named Ji because I'd want to shorten my name like Augustus did or, on second thought maybe I'd break the rules and lengthen it to be Jillustus which I like because it has "lust" in it.

Some Celebrations at August's Door

It's Foot Health Month, Family Eye Care Month, Happiness Happens Month, Family Fun Month, Getting Older and Eager Month , May Your Reading be a Haven Month, Women's Small Business Month, Harvest Month, International Air Travel Month, Peach Month, National Golf Month, National Parks Month, National Catfish Month, National Water Quality Month, Romance Awareness Month

AWe-Manac Invented Events:

August 2 Isabelle Allende's Blender Day
August 10 Shoe Appreciation Day
August 22 Bradbury/Parker Day
August 25 Blue Day
August 27 Light Day

Suggested Ways to Celebrate

1. In 1999 the Secret Society of Happy People declared August National "Admit You're Happy" Month, which was later changed to Happiness Happens Month. I didn't know there WAS a happy secret society; why would they keep such an organization a secret . . . and do they live in a tree? So I did two minutes worth of extensive research and found that Pamela Gail, a business woman in Texas, founded the Secret Society of Happy People in 1998 "to provide a missing voice for those who experience happiness and want to express it without other people raining on their parade." Once, I found my missing happy voice under the chaise lounge out on the porch.

The foolish man seeks happiness in the distance; the wise grows it under his feet. -James Oppenheim

259

AugUsT 1

Name today _____

Daily Soul Vitamin
He who has never failed somewhere, that man can not be great. ~Herman Melville

Toast of the Day
Here's to romancing creativity or romancing creatively.

Dose Of Mirth
A smile is a facelift that's in everyone's price range! ~Tom Wilson

Awe-servances
Happy Birthday to:

Herman Melville, 1819, novelist, essayist and poet. *Moby-Dick* was largely considered a failure during his lifetime; "rediscovered" in the 20th century as a literary masterpiece.

Tom Wilson, 1931, cartoonist, creator of the comic strip *ZIGGY*.

National Night Out and August is Romance Awareness Month.

Aha-phrodisiacs
Create an acronym for ROMANCE or a poem where the first letter of the first word of each sentence spells ROMANCE. Go look for a shooting star outside tonight.

Write from the point of view of an inanimate object with attitude, e.g. a deceitful cereal bowl, a happy alarm clock, a confused candle. Or make a collage of several objects that have attitudes.

Journal Juju
Herman Melville said, "It is not down in any map; true places never are." Make a list of places you would define as true—states of minds, visions, thoughts, feelings, heartfelt places that are not on maps. Extra Credit: Make or doodle a map with those places on it or pick one of them and write how to locate it "from here."

Make up your own meditation technique. How can you customize your meditation according to who you are, where you live, to connect to nature? I live at the top of a steep cement driveway in the high desert. One of my favorite meditations is lying down on the driveway on a summer night; the air is cool but the driveway is still warm. I watch stars and invite the moment to embrace me. The curve of the driveway uncurls my spine for a gentle yoga experience.

Daily Soul Vitamin

Since my childhood I have been creative in weird ways. When I see a gadget, say a blender, I imagine how I can use it for something else. ~Isabel Allende

Toast of the Day

Here's to found object art where the unexpected use of something found makes you smile.

Awe-servances

Happy Birthday to;
Isabel Allende,1942, Chilean novelist.
An *Awe-manac* Generated Observance: Isabelle Allende's Blender Day

Aha-phrodisiacs

Isabel Allende's Soul Vitamin exemplifies the use of *Awe-manac* Viewfinders. Pick one of the following subjects and write about it using three different viewfinders. Or pick one viewfinder and write about three of the following subjects with it: A dinner party, a night out, delivering a package, planting a garden, ambushing a picnic. Viewfinders: paranoid, overly polite, baffled, over-zealous, infomercial, Dr. Seuss, in poetic angst, indifferent, attention to detail, enlightened.

So for example write about an overly polite night out, a Dr Seussian night out or a baffled night out. Or write about planting a garden with attention to detail, in an enlightened way, while doing an infomercial. Or write about unconventional uses for a blender (for instance communicating with extraterrestrials).

Journal Juju

Speaking of gardens, playwright Richard Brinsley Sheridan said, "Won't you come into the garden? I would like my roses to see you." Journal title: *What's in My Garden?* Use it as a metaphor: What do you need to weed out? What do you need to nurture? What do you need to cultivate and harvest? Doodle how it might look.

Today I get to: _____

Name today _____

Daily Soul Vitamin
Without an open-minded mind, you can never be a great success.
~Martha Stewart

Toast of the Day
Here's to when a recipe surpasses your expectations.

Awe-servances
Happy Birthday to:
Martha Stewart, 1941, business magnate, author, editor, and homemaking advocate.

Twins Day Festival, Twinsburg, OH (Aug 3—5), the largest gathering of twins.
In 1492, Chris Columbus set sail in the Santa Maria with the Nina and Pinta in
search of Cathay. Instead they found the Americas.

Aha-phrodisiacs
Write about your imaginary twin. Is she/he like you or opposite? Write about
Martha Stewart's evil or kind twin.
Write about an adventure where, like Columbus, you set out to find one thing
and instead you find another. It can be as simple as looking for a slipper and
finding a photo of an old love or looking for your *Martha Stewart* magazine and
finding your twin. Write a stream of conscious, poem, or haiku about discovery.

Dose of Mirth
*Martha Stewart is getting out of prison so today the terror alert was raised from orange
to pesto.* ~David Letterman

Journal Juju
Narrate one of your daily chores or meal preparations as if you were narrating a
show Martha Stewart-style.

Coffee Twins

AUGUST 4

Name today _____

Daily Soul Vitamin

The memory of things gone is important to a jazz musician. Things like old folks singing in the moonlight in the back yard on a hot night or something said long ago.
~Louis Armstrong

Toast of the Day

HERE'S TO THE FEELING EVOKED by THAT LOUIS ARMSTRONG quote.

Awe-Servances

Happy Birthday to:

Louis Armstrong, 1900 jazz musician.

On this day in 1916 the US acquired the Virgin Islands.

In 1987 a new 22 cent stamp honoring author William Faulkner went on sale in Oxford, MS. He had been fired as postmaster of that same post office in 1924.

Aha-phrodisiacs

Design an island you would like to be marooned on. What would it have? Who would be there? What books, activities, tools would you bring; what band would play on Saturday nights; what seven people would visit once a year? Collage a composite of images into the shape of an island.

Journal Juju

William Faulkner said, "That maybe peace is only a condition in retrospect, when the subconscious has got rid of the gnats and the tacks and the broken glass in experience and has left only the peaceful pleasant things, that was peace. Maybe peace is not *is*, but *was*." What are your gnats and tacks and broken glass?

Today I get to: _____

_____

_____

_____

August 5

Name today _____

Daily Soul Vitamin
Mystery creates wonder and wonder is the basis of man's desire to understand. ~Neil Armstrong

Toast of the Day
Here's to Frederic Lawrence Knowles who said, "The night walked down the sky with the moon in her hand."

SWEET!

STILL LIFE ON THE MOON

Awe-servances
Happy Birthday to:
Neil Armstrong, 1930, astronaut, first man to walk on the moon.

It's also Sisters' Day.
On this day in 1904 the first American traffic light handling traffic in two directions debuted in Cleveland, OH. It had red and green lights with a warning buzzer as the color changed.

Aha-phrodisiacs
Write about the moon walking on you, taking the moon for a walk, being a moon shadow. Write a sister story, real or fictional. Write about traffic lights, real or as metaphors. Make traffic light art out of moons. Make moons out of traffic lights.

Dose of Mirth
On a traffic light, green means go and yellow means yield, but on a banana it's just the opposite. Green means hold on, yellow means go ahead, and red means where the hell did you get that banana at? ~Mitch Hedberg

Journal Juju
Is there a poem or part of a story in what you do or think when waiting at a stop light? Doodle a traffic light and in the bottom green circle write something around which you want to have more "go"; in the yellow circle put names of the things around which you want to slow down, and in the red circle, what you want to stop.

What kind of change would cause you to sound a warning buzzer, or has in the past?

Daily Soul Vitamin
I'd rather regret the things I've done than regret the things I haven't done.
~Lucille Ball

Toast of the Day
Here's to the occasional extravagance.

Awe—servances
Happy Birthday to:
Lucille Ball, 1911, iconic actor, comedian and star of landmark sitcom, *I Love Lucy*.

Halfway Point of Summer and National Smile Week.

Aha—phrodisiacs
Write a fictional history of smiling. How did it get started? Who was the first to smile? When did it catch on?

Invent a summer half-time show. Be extravagant; use any entertainer dead or alive, real or fictional. Any music, any display of imaginative celebration.

Dose of Mirth
The secret of staying young is to live honestly, eat slowly, and lie about your age. ~Lucille Ball

Journal Juju
Write in your journal today as if you were 10 or 15 years younger. Commit to it. Then be 10 or 15 years younger today.

Write about how your summer has been and what magic you hope to find in the second half. Write in poem, prose, letter, announcement, press release, or telegram.

Awe—wakened Inner Messages Public Service Announcement
Think this and feel it in your body: I am patient and satisfied with one small step and I trust the process. What does patience feel like in the body?

Daily Soul Vitamin

God writes a lot of comedy . . . the trouble is, he's stuck with so many bad actors who don't know how to play funny. ~Garrison Keillor

Toast of the Day

Here's to Lake Wobegon and other fictional places.

Awe—Servances

Happy Birthday to:

Mata Hari, 1876, dancer, courtesan and spy. In 1917 she was arrested, convicted, and sentenced to death as a German spy. At her execution she reportedly refused a blindfold and blew a kiss to the firing squad.

Garrison Keillor, 1942, author, humorist, columnist, musician, satirist, and radio personality.

1959 US satellite Explorer VI transmitted the first picture of Earth from space.

Aha—phrodisiacs

Write an ode to or a journal entry on the spy, Mata Hari.

Describe, doodle, or collage the first picture of a planet you invent. Make it your own world.

Dose of Mirth

Kids: they dance before they learn there is anything that isn't music. ~William Stafford

Journal JuJu

Mata Hari said, "The dance is a poem of which each movement is a world." Strike a movement of a dance and then write or make art about how it is a world. Find a picture of a dance move, title it, and write a poem about it.

Subliminal Message Brought to You by the Kindness/Gather Potions

Sometimes kindness to yourself comes in taking care of yourself physically. What stretch could you do just to be kind to your body? Can you take even a 5 minute walk to clear your head or move your limbs? What's one small way you can you spend just 1 to 5 minutes today doing something or thinking about something you love?

AUGUST 8
Name today _____

Daily Soul Vitamin
The two basic items necessary to sustain life are sunshine and coconut milk. ~Dustin Hoffman

Toast of the Day
Here's to the taste of Thai food with coconut milk.

Awe-servances
Happy Birthday to:
Dustin Hoffman, 1937, two-time Oscar-winning actor.

Doodle Auditioning to be a Parade Float

It's also Sneak Some Zucchini onto your Neighbors Porch Night, celebrated by those who have planted too much zucchini.
In 1981, the largest kite was flown, measuring just under 6,000 sq. ft.

Aha-phrodisiacs
Word Pool: benefit, brainstorm, dazzle, zipper, zucchini, kite, bench, roll, flee, pink, whistle, day, shiver, diner, adamant, wiggle, pull, ponderous, free-floating, gather, short, smolder, motorcycle,
    Write a journal entry about sneaking zucchini onto someone's porch. Write a poem, haiku, song, story, or newsflash about a large kite. Write or make art about flying a zucchini.

Dose of Mirth
The first zucchini I ever saw I killed it with a hoe. ~John Gould

Journal Juju
Write about a rebellious time right after college or high school to celebrate Hoffman's role in *The Graduate.*
    Write a list of things you would like to create in your lifetime, from small ideas to large ones.

Body Temple on the Highway
You can make a change in your body even when you are driving by tightening your buns and using your abdominal muscles to press your tummy in. Start in 30 second intervals and work up. Massage your face at stoplights. The circulation it creates is good for keeping the skin looking younger.

August 9
Name today _____

Daily Soul Vitamin
The stars are the street lights of eternity. ~Unknown

Toast of the Day
Here's to sighting a shooting star.

Awe-servances
Happy Birthday to:
P.L. Travers, 1899, author of *Mary Poppins.*

In 1859, the escalator was patented by Nathan Amos.
Meteor Shower Peak time is August 10-12. Get your
   wishes ready.
It's also Popcorn Festival.

Aha-phrodisiacs
Write about shooting popcorn or make art replacing the stars with popcorn constellations.

Garrison Keillor shares that Travers created *Mary Poppins* for her own amusement: "a prim, somewhat ill-humored, magical British nanny who appears at a household in a high wind and floats away when the wind changes." Invent a character for your own amusement, write about having a magical nanny around to help you out, or imagine floating away when the wind changes.

Dose of Mirth
For those of you who like to scarf your popcorn in the sack, the good news is that Newman's Own contains an aphrodisiac. ~Paul Newman

Journal Juju
Write about your first memory of an escalator, or a poem, haiku, or song about an escalator.

Use escalator as a metaphor: what is on the up escalator in your life and what's going down? What's stuck in the steps? What department are you landing in?

Hooray for shoes

Daily Soul Vitamin
Funny that a pair of really nice shoes make us feel good in our heads—at the extreme opposite end of our bodies. ~Levende Waters

Toast of the Day
Here's to the rare pair of shoes that is both comfortable and stylish.

Awe-servances
Happy Birthday to:

Ian Anderson, 1947, singer, songwriter, guitarist, and flautist best known for his
   work as the head of British rock band Jethro Tull— and he wore shoes.

It's also Lazy Day and *The Awe-manac* invented Shoe Appreciation Day
Elvis Week in Memphis, TN.

♥ Aha-phrodisiacs ♥
Ian Anderson has an album called *The Secret Language of Birds*. Put on some comfortable shoes or lazy boys and create a dialog between two birds using the Elvis title pool below. Let Anderson's flute music inspire you while scribbling, painting, doodling, or writing.

   Elvis Title Wave: Heartbreak Hotel, I Was the One, Don't Be Cruel, Love Me Tender, When My Blue Moon Turns to Gold Again, Anyway You Want Me (That's How I Will Be)

   Spend a lazy day doing art and listening to flute music.

   Take a pair of shoes for a walk and imagine they have powers to help you come up with small new ideas or to help you pay attention to small moments of delight.

Dose Of Mirth
Is it time to go home yet? I keep clicking these damn shoes, but nothing happens.
~Robin Hecht

Journal Juju
Repeated completions: "Lazy is. . . " Title a Journal Entry *I Was the One . . .* and see what meaning this has for you related to the past, present, or future.

Daily Soul Vitamin

If your head tells you one thing, and your heart tells you another, before you do anything, you should first decide whether you have a better head or a better heart. ~Marilyn vos Savant

Toast of the Day

Here's to the beauty of a perfect apple, a work of art from nature.

apple queen

Awe—servances

Happy Birthday to:

Alex Haley, 1921, author of *Roots*.

Marilyn vos Savant, 1946, columnist, author, *Highest IQ*.

In 1965, The Beatles proclaimed this "National Apple Week" when they launched their Apple record label.

In 1992, The largest shopping mall in the US opened in Bloomington, Minnesota.

Aha—phrodisiacs

Marilyn vos Savant said, "To acquire knowledge, one must study; but to acquire wisdom, one must observe." Write down three quick observations about apples, malls or your pattern of creating.

Starter Fluid: "I inadvertently had eye contact with a pelican today . . . "

Dose of Mirth

At first, I only laughed at myself. Then I noticed that life itself is amusing. I've been in a generally good mood ever since. ~Marilyn vos Savant

Journal Juju

Write a real or fictional account of your metaphorical or literal roots. Write about your mall experience as a teenager. Get detailed. Make a list of things in your life that could be considered, even in a stretch, as humorous.

Note to Myself: I have used this phrase many times "What doesn't kill me makes me stronger."

August 12

Name today _____

Daily Soul Vitamin

Most of us serve our ideals by fits and starts. The person who makes a success of living is the one who sees his goal steadily and aims for it unswervingly. That is dedication. ~Cecil B. DeMille

Toast of the Day

Here's to sitting in a theater and watching a good movie on the big screen.

Awe—Servances

Happy Birthday to:

Cecil B. DeMille, 1881, one of the most successful film pioneers during the first half of the 20th century.

1851 Elias Howe invented the sewing machine

Aha—phrodisiacs

Word Pool: Sew together these words, add others: discovery, sew, eventually, aura, cupcake, hedge, toast, draw, empty, dud, snapshot, film, amazing, studio, actual, enroll, discreet, meadow, orange, sacred, pocketsize, backdrop, fold, dedicate.

   Use this DeMille quote as Starter Fluid: "Creation is a drug I can't do without." or replace "creation" with the drug metaphor of your choice.

Doses of Mirth

Don't needle the seamstress. ~Author Unknown

Journal Juju

Ellen Birdseye Wheaton said about sewing: "All my scattering moments are taken up with my needle." Make a collage of images that you choose based on your intuition's interpretation of what is you. Let the process of piecing the images together, "peace" you together like a work of restored art.

STILL LIFE INCOGNIITO

Name today _____

Daily Soul Vitamin

*There are few things more sacred than the
moment you come to peace with your pieces.*
~Marney Makridakis

Toast of the Day
Here's to dreams about Flying.

Awe-Servances

Flying Pieces

Happy Birthday to:

Fidel Castro, 1927, former president of Cuba.

Marney Makridakis, 1971, founder of *Artella Magazine* and on-line creative site.

National Aviation Week is around this time.

Aha-phrodisiacs

Write a story or poem that mentions flying cigars.

Write about flying in any form. Write from the point of view of the
bird you would most like to be.

Write about "pieces" however you interpret the word or make a list
of associations.

Dose of Mirth

The knack of flying is learning how to throw yourself at the ground and miss.
~Douglas Adams

Journal Juju

Marney Makridakis said, "People who leave colorful footprints have to walk
through lots of puddles." Use crayons or colored pencils and draw some of the puddles you've walked through in your life in order to have colorful footprints (or
character). Or do a collage.

AUGUST 14
Name today _____

Daily Soul Vitamin
Sometimes, when you aren't sure of something, you just have to jump off the bridge and grow wings on the way down. ~Danielle Steel

Toast of the Day
Here's to growing wings on the way down.

Awe-Servances
Happy Birthday to:
Danielle Steel, 1947, bestselling author.
Steve Martin, 1945, comedian, writer, producer, actor,
    musician, and composer.
Gary Larson, 1950, creator of *The Far Side*, a single-panel dark humor comic strip.

Aha-phrodisiacs
    Far Side title Pool/Starter fluid: It Came From the Far side, The Chickens Are Restless, There's a Hair in My Dirt, Cows of Our Planet. Take the titles apart or use them intact, adding additional words for poetry, prose, or just an amusing piece of writing.

Dose of Mirth
I saw the movie, Crouching Tiger, Hidden Dragon and was surprised because i didn't see any tigers or dragons. And then I realized why: they're crouching and hidden. ~Steve Martin

Journal Juju
Write about the ending of any dispute in your life, including one that hasn't ended—end it in writing as if it ended and see how it happens or how it feels. Write about it in third person for a different perspective.

Herd some recent feelings on the page, brand a few with compassion, then ride one of them out to pasture and have a conversation with it.

August 15

Name today _____

Daily Soul Vitamin
It is a rare and difficult attainment to grow old gracefully and happily. Find something you're passionate about and keep tremendously interested in it. ~Julia Child

Toast of the Day
Here's to this Julia Child quote, "It's fun to get together and have something good to eat at least once a day. That's what human life is all about, enjoying things."

Awe-servances
Happy Birthday to:
Julia Child, 1912, cookbook author and television personality.
National Relaxation Day.

On this day in 1969, Woodstock opened on Max Yasger's farm in upstate NY.
    Twenty-six bands played to 400,000 people.

Aha-phrodisiacs
Get relaxed, hold the pen or pencil loosely, and write or doodle from a relaxed, nonchalant, point of view.

Dose of Mirth
The only time to eat diet food is while you're waiting for the steak to cook.
~Julia Child

Journal Juju
Make a list of all the things that relax you. See if you can then string them together into a poem or prose piece.

    Next time you fix a meal, narrate it like Julia Child even if you're by yourself or for those who are shy, even if you're with others.

    Ask yourself the small question: What one small thing can I do to keep interested in my passions? Do not expect an answer in the moment, just keep asking.

Note to Myself: Keep tremendously interested in art, music, and writing.

August 16

Daily Soul Vitamin

. . . if you're going to try, go all the way, there is no other feeling like that, you will be alone with the gods and your nights will flame with fire, you will ride life straight to perfect laughter. ~Charles Bukowski

Toast of the Day

Here's to sweet watermelon.

Awe-servances

Happy Birthday to:

Charles Bukowski, 1920, an influential Los Angeles poet and novelist. A prolific author, Bukowski wrote thousands of poems, hundreds of short stories, and six novels, eventually having more than 50 books in print.

Steve Carell, 1962, award-winning comedian, actor, and writer.

It is Watermelon Festival Day.

Aha-phrodisiacs

Mark Twain said about watermelon, "When one has tasted it he knows what the angels eat."

Make watermelon art. Draw a bunch of imperfect watermelons (sliced or whole), cut them out and make a collage: watermelons on parade, watermelons laughing, still life and watermelon. Write an ode to watermelons. Carve a piece of watermelon into your first initial.

Starter fluid or Repeated Completions: I will ride life straight to . . .

Dose of Mirth

Nothing to me feels as good as laughing incredibly hard. ~Steve Carell

Journal Juju

See today's Soul Vitamin. Give the world advice about being passionate, committing to it convincingly with a Charles Bukowski perspective.

Note to Myself: Find people to hang out with that make me laugh incredibly hard.

August 17

STILL LIFE IN HOT AIR ORANGE

Daily Soul Vitamin
No person who is enthusiastic about his work has anything to fear from life. ~Samuel Goldwyn

Toast of the Day
Here's to the look of hot-air balloons floating in the sky.

Awe-Servances
Happy Birthday to:
Samuel Goldwyn, 1882, award winning producer.
Cat Nights Begin: An old Irish legend has it that a witch could turn herself into a
     cat 8 times and then regain herself, but on the 9th time, August 17th, she
     couldn't change back. Hence the saying "A cat has nine lives."
On this day in 1978, Maxie Anderson, Ben Abruzzo, and Larry Newman, all of
     Albuquerque, NM, became the first to complete a transatlantic trip by
     hot-air balloon.

Aha-phrodisiacs
Write a journal entry or poem from the ninth life of a cat.
     Write a dialog between Maxie, Ben, and Larry (all of Albuquerque) from the
balloon ride. Write a journal entry from one of them OR continue with this sentence: "High above the Atlantic, I noticed our balloon began to . . ." Or just read
these and think, maybe some day I'll write a response to one of these prompts.

Journal Juju
If you had nine lives to lead, and could have a different occupation in
each, what would you be?

Dose of Mirth
I don't think anyone should write their autobiography until after they're dead.
~Samuel Goldwyn

Brought to You by Body Temple Potion
*The body is an instrument, the mind its function, the witness and reward of its
operation.* ~George Santayana
     Do a yoga stretch today and pay undivided attention to everything that feels
good about it.

August 18

Name today _____

Daily Soul Vitamin
Marianne Moore's definition of poetry: "Imaginary gardens with real toads in them."

Toast of the Day
Here's to a ginger ale and cranberry juice with a twist on the rocks on a summer's eve.

Awe—servances
Happy Birthday to:
Martin Mull, 1943, actor, comedian, painter and recording artist.
It's also Bad Poetry Day.
National Homeless Animals Day, sponsored by the International Society for Animal Rights (ISAR). Have your pet spayed, or take in a stray.

Aha—phrodisiacs
Martin Mull said, "The trouble with jogging is that the ice falls out of your glass." Starter Fluid: The trouble with cleaning the kitchen . . . , The trouble with washing the dog . . . , The trouble with being grown-up . . .

Writing bad poetry is one of my favorite things to do because it's liberating and amusing. Pick a subject and write bad poetry about it: cleaning the kitchen, sitting in shadow, eating ice cream, being a grown-up, writing bad poetry.

Journal Juju
Make an event that happened today or recently into bad poetry.

Repeat Advertising
When you are aware that you are hard on yourself, reply back with whatever is appropriately confident: "So what I'll do it anyway." "It's close enough." "It's all practice." "It's all good."

Today I Get To: _____

Name today _____

Daily Soul Vitamin

It isn't all over; everything has not been invented; the human adventure is just beginning. ~Gene Roddenberry

Toast of the Day

Here's to raspberries, mint leaves, and culinary adventures.

Awe-servances

Happy Birthday to:

Ogden Nash, 1902, poet best known for writing pithy and funny light verse.

Gene Roddenberry, 1921, scriptwriter and producer, best known as the creator of the science fiction universe of *Star Trek*.

Aha-phrodisiacs

Gene Roddenberry said, "If man is to survive, he will have learned to take a delight in the essential differences between men and between cultures. He will learn that differences in ideas and attitudes are a delight, part of life's exciting variety, not something to fear." Take time today to explore a cultural difference on the Internet and then write or make art about it.

Write a pithy and fun verse about space and/or adventure. Begin with: "The trouble with space is . . . " or "My adventure care package came complete with . . . "

Journal Juju

Ogden Nash said, "The most exciting happiness is the happiness generated by forces beyond your control." Make a list of adventures you still plan on taking . . . but don't censor, have fun with it, include all possibilities from the absurd to the highly likely.

Note to Self: It's hard to shut up when you're right, but it rapidly develops character.

Today I Get To: _____

_____

Name today _____

Daily Soul Vitamin
There shall be eternal summer in the grateful heart. ~Celia Thaxter

Toast of the Day
Here's to the essence of summer.

Awe-Servances
1741, Vitus Jonasen Bering discovered Alaska.

In 1985, the first Xerox 914, which had been introduced in 1959, was presented to the Smithsonian Institution's National Museum of American History.

Aha-phrodisiacs
Write an ode to the discovery of Alaska. Write it from a polar bear's point of view.

To honor the Xerox discovery, use one (or more) of these phrases repetitively responding in various fashions each time and watch where the rhythm of repetition leads you: "Close the door . . . " "It's a miracle . . . " "My brain just stopped . . . "

Midsummer's Night Word Pool: sofa, nightmare, excuse, audience, black, gastronomic, underneath, wrong, glad, sly, meander, bless, genius, suspicious, night attendant, popsicle, Xerox, fantasy, discover, okay then.

Dose of Mirth
A perfect summer day is when the sun is shining, the breeze is blowing, the birds are singing, and the lawn mower is broken. ~James Dent

Journal Juju
Write a list of images, feelings and words about summer. Then string them together using this formula: It was_____, _____, and _____.

Or title a journal entry: *Restless Thoughts of a Random Mind Toward Summer's End*

Subliminal Message Brought to You by the FOOOF potion
Lighten up: look at something you are taking too seriously through the perspective of someone you know could frame it lightly like Robin Williams, Ellen DeGeneres, Paula Poundstone, John Stewart, Stephen Colbert, or Bugs Bunny.

August 21

Name today _____

Daily Soul Vitamin

A horse is the projection of peoples' dreams about themselves—strong, powerful, beautiful—and it has the capability of giving us escape from our mundane existence. ~Pam Brown

Toast of the Day

Here's to the art, grace, and beauty of a pasture of horses.

Awe-servances

Happy Birthday to:
Kenny Rogers, 1938, singer.

Southern Hemisphere Hoodie-Hoo Day: at noon people in the
southern hemisphere should go outdoors and shout
"Hoodie-Hoo" to chase away winter.

Aha-phrodisiacs

Use the Kenny Rogers song title, "She Rides Wild Horses", as Starter Fluid.

Decide what it is in your life that you need to get rid of and come up with something to shout in order to chase it away.

Dose of Mirth

Horses are uncomfortable in the middle and dangerous at both ends. ~Ian Fleming

Journal Juju

Find 21 (since it's the 21st) words in books, on cereal boxes, brochures, and dictionaries and use them in poem, story, or nonsense verse. Try to see if the words can be modified to make sense as a real journal entry. Use your imagination to embellish your existence if it is mundane.

And Now a Question from Awe-wakened Moment Potion

Without expecting an immediate answer, keep asking yourself: "How will I be inspired today?"

A MID-SUMMER NIGHT'S STEAM

August 22

Name today _____

We are cups, constantly and quietly being filled. The trick is knowing how to tip ourselves over and let the beautiful stuff out. ~Ray Bradbury

The Awe-manac Staff liked so many of Ray Bradbury's thoughts that they proclaim his birthday RAY BRADBURY DAY.

Daily Soul Vitamin

If you enjoy living, it is not difficult to keep the sense of wonder. ~Ray Bradbury

Toast of the Day

Here's to the wise people that inspire us, here's to the wisdom in ourselves.

Awe-servances

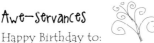

Happy Birthday to:

Ray Bradbury, 1920, literary, fantasy, horror, science fiction, and mystery writer.

Aha-phrodisiac

Use this Ray Bradbury quote as Starter Fluid for writing or collage: "Every morning I jump out of bed and step on a landmine. The landmine is me. After the explosion, I spent the rest of the day putting the pieces together."

Journal Juju

Pick one or more of these Ray Bradbury quotes and write where you are with it or how it might inspire you:

"Don't think. Thinking is the enemy of creativity. It's self-conscious and anything self-conscious is lousy. You cannot try to do things. You simply must do things."

"I know you've heard it a thousand times before. But it's true, hard work pays off. If you want to be good, you have to practice, practice, practice. If you don't love something, then don't do it. "

"If we listened to our intellect, we'd never have a love affair. We'd never have a friendship. We'd never go into business, because we'd be cynical. Well, that's nonsense. You've got to jump off cliffs all the time and build your wings on the way down."

Question from Awe-vanced Inner Messages

What quote or phrase can strengthen you when discouraging self messages flare up?

August 23
Name today _____

Daily Soul Vitamin
The soul that is within me no man can degrade.
~Frederick Douglass, author and former slave

Toast of the Day
Here's to freedom in all of its forms.

Awe-Servances
Happy Birthday to:
Gene Kelly, 1912, actor, dancer, and star of *Singin' in the Rain*.

In 1609, the telescope was demonstrated by Galileo.
Virgo begins.
U.N. International Day for the Remembrance of the Slave Trade and *its* Abolition.

Aha-phrodisiacs
Starter Fluid: "Sometimes I sing in the rain, other times I . . . "

Imagine looking through your high-powered metaphorical telescope and report your findings in poem, haiku, scientific report, or song: the inside of a poem? the middle of a dream? the makeup of a peaceful feeling?

Write about dancing, the soul, or freedom from one or more of these Virgo traits: practical, responsible, analytical, highly discriminating, helpful, dedicated, perfectionist.

 ## Dose of Mirth
A poet is someone who stands outside in the rain hoping to be struck by lightning. ~James Dickey

Journal Juju
Write about anything you are a slave to and how you might free yourself.

Brought to You by the Kindness and Gathering Potions
William Brown, PhD, a lecturer of psychology at Brunel University, studied people in Brooklyn, NY. Those who had a developed social network and gave more to their friends and family than they received—whether in the form of money, food, advice, or time—reported feeling healthier than others, even when activity levels were lower.

August 24

Daily Soul Vitamin

Clouds come floating into my life, no longer to carry rain or usher storm, but to add color to my sunset sky. ~Rabindranath Tagore

Toast of the Day

Here's to colorful summer sunsets.

Awe-Servances

Mason Williams, 1938, guitarist, composer, poet and lyricist best known for "Classical Gas."

In 1897, newspaper editor Charles Dudley Warner said, "Everybody talks about the weather, but nobody does anything about it."

Aha-phrodisiacs

Write about having the ability to do something about the weather and doing it.

Dose of Mirth

What dreadful hot weather we have! It keeps me in a continual state of inelegance. ~Jane Austen

Journal Juju

If your mood could be described in weather terms, what kind of weather would it be today?

AUGUST 25
Name today The Awe-manac Day of Blue

Every once in a blue moon, something new comes along that scrambles your preconceptions. ~Unknown

Daily Soul Vitamin
If the sight of the blue skies fills you with joy, if a blade of grass springing up in the fields has power to move you, if the simple things of nature have a message that you understand, rejoice, for your soul is alive. ~Eleonora Duse

Toast of the Day
Here's to all the shades of the color blue.

Awe-Servances
Happy Birthday to:
Elvis Costello, 1954, musician, singer, and songwriter

Aha-phrodisiacs
Elvis Costello Title Pool or Starter Fluid: 15 Petals, Dust, My Little Blue Window, Episode of Blonde. This is part of a Samuel Taylor Coleridge quote. Use it for Starter Fluid: "The blue sky bends over all . . ." Use a variety of blue shade to make a collage or painting.

Dose of Mirth
Blue color is everlastingly appointed by the Deity to be a source of delight.
~John Ruskin

Journal Juju
Make a dream board as a blueprint: Cut out images from cards and magazines and make prints from the Internet of the things, people, and energy that you want to manifest in your life.
    Write about the color blue in poetry or prose, song or silliness.

Today I Get To: _____

August 26

Daily Soul Vitamin

Every time you smile at someone, it is an action of love, a gift to that person, a beautiful thing. ~Mother Teresa

Toast of the Day

Here's to little things that bring great joy, like butterflies, comfortable shoes, and lying on a blanket in the sand.

Awe-servances

Happy Birthday to:

Mother Teresa, 1910, Nobel Peace Prize-winning humanitarian and advocate for the poor and helpless.

Women's Equality Day, in commemoration of the 19th amendment, which gave women the right to vote. This day is celebrated as a day of achievement for women nationwide.

Aha-phrodisiacs

Mother Teresa said, "Little things are indeed little, but to be faithful in little things is a great thing." Write or make art about little things. Doodle little doodles.

Dose of Mirth

"Smile, It's the second best thing you can do with your lips." ~Unknown

Journal Juju

Write about your lips.

Write about an achievement you or a woman friend has made. Write in a style that is poetic or journalistic, or write in prose. Imagine your are an authority and give 5 tips on How to be a Woman of Achievement.

Note to Myself: Explore this smiling phenomenon.

Today I Get To: _____

Daily Soul Vitamins

When you possess light within, you see it externally. ~Anaïs Nin

> *You can owe nothing, if you give back its light to the sun.* ~Antonio Porchia
> *I will love the light for it shows me the way, yet I will endure the darkness for it shows me the stars.* —Og Mandino

Confucius said, *"It is better to light one small candle than to curse the darkness."*

Toast of the Day

Here's to "light" in all of its many uses.

Awe-servances

The Awe-manac day of Light, brought to you by Anti-aging Potion Inner Elixir.

Aha-phrodisiacs

Eat light today. Let light shine through your eyes. Use one of today's Soul Vitamins as inspiration for collage or other art. Write something that plays with the word "light."

Dose of Mirth

In the beginning there was nothing. God said, "Let there be light!" And there was light. There was still nothing, but you could see it a whole lot better.
~Ellen DeGeneres

Journal Juju

Be light in your journal tonight. Write light, make light of something, go into the light, let your light shine, have a lite beverage while writing.

Use the metaphor of lighting one small candle vs. cursing the dark. How does that look in your life? What one small thing can you do to bring light to a place of darkness in your life?

August 28
Name today _____

Daily Soul Vitamin
A creation of importance can only be produced when its author isolates himself, it is a child of solitude.
~Johann Wolfgang von Goethe

Awe-servances
Happy Birthday to:

Johann Wolfgang von Goethe, 1749, German poet, dramatist, novelist, philosopher, humanist, scientist, and painter.

In 1907, teenagers Jim Casey and Claude Ryan started a local delivery service in Seattle. It later became United Parcel Service.

Toast of the Day
Here's to enjoyable moments of solitude focused on a creation.

Aha-phrodisiacs
If you had special powers to deliver something to everyone or a select number of people, what would it be and who would you select?

Write 26 positive words about being alone, one for each letter of the alphabet. Or do 13 today and 13 tomorrow. Or 6 today, 6 tomorrow, and 7 the day after tomorrow and the rest on Sunday.

Dose of Mirth
What a lovely surprise to finally discover how unlonely being alone can be.
~Ellen Burstyn

Journal Juju
Goethe said, "As soon as you trust yourself, you will know how to live." Repeated completions: "I trust . . . " Write about what you trust about yourself and what you do not.

Schedule some solitude for yourself.

Note to Myself: Find a place in nature for some solitude.

August 29

Name today _____

Daily Soul Vitamin
Be yourself. The world worships the original.
~Ingrid Bergman

Toast of the Day
Here's to being around someone who is
completely comfortable being his or herself.

Awe-servances
Happy Birthday to:
Oliver Wendell Holmes, 1809, physician, writer; regarded as one of
    the best poets of the 19th century.
Ingrid Bergman, 1915, award-winning Swedish actress.

More Herbs, Less Salt Day.

Aha-phrodisiacs
Oliver Wendell Holmes said, "Man's mind, once stretched by a new idea, never
regains its original dimensions." Draw, doodle or collage a mind and title it
Stretched by a New Idea.

    Explore a recipe that uses herbs you do not usually use.

Dose of Mirth
A kiss is a lovely trick designed by nature to stop speech when words become superfluous.
~Ingrid Bergman

Journal Juju
Write about your kiss history. Write a list of the things in your life to which you
would like to send a kiss. Where is there the most spice in your life right now?

Anti-aging Thought
*To be 70 years young is sometimes far more cheerful and hopeful than to be
40 years old.* ~Oliver Wendell Holmes

August 30

Name today _____

Double Dose Daily Soul Vitamin

Great minds discuss ideas; Average minds discuss events; Small minds discuss people. ~Eleanor Roosevelt

You can chain me, you can torture me, you can even destroy this body, but you will never imprison my mind. ~Mahatma Gandhi

Toast of the Day

Here's to the amazing mind.

Awe-Servances

Happy Birthday to:

Mary Wollstonecraft Shelley, 1797, author of *Frankenstein*.

It's Mind Day.

Aha-phrodisiacs

Mary Wollstonecraft Shelley said, "My dreams were all my own; I accounted for them to nobody; they were my refuge when annoyed, my dearest pleasure when free." Use the attitude of this quote to continue with your own writing.

Play with the word and meanings of "mind" in poetry, prose, haiku, or nonsense verse.

Dose of Mirth

The mere thought hadn't even begun to speculate about the merest possibility of crossing my mind. ~Douglas Adams

Journal Juju

Mary Wollstonecraft Shelley also said, "Nothing contributes so much to tranquilize the mind as a steady purpose, a point on which the soul may fix its intellectual eye." Write in your journal how you relate to this quote.

August 31

Name today _____

Daily Soul Vitamin
Meditation is such a more substantial reality than what we normally take to be reality. ~Richard Gere

Toast of the Day
Here's to the inner smile that is discovered and embodied during meditation.

Awe-servances
Happy Birthday to:
Van Morrison, 1945, singer and songwriter.
Itzhak Perlman, 1945, virtuoso violinist and teacher.
Richard Gere, 1949, actor, practicing Buddhist and active supporter of the Dalai Lama.

Aha-phrodisiacs
Nourish your inner world with 5 to 30 minutes of meditation today.

Van Morrison Starter Fluid: "Can you feel the silence?"or "The wild night is calling . . . "

Word Pool: meditation, a useful lesson, open, journey, submit, clock, in action, rain, hut, prolong, find another, steal, listen, exquisite, mischief, beginning anew

Dose of Mirth
My sole literary ambition is to write one good novel, then retire to my hut in the desert, assume the lotus position, compose my mind and senses, and sink into meditation, contemplating my novel. ~Edward Abbey

Journal Juju
Itzhak Perlman said, "I am playing the violin, that's all I know, nothing else, no education, no nothing. You just practice every day." Imagine and write about being as singularly focused as Itzhak Perlman about one of your creative passions. Or write about your experience with meditation.

A word from Inner Awe-Lixir
Meditate on words that evoke calm and invite them to shift your body into their meaning: Examples: feel the word compassion with your mind and your body. Try peace, love, calm, surrender, grounded beauty, serene trust, pleasing moment.

Arpeggio

Ah, music. A magic beyond all we do here! ☐ J. K. Rowling

If I were to begin life again, I would devote it to music. It is the only cheap and unpunished rapture upon earth.
~Sydney Smith

You don't need to begin life again to imbibe in the creative, healing, anti-aging power of music — turn up the volume now. Things go better with music. It heals us, lifts us, we transcend into a different space by listening to music that moves us. Lyrics validate our feelings, harmonies shift our mood, melodies bring back memories, and soundtracks deepen the power of an experience. Consider Rocky, there's no way he would have made it up those stairs without his theme song. Music keeps the staff of *The Awe-manac* on their treadmill for fifteens of minutes longer than they would usually stay on, with a foolishly blissful expression on their faces.

Music encompasses so many things that are creative . . . writing, storytelling, poetry, imagery. When music is integrated into other art, it can totally change the perception of that art. . . . it can guide us so emotionally . . . it can make us dance, it can make us cry . . . all within the same piece. And no other art form remains so glued to the moments of our life than music. ~Royce Addington

Music is what feelings sound like.
~Author Unknown

Music is the poetry of the air.
~Richter

Why waste money on psychotherapy when you can listen to the B Minor Mass?" ~Michael Torke

POSSibLE EFFectS: inspiration, transcendence, repose, freedom, toes-a-tapping, a spontaneous mambo.

Side EFFectS: Consult your doctor if you get a song stuck in your head for longer than four hours—singing a Scottish ballad helps. Side effects may include dancing the night away. You may get an urge to play a violin—if you do, sequester yourself to the barn in the lower forty. Caution: Do not whistle or play a kazoo while on Arpeggio. Thanks.

SEPTEMBER'S ENTRY WAY

September is from *septem* meaning "seven;" so called because it was the seventh month of the old Roman calendar, which began the year in March; Julian calendar reform (46 B.C.E.) shifted the new year back two months.

A Few Things at September's Door

It's Be Kind to Writers and Editors Month, Autumn Month, Classical Music Month, Library Card Sign-Up Month, Read-A-New-Book Month, National Sight Saving Month, National Sewing Month, National Chicken Month, National Honey Month, National Piano Month, Organic Harvest Month, National Mind Mapping Month, National Papaya Month, National Biscuit Month, Pleasure Your Mate Month, Self-Improvement Month, National Hispanic Heritage Month (Sep 15-Oct 15), National Mushroom Month, Better Breakfast Month Self-Improvement Month.

From all of this, I think it's most important to be polite to papayas. Let your chicken play the piano. Play some more with combinations, it's a good practice for creative thinking. Play can be the frivolous amusement we sometimes need when our brains are all stressed out.

Writing is a kind of double living. The writer experiences everything twice. Once in reality and once in that mirror which waits always before or behind.
—Catherine Drinker Bowen

Suggested Ways to Celebrate

1. For Be Kind to Writers and Editors Month: Many of you are writers. If you clean your refrigerator or weed your garden, in a sense you are an editor. If you write in your journal or on "get-to-do lists," I give you permission to call yourself a writer—so you now you have no excuse not to be kind to yourself this month.

2. Write about writing and then edit it: Be kind to yourself, being a writer is hard. Start with one of these unfinished sentences:

   In this moment. . . , I was just thinking. . . , Instead of doing something creative I. . . , The reason I'm not going to finish any of these unfinished sentences is . . .

3. Self-Improvement Month

   Let's use a creative principle and break the rules. Take the whole first week off from self-improvement and every day appreciate the qualities about yourself that are fine just the way they are.

Astrological Spells

All Signs: The planets have converged and all of them advise you to think a kind thought about yourself at least 21 times this month (22 for Virgos). Or follow these forecasts:

Aries: Try enjoying autumn 25 percent more than you usually do.

Taurus: Listen to classical music while doodling, make 5 pictures this way.

Gemini: Go to the library. Pay attention, there is an answer somewhere there for you.

Cancer: Read-A-New-Book, one different than you're used to reading.

Leo: Close your eyes often and let your other senses have a party this month.

Virgo: Sew.

Libra: Try a new recipe for a gourmet chicken dish.

Scorpio: This is your month to find a honey or take your relationship to a deeper level.

Sagittarius: Go listen to live piano music and be aware of an answer during the performance.

Capricorn: Eat more organic food this month.

Aquarius: Pick a subject and do a mind map. Look mind-mapping up on the Internet.

Pisces: Discover papaya.

Just Write

start where you are, believe in practice, don't stop

Tides

Ebbing:

Flowing:

Vessel of Strength:

GardeNiNg INFoRMatioN:

Flower: Aster
Monthly Awe-manac crop: Books
Planting Tips: Sit down and write.

Daily Soul Vitamin

The Soul would have no rainbow if the eyes had no tears. ~Native American Proverb

Toast of the Day

Here's to Native American proverbs that soothe the soul.

Awe-Servances

Happy Birthday to:

Conway Twitty, 1933, country western singer

Lily Tomlin, 1939 actor, comedian, writer and producer.

C. J. Cherryh, 1942 science fiction and fantasy author.

Aha-phrodisiacs

Use one of Lily Tomlin's quotes as Starter Fluid: "I always wanted to be somebody, but I should have been more specific." or "I personally think we developed language because of our deep need to complain."

Journal Juju

C. J. Cherryh began writing stories at the age of ten when she became frustrated with the cancellation of her favorite TV show, Flash Gordon. What is something that frustrates you and into what creative endeavor can you channel that energy?

Dose of Mirth

I worry that the person who thought up Muzak may be thinking up something else. ~Lily Tomlin

Message from the Body Temple Potion

Eat a rainbow of fruit and vegetables daily. Start the habit a little at a time, as trying to eat the recommended dose of nine servings may discourage you if you haven't been eating close to that. As you get used to it, it will be easier, more desirable, and automatic

Today I get to: _____

writingfreesmereadingenrichesmeeditinggetsridofstuffwedon'tneed writingfreesmereadingenrichesmeeditinggetsridofstuffwedon'tneed

297

Soul Vitamins to Fortify Friendships

The best kind of friend is the kind you can sit on a porch swing with, never say a word, then walk away feeling like it was the best conversation that you ever had. ~Unknown

Friends are relatives you make for yourself. ~Eustache Deschamps

If a friend is in trouble, don't annoy him by asking if there is anything you can do. Think up something appropriate and do it. ~Edgar Watson Howe

Nothing but heaven itself is better than a friend who is really a friend. ~Plautus

Toast of the Day

Here's to the company and comfort of a good friend. Here's to _____ (fill in a name of a good friend).

Awe-Servances

It is a day to cherish friendships... including the one with yourself.

Aha-phrodisiacs

Take a dose of the potion Kindness and let your creative juices go into extreme-friend mode. Send a pressed periwinkle with a note that shares the sentiment of precious friendship. Do not let skip appreciating kindred connections. Life is short. Surprise a friend with a home visit and a delivery of bath salts and soothing eyepads or a jar of relaxing mud mask or a friendship candle.

Put "Dr." in front of your name and write about friendship as if you were an expert on what works.

Journal Juju

Write the names of some of your friends and the qualities you admire about them. Realize they are a mirror for qualities you may have your self and pause to be a friend to yourself. Make a list of other qualities you would like to find in a friendship . . . think outside of your usual friendship qualities— what is some new trait you would like to have in a friend?

September 3

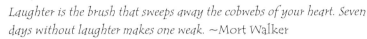
Daily Soul Vitamin

Laughter is the brush that sweeps away the cobwebs of your heart. Seven days without laughter makes one weak. ~Mort Walker

Toast of the Day

Here's to favorite comic strips and the lightness they evoke.

Awe—servances

Happy birthday to:

Mort Walker, 1923, comic artist, best known for *Beetle Bailey* and *Hi and Lois*.

In 1951, the soap opera *Search for Tomorrow* premiered and ran for 35 years.

Alison Lurie, 1926, Pulitzer Prize-winning novelist and author of *Foreign Affairs*, *Imaginary Friends* and *Real People*.

Aha—phrodisiacs

Write in prose or poetry, or make a collage entitled *Imaginary Friends*.

Word Pool: hemisphere, parole, totally, imprint, handlebar, green, bunk bed, expressive, hostess, shimmy, clock, protect, subterranean, escape, triumph, imagine, crinkle, slide, aroma, billowing, kite, tinker, exaggerate, pie, never-neverland, gift, impish, turtle, peanut butter, high-ball. (extra credit: Begin the word pool with "When the window is open . . . ")

Today I get to:

Journal Juju

Pick a title for today's entry: *Search for Today, Finding the Real People, Imaginary People with Real Problems,* or *An Affair with an Imaginary Tomorrow.*

For a fresh approach to writing in your journal, write your entries in the form of poems. Break up paragraphs into lines like a poem and eliminate extra words. Watch how images stand out, and how with just these techniques, rambling turns into rhythm and richness.

September 4

Daily Soul Vitamins

Men can starve from a lack of self-realization as much as they can from a lack of bread. ~Richard Wright

Toast of the Day

Here's to the convenience of flipping a switch for heat and air conditioning.

Awe-servances

Happy Birthday:

Richard Wright, 1908, author of novels, short stories and non-fiction.

Barney Flaherty, 1833. After answering an ad in the *NY Sun*, he became the first paper boy.

1904, the St. Regis Hotel in NYC became the first to have air conditioning and heating in each room.

Aha-phrodisiacs

Write a paperboy haiku or poem. Write about taking things for granted like heat or air conditioning.

Let your intuition pick a picture out of a magazine. Paste it in your writing journal and write about it: what happens next? Write from the point of view of the subject, provide a caption, or narrate it. Pick two or three images and write about how they work together. Pick five or six images, arrange them from left to right, and write how one image progresses to the next.

Journal Juju

Richard Wright said, "The artist must bow to the monster of his own imagination." Have a dialog in your journal with your imagination, ask it questions—modify the way your writing looks for its answers. Have your imagination write a journal entry. Time for a Credit Report. (Write a list of things you're glad you did).

Dose of Mirth

The function of the imagination is not to make strange things settled, so much as to make settled things strange. ~G. K. Chesterton

Today I Get to: _____

Daily Soul Vitamin

Procrastination is the thief of time. ~Edward Young

Toast of the Day

Here's to the concept of breaking creative pursuits down into small steps to make them easy and pleasurable to get to.

PAINT A PICTURE
By AUGUST 31

Awe—servances

Today is Be Late for Something Day, sponsored by the Procrastinators' Club of America, whose goal is to promote "the positive aspects of procrastination."

In 1698, the first tax on beards was imposed by Russian Czar Peter the Great.

In 1991, the USSR was dissolved by the congress of people's deputies.

Aha—phrodisiacs

Write a Dr Seuss-like poem, a sports commentary, or any style writing about procrastination.

Have you ever procrastinated? Write about one of those many events as if it were a good thing. Stretch your rationalization skills and list some positive aspects of procrastination.

Write a tongue-in-cheek essay about beards or a beard you know personally.

Dose of Mirth

I believe that if ever I had to practice cannibalism, I might manage if there were enough tarragon around. ~James Beard

Journal Juju

Write about something in your life you are tightly controlling and explore what it would be like to release control or set it free. A relationship? A desire? Your thoughts? A creative endeavor? Your steering wheel (real or metaphorical)?

Write about arresting the thief of time, procrastination, and getting your time back.

Note to Myself

Just begin without thinking, without care for quality; go for quantity and fascination. You take care of the quantity and the quality will just happen in the process.

Daily Soul Vitamin

Imagination will often carry us to worlds that never were. But without it, we go nowhere. ~Carl Sagan

Toast of the Day

Here's to being liberated, transported and restored, all for free in our imagination.

Awe-servances

Happy Birthday to:
Jane Curtin, 1947, actress, comedian.
Jeff Foxworthy, 1958, comedian, actor and game show host.

In 1959, the first Barbie doll was sold on this date by the Mattel Corp.
It's Read A Book Day and National Do It Day.

Aha-phrodisiacs

Write or make art with the theme "do it." Write or make a collage about reading. Read for 10 minutes. List 6 things you like about September and then weave them together into poetry using short choppy sentences and coming up with a phrase you can repeat.

Dose of Mirth

Did you know babies are nauseated by the smell of a clean shirt?
~Jeff Foxworthy

Journal Juju

Repeated Completion: "I did it, I . . . "

Jane Curtin said, "I'm easy. Put me in an interesting location with good people and I'm there." Title a journal entry "I'm easy" and see what comes out.

Subliminal Message Brought to You by the Aha-phrodisiacs Potion

When you write you illuminate what's hidden. When you create you liberate originality. As a creator you connect yourself to a divine human ability. When you share, you touch, free, inspire, amuse, and teach others.

September 7

Name today _____

Daily Soul Vitamin
Life is what we make it, always has been, always will be. Painting's not important. The important thing is keeping busy. ~Grandma Moses

Toast of the Day
Here's to people over 70 who are living inspirations.

Awe—servances
Happy Birthday to:
Grandma Moses, 1860, the painter who started her career at 78 years old.
Buddy Holly, 1936, singer, songwriter, and a pioneer of rock and roll.

In 1967, The TV show *The Flying Nun* premiered. Sally Field played Sister Bertrille.

Aha—phrodisiacs
Buddy Holly Title Wave. That'll Be The Day, Everyday, Not Fade Away, Listen To Me, Heartbeat, Think It Over.

What if you had some kind of hat that made you able to fly? Write about your adventures.

Dose of Mirth
The 1960s were when hallucinogenic drugs were really big. And I don't think it's a coincidence that we had the shows then like The Flying Nun. ~Ellen DeGeneres

STILL LIFE WITH FLYING NUN HATS

Journal Juju
Write about what new lease on your life you will have when you are 70 as if it were that moment now.

Brought to You by Inner Awe—lixir Potion
Publisher Ralph Marston said, "Patience expands your options. If you insist on immediate gratification, your choices are severely limited. When you are willing to work patiently and steadfastly toward your goals, those goals can realistically be just about anything you choose." Feel or imagine the sensation of patience in body, mind and spirit and then see what you are inspired to write, or have Patience write you a letter.

Daily Soul Vitamin
In between goals is a thing called life that has to be lived and enjoyed. ~Sid Caesar

Toast of the Day
Here's to double-stick Scotch tape.

Awe—servances
Happy Birthday to:
Sid Caesar, 1922, Emmy-winning comic actor
   and writer.

On this day in 1921, Scotch tape was developed by Richard Drew. In 1930
   Margaret Gorman of Washington DC was crowned the first Miss America.

Aha—phrodisiacs
Tape quotes that inspire you to the inside cabinet drawers and on the ceiling above your bed. Use one of the many meanings of the word "stick" to trigger writing of any kind. Examples: Stick your neck out, sticking with a project, making a house out of sticks.
   Write a short but fun acceptance speech from the first Miss America.

Dose of Mirth
The guy who invented the first wheel was an idiot. The guy who invented the other three, HE was a genius. ~Sid Caesar

Journal Juju
Referring to today's Soul Vitamin, write about what you are enjoying in between goals.
   Try a new twist in journal writing and use the letters of the alphabet to start each line. Example:
   Always thinking about creativity, I decided
   Before breakfast to
   Create a
   Drawing.
   Evidently I need coffee
   First.

September 9

Daily Soul Vitamin

Grandmas are moms with lots of frosting. ~Author Unknown

Toast of the Day

Here's to biscuits and gravy every once in a while.

Awe—servances

Happy Birthday to:
Adam Sandler, 1966, actor, comedian, producer, and musician.

Also it's National Grandparents Day.
Biscuits and Gravy Week—Recognizes the culinary marriage of biscuits and gravy.
Protecting Your Home Furnishings Week (who thinks of these things?!).

Aha—phrodisiacs

If you could marry two kinds of foods what would they be? I would marry dark chocolate and angel food cake or dark chocolate and nectarines or dark chocolate and dark chocolate.

Adam Sandler has an album titled *What the Hell Happened to Me?* Start some writing with that line or make a doodle, painting, or collage that epitomizes that title.

Dose of Mirth

I sing seriously to my mom on the phone. To put her to sleep, I have to sing "Maria" from West Side Story. When I hear her snoring, I hang up.—Adam Sandler

Journal Juju

Write a story about your grandparents or a grandparent. What influence did your grandparents have on you? How did they change your life? What habit does or did one of them have?

What is your favorite piece of furniture? If you could be a piece of furniture what would you be? Write from its point of view.

Note to Myself: Imagine being a recliner.

Daily Soul Vitamin
This is a place where you can hear fall coming for miles.
~Charles Kuralt

Toast of the Day
Here's to imagining being in a place where you can
hear fall come for miles.

Awe–servances
Happy Birthday to:
Charles Kuralt, 1934, award-winning journalist.

It's also Swap Ideas Day.
On this day in 1953, Swanson sold its first TV dinner. In 1966, *The Road Runner
Show* premiered.

Aha–phrodisiacs
Swap ideas: Open *The Awe-manac* to any other page and pick an Aha-phrodisiac
and complete it again or for the first time. Open another book and pick out
words and phrases and do a Word Collage. If you could run as fast as the Road
Runner where would you run and who would you run from? Continue with this
sentence: "I can hear fall coming for miles . . . "

Dose of Mirth
Meep Meep! ~Road Runner

Journal Juju
Talk about your relationship to or any memories of TV dinners.

Message brought to you by Arpeggio Potion
Exposing yourself to music can help boost your immune system: In a study
done by Robert Beck, PhD, at the University of California, Irvine, levels of an
infection-fighting antibody increased 240 percent in choral members performing
Beethoven's *Missa Solemnis*. When you feel a sense of delight listening, playing,
or singing music, endorphins, the body's anti-aging, feel good chemicals, are
often released as well.

September 11

Name today _____

Daily Soul Vitamins

*It is no good casting out devils. They belong to us, we must accept them and be
at peace with them.* ~D.H. Lawrence

Thus shadow owes its birth to light. ~John Gay

*Thoughts are the shadows of our sensations—always darker, emptier, simpler
than these.* ~Friedrich Nietzsche

Toast of the Day

Here's to making it through the shadows to morning.

Awe—Servances

Happy Birthday to:

D.H. Lawrence, 1885, influential writer of all forms, and painter.

Aha—phrodisiacs

D.H. Lawrence had his character in *The Rainbow* write in her diary: "If I were the
moon, I know where I would fall down." Use this as a title for a collage, painting,
or doodle.

Make a lightning-fast (15 minutes) collage of your shadow side, ripping and
tearing images that your intuition translates as a dark side of yourself, and then
write a poem from its point of view about what it wants to say to you.

Dose of Mirth

*In times like these, it is helpful to remember that there have always been times like
these.* ~Paul Harvey

Journal Juju

Write what a day of shadows means to you in poetry, haiku, song, or stream
of consciousness.

List the qualities of some of your shadow sides, then have them
write to you telling you what they need in order to be whole.

Daily Soul Vitamin

"At worst, a house unkept cannot be so distressing as a life unlived."
~Rose Macaulay

Toast of the Day

Here's to the way your house feels after somebody else cleans it.

Awe-servances

Happy Birthday to:
H. L. Mencken, 1880, journalist, satirist, social critic, cynic, and freethinker.

Video Games Day.
International Housekeepers Week is around now.

Aha-phrodisiacs

Write about a video game of housekeepers. What's the objective?
Create a character who is a housekeeper; list a desire, conflict, a few personality characteristics and quirks, and then write from his or her point of view.

   Appreciate your housekeeper by calling him or her on the phone and saying, "I just wanted to let you know that I appreciate you. Thanks for cleaning my house so well. Okay, then, bye now."

   Buy some peanut butter for tomorrow.

Dose of Mirth

An idealist is one who, on noticing that roses smell better than a cabbage, concludes that it will also make better soup.
~H. L. Mencken

Journal Juju

H. L. Mencken said, "Love is the triumph of imagination over intelligence." Ponder your opinion about this quote in your journal. Tackle it from a variety of point of views from the serious to the tongue-in-cheek. Dispute it, side with it, go off on a tangent with it. Go on.

September 13

Name today _____

Daily Soul Vitamin

A person is a fool to become a writer. His only compensation is absolute freedom. ~Roald Dahl

Peanut Butter and Jelly Night

Toast of the Day

Here's to the first bite of a peanut butter and banana sandwich.

Awe—servances

Happy Birthday to:

Roald Dahl, 1916, novelist, short story author, and screenwriter, famous for
    Charlie and the Chocolate Factory, and *James and the Giant Peach*
Judith Martin, 1938, Miss Manners.

On this day in 1976, *The Muppet Show* premiered with Kermit the Frog, Miss
    Piggy, and Fozzie Bear.
National Peanut Butter Day.

Aha—phrodisiacs

Write a letter to and from your version of Miss Manners, seriously or funnily.
Complain to Miss Manners about living with a Muppet or growing giant peaches.
    Roald Dahl said, "A little nonsense now and then is relished by the wisest men." Write or make art using nonsense as your catalyst, make up words, absurd situations, a peanut butter moon, a Bliss-mas Factory.

Dose of Mirth

Nothing takes the taste out of peanut butter quite like unrequited love.
~Charlie Brown

Journal Juju

Have a peanut butter sandwich as you write in your journal today. Write about your favorite tastes in simple foods. Write about peanut butter memories. Write about a memory that sticks to the roof of your mind.

Roald Dahl, Spokesman for Aha—phrodisiacs

Roald sez, The writer has to force himself to work. He has to make his own hours and if he doesn't go to his desk at all there is nobody to scold him.

September 14

Name today _____

Daily Soul Vitamin

It is better to take many small steps in the right direction than to make a great leap forward only to stumble backward.
~Old Chinese Proverb

Toast of the Day

Here's to finding quotes that say exactly what you want to get across to your readers.

The September 1st Rainbow Flies Through September 14

Awe-servances

Happy Birthday to:

Ivan Pavlov, 1849, Nobel Prize-winning scientist. Pavlov is known for describing classical conditioning. In his experiments, he conditioned dogs to drool in anticipation of eating when a bell was rung.

Aha-phrodisiacs

Ivan Pavlov said, "While you are experimenting, do not remain content with the surface of things." Apply this to writing: Do not be content with generalities—go back to a draft you have written and change some of the more general words to specific words. Change "I went to the store" to "I went to the Kate's Card Haven where the scent of lavender seduced my nose and the bells on the door triggered my adrenalin."

Dose of Mirth

Does the name Pavlov ring a bell?—bumper sticker

Journal Juju

Pavlov also said, "Gradualness . . . From the very beginning of your work, school yourself to severe gradualness in the accumulation of knowledge." Moving forward little by little to change our thoughts and actions is a strategy vital to our creative success. Write a thought you believe will serve your creativity or the creation of contentment, such as "Each moment I believe more in my creative

brilliance" and gradually practice feeling it in body, mind, and spirit 15 seconds at a time. Over time its gradual influence will accelerate your creative movement (mileage may vary).

September 15

Name today _____

Daily Soul Vitamin

It took me fifteen years to discover that I had no talent for writing, but I couldn't give it up because by that time I was too famous. ~Robert Benchley

Toast of the Day

Here's to wisdom that can be framed humorously.

Awe-servances

Happy Birthday to:

Robert Benchley, 1889, humorist, newspaper columnist, film actor, and literary editor.

Agatha Christie, 1890, crime fiction writer. She is chiefly remembered for her 66 detective novels.

International Eat an Apple Day.

Born to be Wild Day.

Someday—You know all those things you're going to do "someday"? Well, this is it.

BORN TO BE MCINTOSH

Aha-phrodisiacs

Take a recent event and rewrite it in a detective genre. Add fictional characters who are murdered.

Write about or make into art a suspicious or wild apple.

Write poetry or prose about a character who was born to be tame, orderly, or gentle.

Double Dose of Mirth from Robert Benchley

A boy can learn a lot from a dog: obedience, loyalty, and the importance of turning around three times before lying down.

I can't bring myself to say, "Well, I guess I'll be toddling along." It isn't that I can't toddle. It's just that I can't guess I'll toddle.

Journal Juju

List or expound upon some things you have learned from your pet.

Repeated Completions: "I'm born to be . . .", Today is "someday."

September 16

Name today _____

Daily Soul Vitamin

I think your whole life shows in your face and you should be proud of that.
~Lauren Bacall

Toast of the Day

Here's to a friend whose concern for you touches your soul.

Awe-Servances

Happy Birthday to:

Lauren Bacall, 1924, award-winning film and stage actress.

Peter Falk, 1927, actor, best known for the title role of Columbo, a shabby and
    ostensibly absentminded police detective.

It's also Women's Friendship Day.

Aha-phrodisiacs

In reality, Columbo possessed a keen mind and solved his cases by paying close
attention to tiny inconsistencies in a suspect's story. Write about a character who
explains an event with slight inconsistencies. Write a poem about a friend of
yours, send it or not.

   Columbo-inspired Repeated Completion: "One more thing..." Write instructions about something as if you were absentminded. Ideas: how to get ready in
the morning, how to find happiness, how to impress someone.

Dose of Mirth

Being chased by Columbo is like being nibbled to death by a duck. ~Peter Falk

Journal Juju

Talk in your journal about some inconsistencies in your life.

Repeated Completions: "I will be…" "My friend is…"

And Now an Application from Awe-vanced Inner Messages Potion

What questions can I ask myself that will set my creative subconscious in motion?

September 17

Name today _____

Daily Soul Vitamin
Life is all about timing . . . the unreachable becomes reachable, the unavailable become available, the unattainable . . . attainable. Have the patience, wait it out. It's all about timing. ~Stacey Charter

Toast of the Day
Here's to the rewards of patience.

Awe-Servances
Happy Birthday to:
Rita Rudner, 1956, comedienne and writer.

1963 *The Fugitive* premiered, 1964 *Bewitched* premiered, 1966 *Mission: Impossible* premiered

Aha-phrodisiacs
Write about having plant tendencies. Draw, doodle, or collage a plant with human tendencies.

Write about a fugitive witch who encounters a CIA agent.

Write to-do lists from a certain character or attitude: a UFO, a feng shui expert, a consultant, a housewife witch, a fugitive, a grumpy person, a nerd, someone with very little to do, an elated person, a clown, a magician, a disorganized person, a porno star, an artist.

Pick a character above and make a to-do list that is just doodled or collaged pictures.

Dose of Mirth
I was a vegetarian until I started leaning toward the sunlight. ~Rita Rudner

Journal Juju
Write about the influence TV shows from the 60s might have had on you or the influence any TV show has on you.

Today I Get to: _____

September 18

Name today _____

Go Ahead. Make Something.

Daily Soul Vitamin

I don't know where my ideas come from. They just come, usually when I'm mowing the lawn, driving to work, or walking my hound. ~Ron Kofron

Toast of the Day

Here's to the look and feel of a newly cleaned carpet.

Awe-servances

Happy Birthday to:
Greta Garbo, 1905, actress during Hollywood's silent film period and Golden Age.
Ron Kofron, 1959, geologist and craftsman.

On this day in 1876, Melville R. Bissell patented the carpet sweeper.
National Play-Doh Day.

Aha-phrodisiacs

Use the verb "sweep" or its variations in poetry or prose. Write a list of images that come to mind.

Write a list of random words and phrases and then write what those words or phrases might be answers to. Go buy some Play-Doh. Make a number of little abstract shapes, title them, and then use the titles as writing prompts together or separately like a Title Wave.

Dose of Mirth

New ideas pass through three periods: 1) It can't be done. 2) It probably can be done, but it's not worth doing. 3) I knew it was a good idea all along! ~Arthur C. Clarke

Journal Juju

If you are feeling unfocused, one way to calm and focus the mind is to trace around your hand, then color it in with various pictures and colors. You can do the same with a circle or heart shape.

Greta Garbo said: "There seems to be a law that governs all our actions so I never make plans." Imagine that you know a law that is governing our actions and write about it as if you were an expert. Starter Fluid: "My research indicates that there is a law that governs . . . "

September 19

Name today _____

Daily Soul Vitamin

My yesterdays walk with me. They keep step,
they are gray faces that peer over my shoulder.
~William Golding

Toast of the Day

Here's to the visual art of laundry hanging in
the sun and breeze.

Awe—Servances

Happy Birthday to:

William Golding, 1911, Nobel Prize winning
    novelist and poet, best known for
    Lord of the Flies.

James Lipton, writer, poet, dean emeritus of the Actors Studio Drama School, and
    host of the Bravo cable television series, *Inside the Actors Studio.*

National Vision Rehabilitation Day.

1849, the first commercial laundry is established in Oakland, CA.

Aha—phrodisiacs

Here are the ten questions (compiled by Bernard Pivot) that James Lipton asks
every famous actor he interviews on *Inside the Actors Studio.* Have fun answering
them: 1. What is your favorite word? 2. What is your least favorite word?, 3.
What turns you on?, 4. What turns you off?, 5. What is your favorite curse word?
6. What sound or noise do you love?, 7. What sound or noise do you hate? 6.
What profession other than your own would you like to attempt?, 9. What profession would you not like to attempt? 10. If Heaven exists, what would you like
to hear God say when you arrive at the Pearly Gates?

Journal Juju

Vision Rehab: Starter Fluid or Repeated Completions: "I better see . . . "
    Define the spin cycle of your life.

Today I Get to: _____

Daily Soul Vitamin

There is a fountain of youth; it is your mind, your talents, the creativity you bring to your life and the lives of people you love. When you learn to tap this source you will have truly defeated age. ~Sophia Loren

Toast of the Day

Here's to staying young for our whole life by tapping into our soul's expression.

Awe-servances

Happy Birthday to
Joyce Brothers, 1928, leading family psychologist and advice columnist.
Sophia Loren, 1934, award-winning actress.

Aha-phrodisiacs

Take some time today, even if it is 5 minutes, to fill your fountain of youth: Prepare to step-up your creativity. Look for a class to take, get supplies ready for painting, read something about writing, but then APPLY it: take one small step toward integrating more creativity into your life.

Dose of Mirth

Everything you see I owe to spaghetti. ~Sophia Loren

Journal Juju

Create a travel article about a side-trip in the journey of your life—chronicle some turning point or insignificant moment. Extra credit: add pictures, actual or fictional.

Joyce Brothers said, "Trust your hunches. They're usually based on facts filed away just below the conscious level." Starter Fluid or Repeated Completions: "I have a hunch . . . ."

Brought to You by the Makers of the FOOOF

To summon new playful, rejuvenated, or enlightening insight into a creative pursuit or an issue you are dealing with, write as if you were explaining it to a class of kids.

September 21

Name today _____

Daily Soul Vitamin
Poetry is just the evidence of life. If your life is burning well, poetry is just the ash.
~Leonard Cohen

Toast of the Day
Here's to a life that is ignited, burning, and fueled with creative passion.

Awe-servances
H. G. Wells, 1866, author whose books include *The Invisible Man*, and *The War of the Worlds*.
Leonard Cohen, 1934, poet, novelist, and singer-songwriter.
Stephen King, 1947, author of over 50 bestselling horror novels.

Office Olympics in Shreveport, LA: 100 teams of office employees compete in such events as The Water Break Relay, The Office Chair Roll-off, Toss the Boss, and the Human Post-it-Note.

Aha-phrodisiacs
Write a piece as the sports announcer or write a dialog between two sports announcers of Office Olympics: Use any of the topics above or go with Fixing the Copier.
     Write about your day as the invisible man or woman. Include: frustrations, advantages, desires, conflict, relationships, a visit to a locker room.

Dose of Mirth
 I like to tell people I have the heart of a small boy. Then I say it's in a jar on my desk. ~Stephen King

Journal Juju
Write a list of the things you'd do if you were invisible. Write a poem about being visible.
     Write about keeping your own or anyone's heart in a jar on your desk, metaphorically or for real.
     Add an amusing horror element to a journal entry.

September 22

Daily Soul Vitamin

I doubt whether the world holds for anyone a more soul-stirring surprise than the first adventure with ice cream. ~Heywood Campbell Brown

Toast of the Day

Here's to elephants.

Awe-Servances

1903, Italo Marchiony invented the ice cream cone, served from his pushcart in New York City.
Elephant Appreciation Day (I didn't make this up).
Autumnal Equinox.
Jewish holidays are around this time.

Aha-phrodisiacs

Write a poem or haiku about elephants. Doodle an elephant. Write a poem, song or run-on sentence about ice cream. Take your favorite flavor and write a love poem to it.

Keep going with this Jewish Proverb, "Never trust the man who tells you all his troubles but keeps from you all his joys."

Doses of Mirth

If at first you don't succeed, destroy all evidence that you tried. ~Susan Ohanian

Journal Juju

Write unsent letters whenever you need to in your journals. Tell old lovers what you'd like them to know now that you are older and wiser or dumber. Tell family members or friends something you never told them before. Tell a younger or older version of yourself something that you'd like her or him to know. Write to a memory or to a goal. For an often enlightening exercise, try writing letters back to yourself from any of these people or things.

September 23

Daily Soul Vitamin

I never feel age . . . If you have creative work, you don't have age or time. ~Louise Nevelson

Toast of the Day

Here's to making art out of found objects and to never feeling age.

Umbrella with Found Objects

Awe-servances

Happy Birthday to:

Walter Lippmann, 1889, writer, journalist, and political commentator.

Louise Nevelson, 1900, assemblage artist. Nevelson is known for her abstract expressionist "boxes" grouped together to form a new creation.

Libra begins.

Aha-phrodisiac

Use the point of view of the following Libra characteristics to write four short versions having to do with anything about boxes: bossy, loves art, loves public service, dresses up for the occasion.

Louise Nevelson said, "When you put together things that other people have thrown out, you're really bringing them to life, a spiritual life that surpasses the life for which they were originally created." Compile a number of found objects and group them together to form a new creation. Use wire or a glue gun to adhere them. Then have it write about itself from its point of view

Dose of Humor

Our business in life is not to succeed, but to continue to fail in good spirits. ~Robert Louis Stevenson

Journal Juju

Walter Lippman said, "Where all think alike, no one thinks very much." Repeated completions: "I think . . . " "No one thinks . . . "

Antiaging Application

Review the above Louis Nevelson Soul Vitamin 14 or 15 times.

September 24

Name today _____

Daily Soul Vitamin
You can play a shoestring if you're sincere ~John Coltrane

Toasts of the Day
Here's to the unconditional love of dogs and here's to people who treat their pets well.

Awe–Servances
Happy Birthday to:
John Coltrane, 1926, jazz saxophonist and composer.

Fall begins.
National Dog Week.

Aha–phrodisiacs
Use "fall" in one or more of these forms: fall into a rut, falling short, waterfall, fall away, fall under, fall to pieces, fall into one's hand, downfall; fall out, fall of day,
    Write a tribute to dogs.

Doses of Mirth
Properly trained, a man can be a dog's best friend. ~Corey Ford
    I wonder what goes through his mind when he sees us peeing in his water bowl. ~Penny Ward Moser
    I wonder if other dogs think poodles are members of a weird religious cult. ~Rita Rudner

Journal Juju
Close your eyes and visualize fall memories and sensations. Write a stream of conscious with this Starter Fluid: "I know what you're thinking . . . "
    Coltrane said, "I've found you've got to look back at the old things and see them in a new light." Make a list of things in your life, then go back and make notes about how you can see them in a new light if you looked through the following Viewfinders: calm, simplistic, confident, nonchalant, big-shot, imaginative, resourceful, accepting, compassionate, upside down, imperfect, quick.

Today I get to: _____

Name today _____

Daily Soul Vitamin

Always dream and shoot higher than you know you can do. Don't bother just to be better than your contemporaries or predecessors. Try to be better than yourself.
~William Faulkner

Toast of the Day

Here's to feeling like "a wet seed wild in the hot blind earth." (Faulkner quote).

Awe-servances

Happy Birthday to;
William Faulkner, 1897, Nobel Prize-winning novelist and poet.
Barbara Walters, 1931, journalist and well-known media personality.

On this day in 1676, Greenwich Mean Time became standard in
    England and in 1884 for the world.

Aha-phrodisiacs

Make some time to write or make art about time. A haiku, a poem, a run-on sentence, a story about a time machine, a story about being on time.
    Faulkner said, "Clocks slay time . . . time is dead as long as it is being clicked off by little wheels; only when the clock stops does time come to life." What the heck does that mean?

Dose of Mirth

Deep breaths are very helpful at shallow parties. ~Barbara Walters

Journal Juju

Barbara Walters also said, "To feel valued, to know, even if only once in a while, that you can do a job well is an absolutely marvelous feeling." Write a list of or talk at length about times when you felt valued. Bring the feeling of being valued into the present moment.

Repeat Advertising from Awe-wakened Moment

Can you believe that everything is unfolding just the way it is supposed to? How can you acknowledge, feel, and embody the fact that many parts of your dream are already happening now?

Daily Soul Vitamin

Only those who will risk going too far can possibly find out how far one can go. ~T. S. Eliot

Toast of the Day

Here's to acknowledging our moments of willpower.

Awe-servances

Happy Birthday to:

T. S. Eliot, 1888, Nobel prize-winning poet, dramatist, and literary critic.

Jack LaLanne , 1914, fitness, exercise and nutritional expert.

On this day in 1969, the Beatles released *Abbey Road*. It was their 13th and last album.

Aha-phrodisiacs

Abbey Road Title Wave for writing or art: Come Together, Something, Oh! Darling, I Want You, Here Comes The Sun, Because, She Came In Through The Bathroom Window, Carry That Weight, The End.

Journal Juju

Jack LaLanne said, "I hate to work out! I'd rather take a beating. So I get it out of the way, and the next thing I know, I look in the mirror and say, 'Jack, you've done it again.' And if I've got the will power to do that, everything else is easy by comparison." Congratulating ourselves daily for what we do, motivates us to do more. It's time for another credit report. Start working out one minute a day.

Note to Self

Workout by dancing to Motown music. **Still Life Doing Jumping Jacks**

Today I get to: _____

September 27

Name today _____

Daily Soul Vitamin
All appears to change when we change. ~Henri-Frédéric Amiel

Toast of the Day
Here's to our ancestors.

Awe-servances
Happy Birthday to:
Henri-Frédéric Amiel, 1821, philosopher, poet and critic.
Peter Sellers, 1925, comedian, actor and performer, starred
   in early Pink Panther films.

Ancestor Appreciation Day.

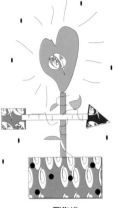

THING

Aha-phrodisiacs
There is an African ritual where you set a place at the dinner table for selected
ancestors. Today would be a good day to do that. What decoration would your
selected ancestor like? Have their favorite meal if you know what it was. Set a
place for them and eat as if their spirit were with you.

Write a list of questions from the absurd to the profound. The faster you
write the better. Then check and see if any of those questions would trigger
writing, doodling, or art.

Dose of Mirth
*If there's an exception to every rule, is there an exception to that rule? If you say some-
thing is indescribable, isn't that describing it?* ~Stephen Wright

Journal Juju
Peter Sellers said, "I'm a classic example of all humorists—only funny when I'm
working," and "I feel ghostly unreal until I become somebody else again on the
screen." Write in your journal about how are you different when you are working or are around others than when you are in solitude.

Brought to You by the Kindness/Gather Potions
Can you dedicate whatever you are doing to a purpose higher than yourself,
even if only you know about the dedication? Can you dedicate it to someone
important who has passed away? When you do this, new forces and a different
kind of motivation often enter in, to energize and direct you.

September 28

Name today _____

Daily Soul Vitamin
Success is following the pattern of life one enjoys most.
~Al Capp

Toast of the Day
Here's to the novelty, ease, and delight of take-out Chinese food.

Awe-servances
Happy Birthday to:

Confucius, 551 BCE, Chinese thinker and social philosopher, whose teachings
and philosophy have deeply influenced Chinese, Japanese, Korean, and Viet-
namese thought and life.

Ed Sullivan, 1901, entertainment writer and television host.

Al Capp, 1909, creator of the comic strip, *Li'l Abner.*

Aha-phrodisiacs
Write a number of wise phrases you have learned in your life as if you were
channeling Confucius. Repeated Completions: "_____(your name) says . . . .."

 ## Dose of Mirth
*Abstract art is a product of the untalented, sold by the unprincipled to the
utterly bewildered.* ~Al Capp

Journal Juju
Explore in your journal what associations you have to this Confucius quote:
"We should feel sorrow, but not sink under its oppression."

An Application of the Kindness Potion
Ed Sullivan said, "If you do a good job for others, you heal yourself at the same
time, because a dose of joy is a spiritual cure. It transcends all barriers." Buy some
fortune cookies, remove fortunes with tweezers, and put in your own positive
quotes or soul vitamins—deliver them to a friend, co-worker, or boss.

Today I get to: _____

September 29

Name today _____

Daily Soul Vitamin

Friendship: It's like having a tiny apartment and somebody moves in with you. But instead of becoming cramped and crowded, the space expands, and you discover rooms you never knew you had until your friend moved in with you. ~Steve Tesich

Toast of the Day

Here's to people who expand our space.

Awe-Servances

Happy Birthday to
Mihály Csíkszentmihályi, 1934, author of books on
     what makes people truly happy and fulfilled.
Jerry Lee Lewis,1935, a rock and roll and country
     music singer, songwriter, and pianist.
Steve Tesich, 1942, award winning screenwriter, playwright, and novelist.

Family Health and Fitness Day.

Aha-phrodisiacs

Steve Tesich wrote a play called *Square One*. Write a poem or make some art that uses this title as inspiration.
     Begin some poetry or prose with this Jerry Lee Lewis song title: "I'm Walking."

Dose of Mirth

My grandmother started walking five miles a day when she was sixty. She's ninety-seven now, and we don't know where the hell she is. ~Ellen DeGeneres

Journal Juju

John Kennedy said, "Physical fitness is not only one of the most important keys to a healthy body, it is the basis of dynamic and creative intellectual activity." Write about your relationship to physical fitness and if it's not good, start with two minutes of exercise a day.

September 30

Daily Soul Vitamin

To me, the greatest pleasure of writing is not what it's about, but the inner music that words make. ~Truman Capote

Toast of the Day

Here's to the smell of coffee.

Awe-Servances

Happy Birthday to:

Truman Capote, 1924, writer whose nonfiction, stories, novels, and plays are literary classics.

Johnny Mathis, 1935, award-winning singer and songwriter.

Fran Drescher, 1957, film and television actress, famous for her nasal voice.

Aha-phrodisiacs

Johnny Mathis song title for Repeated Completions: "It's Not for Me to Say . . . "

Write about from the point of view of an angel, have a dialog with one asking advice and getting it from one or more of these 'tudes: angry, argumentative, articulate, at wit's end, baffled, belligerent, boastful, brave, bumbling, nosey, overpolite, overprotective, overzealous.

Dose of Mirth

The reason angels can fly is because they take themselves lightly. ~G.K. Chesterton

Journal Juju

Fran Drescher is a cancer survivor, and she said, "Once you wake up and smell the coffee, it's hard to go back to sleep. Since my illness, I've felt the presence of my angels." If you are not awake yet, WAKE UP! Life is short and every day there is an element of magic, miracle and mirth to be deeply embraced (5 percent at a time; mileage may vary). Write a How-to for yourself: *Five Ways to Wake Up.*

A TWO POTION SET

When I was young, I admired clever people. Now that I am old, I admire kind people.
~Abraham Joshua Heschel

My religion is very simple. My religion is kindness.
~The Dalai Lama

aNd

Agelessness, fulfillment and creativity work so much better when we make connections with others, whether it's service, spending time with people on our wavelength, or reaching out to ask for support. We are pack animals. Being with people, asking for help, and immersing ourselves in situations where the synergy bounces off like-minds is just evolutionarily correct. And we look our best when we are kind and when we are helping others. It's kind of easy. And the place to begin with kindness is to be kind to yourself.

I will show you a love potion without drug or herb or any witch's spell; if you wish to be loved, love. ~Hecato

POSSibLe EFFectS: Joy, inspiration, reward, feelings of contentment, good karma, health, support, a ride home, a casserole, feedback, compassion, a shoulder, a hand.

Side EFFectS: Apply Kindness and Gathering liberally. If kindness is sustained longer than four hours you will either feel better about yourself than you ever thought possible or turn into a grape pixy stick. Side effects may include diminished angst drive. You may need to change friends as you detect unsupportive, chronically cranky or moldy traits.

OCTOBER ENTRY WAY

October is from the Latin octo meaning "eight." It was the eighth month of the old Roman calendar, which began with March. Quickly write eight things you like about October or, if you are in a reading mode, stop and do an exercise for imagination and amusement: think of at least four favorite October things, and in your imagination. Blow those four things up like balloons in the Macy's Thanksgiving Day Parade (even if they are intangible like weather). When you DO sit down with your trusty journal, continue to upgrade your mind for creative confidence and write eight things you like about yourself.

October is Popular.
Here Are Just a Few of the Events:

National Clock Month, Fantasy Month, National Popcorn Poppin' Month, Right Brainer's Rule Month, Adopt-A-Shelter-Animal Month, Diversity Awareness Month, Month of the Dinosaur, National Communicate With Your Kid Month, National Depression Education Awareness Month, National Pasta Month, National Roller Skating Month, National Apple Month, National Pizza Month, National Pretzels Month, National Cookie Month, National Vegetarian Awareness Month, Self-Promotion Month, National Country Music Month, Dryer Vent Safety Awareness Month, Family History Month, Gay and Lesbian History Month, Listen to Your Inner Critic Month, Month of the Dinosaur, National Sarcastic Awareness Month (great, just what we need), International Fired Up Month, where people learn what gets them fired up and incorporate it into their lives..

AWe-Manac Invented Days:
October 11 Courage Day
October 23 Inner Awe-lixir Day

Suggested Ways to Celebrate

There is a magic to the month of October. It is the month of permission to be someone different, something creative, and somewhat outrageous. The weather's turning to crisp, we are turning inward, and it is the shadow's turn to emerge. If you could be four different characters, who would they be? Make a list of small ways to bring the magic of these characters into each of the weeks of October, even if the action or thought is distantly related or associated with your character.

Astrological Word Pools Do-it-Yourself

Create your horoscope by adding words to the ones provided with your sign.

Aries: donate, money, local animal shelter.

Taurus: loved, things, isle, two, places, lost, believe, add.

Gemini: talk, kid, more, great, instructions, point, look, willingly, truth.

Cancer: compelled, pasta, share, help, watch, artist, delude, let it go.

Leo: popcorn, loved one, mirror, shore, noise, reveal, differently.

Virgo: apple pie, before, ridiculous, expand, care, fifty, open, about, contribution, reality.

Libra: pizza, done, fall, towards, overhear, compose, decision, making, infinitely.

Scorpio: bake, cookies, and, take, them, to, a, retirement, home.

Sagittarius: cook, know, careful, precisely, thirty, home, foray, draw.

Capricorn: treat, around, tear up, plant, change, sign ability, some, dust, doorway, mysterious, wardrobe.

Aquarius: rest of your life, equally, important, elusive, matters, escape, blank, seems, going.

Pisces: walk, epiphany, every, possible, moonlight, rainy, dog, incident, basis, delightful, wonder, aborigine.

Tides:

Ebbing: What are you letting go of this month (just a little bit)?

_____

Flowing: Where are you expanding this month (just a little bit)?

_____

Vessel of strength: What saying or quote will navigate you and keep you afloat through the month (See Awe-wakened Inner Messages)?

_____

Gardening Information

Flower: Calendula

Monthly Awe-manac Crop: Clocks

Planting Tips: Add 60 tics and 60 tocks, rush with water, plant next to thyme, space 30 seconds apart, and hire some hands. Hit "snooze" if they come up too soon.

Daily Soul Vitamin
Perseverance is failing nineteen times and succeeding the twentieth. ~Julie Andrews

Toast of the Day
Here's to songs from the movie *Mary Poppins*

Awe-servances
Happy Birthday to:

Julie Andrews, 1935, multi-award winning actress, singer, and author.

Naval Officer James Lawrence, 1781. Although his last battle was a defeat, while being carried off the ship mortally wounded, he uttered, "Don't give up the ship."

It's also International Day of Older Persons and National Heart Magic Day.

Aha-phrodisiacs
Word Pool: cleansing, out of order, give, utter, tears, success, nomad, begin, haunt, top of the refrigerator, expansive, keep going, chair, noise, order, stairs, spoon full of sugar, umbrella.

Heart Magic: If your heart could whisper to you today, what would it say? Write down a list of associations to the word heart. Write fast and have no care that any of it makes sense. Draw, doodle, or paint how your heart is feeling today and then do a second picture of how you would like it to feel.

Journal Juju
Write about what "Don't give up the ship" means in your life.

For International Day of Older Persons: Ask your 85 year old self a question and answer it.

Have a dialog with Mary Poppins or another fictional character as if they were working or doing chores with you today.

Dose of Mirth
The elevator to success is out of order. You'll have to use the stairs . . . one step at a time. ~Joe Girard

Today I get to:

Daily Soul Vitamin

Everyone who wills can hear the inner voice.
It is within everyone ~Mahatma Gandhi

Toast of the Day

Here's to that feeling of fall in the air.

Awe-servances

Happy Birthday to:

Mahatma Gandhi, 1869, major political and spiritual leader
of India; the Father of the Nation.

1959 'There is a fifth dimension, beyond that which is known
to man . . .' Another thriller *The Twilight Zone* premiered
on this date with Rod Serling, it's host and creator.

It's also Name Your Car Day and World Farm Animals Day.

Aha-phrodisiacs

Start with this unfinished sentence: "When I opened my dryer I
noticed another dimension . . ."

Write about meeting up with farm animals driving cars with names in the
Twilight Zone.

Journal Juju

Gandhi lived simply—what's one way you could live more simply than you are now?

Write, collage, paint, doodle, or dance about another dimension in your life.
Name it first. Suggestions: *The Imagination Dimension, The Escape Dimension,*
The Place I'd Like to Be, The Dimension of Peace, The Dimension I Forgot About But Now
Remember, or maybe just, *Edna.*

Dose of Mirth

You know, somebody actually complimented me on my driving today. They left a little
note on the windscreen, it said "Parking Fine". ~Tommy Cooper

Today I get to: _____

Daily Soul Vitamin

A free spirit is an archetype. It refers to a human being who feels unconstrained by convention; rather, the spirit of liberty is paramount to that person. ~Neural Gourmet blog

Toast of the Day

Here's to a feeling of freedom.

Awe-servances

Happy Birthday to:
Gore Vidal, 1925, author of novels, stage
     plays, screenplays, and essays.

It is also Feast of Free Spirits
1893, The first motor-driven vacuum cleaner is patented by J.S. Thurman of
     St. Louis, MO.

Aha-phrodisiacs

Make a free spirit collage: Consider putting quotes on it from Isadora Duncan, John Lennon and William Blake.

     Word Pool: mistaken, attempt, star, polished, underneath, today only, cat, happen, smooth, stop, plant, wondering how, extraordinary, wander, surround, horn, mystery, hide, loud, free spirit, liberated.

Dose of Mirth

There is no human problem which could not be solved if people would simply do as I advise. ~Gore Vidal

Journal Juju

Repeated completion: "I feel liberated when . . ."

Awe-vanced Inner Message Propaganda

When you wake up today, tomorrow, next Tuesday or all of the above say to yourself: I can't wait to see what I say and do today.

October 4

Daily Soul Vitamin

Start by doing what's necessary; then do what's possible; and suddenly you are doing the impossible. ~St. Francis of Assisi

Toast of the Day

Here's to the sound of the wind when you're inside, under the covers.

Awe—Servances

International Toot Your Flute Day, a day to sell yourself.
It's also Ten-Four Day, a day of recognition to radio operators.
St. Francis of Assisi Day: The saint who preached kindness and gentleness to animals.
1959: Luna 3 (USSR), the first space probe to photograph the dark side of the moon was launched
1957: Leave it to Beaver premiered.

Aha—phrodisiacs

Write a radio transmission from June Clever or you from the dark side of the moon. Write what you see and do. Toot a flute. End it with 10-4. Collage the dark side of your metaphorical moon and then do another picture of your "full" moon.

Dose of Mirth

When in doubt, make a fool of yourself. There is a microscopically thin line between being brilliantly creative and acting like the most gigantic idiot on earth. So, what the hell, leap! ~Cynthia Heimel

Journal Juju

National Toot Your Flute Day: write a short little article about yourself as if all the things you want to accomplish have been done. Update your business card. Now write a list of what has been working for you.

More A.I.M. brainwash

Think to yourself: "I can do this."

Note to Myself: I have leaper's knee, I make a fool of myself quite often.

October 5

Name today _____

Daily Soul Vitamin
I have had dreams, and I've had nightmares. I overcame the nightmares because of my dreams. ~Jonas Salk

Toast of the Day
Here's to quick and clever banter.

Dose of Mirth
Nobody can be exactly like me. Even I have trouble doing it. ~Tallulah Bankhead

Awe-servances
Today is National Denim Day, World Smile Day, and National Come and Take It Day.

Aha-phrodisiacs
Write about how we should celebrate Come and Take it Day as if you were its inventor. What ritual happens on this day? What food is served and what kind of parade is there?

Wear denim or do a collage that uses pictures of denim in a quilt or tapestry.

Journal Juju
Today's journal title: *My Take on the Smiley Face* or *Dreams That Make my Soul Smile.* Or write about what the phrase "Come and take it . . ." evokes in you.

Write about something currently happening in the news and your thoughts or feelings about it. Write about something in your life as if it were a news report.

Acting as if you were an expert, write a numbered how-to essay about something that would help you solve a problem.

Question from Awe-wakened Moment Potion
Can you believe that everything is unfolding just the way it is supposed to? How can you acknowledge, feel, and embody the fact that many parts of your dream are already happening now?

October 6

Name today _____

Daily Soul Vitamin

I put a piece of paper under my pillow, and when I could not sleep, I wrote in the dark
~Henry David Thoreau

No one realizes how beautiful it is to travel until he comes home and rests his head on his old, familiar pillow. ~Lyn Yutang

Toast of the Day

Here's to the feel of your head sinking into your pillow after a long, tiring day.

Awe-servances

Today is *Awe-manac* Pillow Appreciation Day.

Aha-phrodisiacs

Buy a new special pillow case or wash a current one and dry in a pleasant smelling fabric softener or hang on a clothesline for that outdoorsy smell (unless you live close to a sewer plant).

Make a collage that includes pillows as clouds, flying carpets, or toadstools.

Journal Juju

With your head on a pillow, daydream about an inner golden energy that is your creativity. Breathe into it and allow it to deepen. Listen to a bit of wisdom it would like to tell you. If nothing comes, imagine what it would say if it did. Write using the Starter Fluid: "The golden energy of my creativity tells me . . . "

Write a note with three small questions and put it under your pillow tonight. In the morning, use a stream of consciousness and an attitude (even if it's pretend) of knowing the answer. Write away without concern for being right, perfect or grammatically correct.

Dose of Mirth

Corduroy pillows: They're making headlines! –Unknown

Today I get to: _____

October 7

Daily Soul Vitamin

. . . you must have a reason to be in the places to which you go, and you must do only things that you really care about. ~Yo-Yo Ma

Toast of the Day

Here's to a shared laugh with a complete stranger at something unexpected.

Awe–servances

Happy Birthday to:
Yo-Yo Ma, 1955, cellist.
John Mellencamp, 1951, singer.

And it's Women's Herbal Health Day.

Aha–phrodisiacs

John Mellencamp Title Wave: *Just Another Day, Empty Hands, French Shoes, Hard to Hold On To, Down and Out in Paradise, Circling Around the Moon.*

Try a new herbal tea today, then write about it or make art to represent the taste.

Journal Juju

Using Yo-Yo Ma's quote as inspiration, write a list of things, people, ideas, and beliefs you really care about. For extra credit, choose one or more items from that list and write lists about those things, then weave words from your lists together in a way that sounds pleasing to you.

Dose of Mirth

Black holes are where God divided by zero.

Subliminal Message Brought to You by the Potions Kindness and Sharing

How can you make life tomorrow just a little easier with 5 minutes of your time today?

Can you practice for 15 seconds believing that you are good enough? If you notice that you are comparing yourself to others, can you stop and honor your own path, uniqueness and process by saying: HEY, FOCUS OVER HERE [pointing to yourself]?

October 8

Name today _____

Daily Soul Vitamin
It comes from saying no to 1,000 things to make sure we don't get on the wrong track or try to do too much. ~Steve Jobs

Toast of the Day
Here's to making up your own toast of the day today [instructions: make up your own toast of the day today].

Awe-servances
Happy Birthday to:
Thomas Moore, 1940, the author of *Care of the Soul*,
   Jungian psychotherapist.
Rona Barrett, 1936, gossip columnist.

National Pet Peeve Week and National Children's Day.

Aha-phrodisiacs
Write about a pet peeve. (Tailgating? People eating with their mouth open?) Write from your pet peeve's point of view.
   Write about your day, your work, your relationship as if you were a child.

Dose of Mirth
The most powerful force in the universe is gossip. ~Dave Barry

Journal Juju
Write a short, short story about you writing a short, short story. Give yourself permission to not avoid this task: Doodle or sketch (rough sketches especially invited) a self-portrait of you engaged in 1) a habit you use for avoidance 2) an activity that brings you reward and enjoyment.
   Make this word pool work for one of your journal entries: things, gossip, pet peeve, soul, child-like, escape, blessing, formidable, understand, limb, brush, power.

A.I.M. Break
Take a moment and imagine how your body would feel and what your mind would think if you believed in yourself five times more than you do right now. Imagine thinking "So what, I believe in myself" anytime you feel yourself comparing yourself to someone else.

Daily Soul Vitamin
Pain is such an important thing in life. I think that as an artist you have to experience suffering. It's not enough to have lived it once; you have to relive it. ~Naomi Watts

Toast of the Day
Here's to the taste of your favorite cheese on your favorite cracker when you're hungry.

Awe-Servances
Happy Birthday to:
John Lennon, 1940, composer, musician, and member of The Beatles

Moldy Cheese Day.

Dose of Mirth
Age is something that doesn't matter, unless you are a cheese. ~Billie Burke

Aha-phrodisiacs
John Lennon Title Wave: Imagine, Crippled Inside, It's So Hard, Give Me Some Truth.

   Write an ode to moldy cheese.

Journal Juju
Starter Fluid: "If nothing ever changed . . . "
Title your entry today with one of Lennon's song titles and see what associations from your own life come out.

Repeat Advertising from to You by the A.I.M. Potion
What little 1-to-5 minute step can you take today toward building a creative commitment or habit? The habit can be practice feeling and thinking differently in a way that better serves you too. What would 15 percent more creative confidence feel like? What would it make you think? What small thing can you do to believe in yourself? Imagine for 20 seconds, really believing you can surpass your limitations.

October 10

Name today _____

NATIONAL WILDLIFE WEEK

Daily Soul Vitamin

Each friend represents a world in us, a world possibility not born until they arrive, and it is only by this meeting that a new world is born. ~Anaïs Nin

Toast of the Day

Here's to the warm, velvety softness of dogs' ears.

Awe-servances

National Bring Your Teddy Bear to Work Day, a celebration of the help, stress relief and joy that teddy bears bring into the lives of people. (I didn't make this up.)

National Wildlife Week.

In 1973, Spiro Agnew became the second person to resign the office of Vice President of the US. He entered a plea of no contest to a charge of income tax evasion.

Aha-phrodisiacs

Write about a character who takes his or her teddy bear to work and what happens. Or write about a work environment where bringing in one's teddy bear is expected.

Write a piece that includes the word "wildlife," a bunch of other "w" words, and other words that start with any letter.

Journal Juju

Write about resignation. Start with a list of any associations you have with the word and either weave them together or write about one that seems to have the most juice for you.

Dose of Mirth

I don't think my parents liked me. They put a live teddy bear in my crib. ~Woody Allen

Questions from A.I.M

Answer these questions quick: I feel stronger when . . . , If I were true to myself I would . . . , If nothing were standing in my way I would . . . (And then keep asking yourself how you might answer these differently throughout the day without expecting immediate answers).

October 11

Name today _____

Soul Vitamin Regimen for Courage

*You gain strength, courage and confidence
by every experience in which you really stop
to look fear in the face. You are able to say to
yourself, I lived through this horror. I can take the next thing that comes along. . . .
You must do the thing you think you cannot do.* ~Eleanor Roosevelt

*Courage is not the absence of fear, but rather the judgment that something else is
more important than fear.* ~Ambrose Redmoon

*Patience and perseverance have a magical effect before which difficulties disappear
and obstacles vanish.* ~John Quincy Adams

*With courage you will dare to take risks, have the strength to be compassionate, and
the wisdom to be humble. Courage is the foundation of integrity.* ~Keshavan Nair

Courage is going from failure to failure without losing enthusiasm. ~Winston
Churchill

Life shrinks or expands in proportion to one's courage. ~Anais Nin

*I count him braver who overcomes his desires than him who conquers his enemies,
for the hardest victory is over self.* ~Aristotle

Awe-servances

Happy Birthday to:
Eleanor Roosevelt, 1884, author, speaker, political leader, wife of FDR.
Ambrose Redmoon, 1933, a beatnik, writer, and rock music manager.

Aha-phrodisiacs

Act confidently and soon you'll feel confident. It works. Just start a little a day and
give yourself a margin of retreating without self-criticism every once in awhile.

Journal Juju

Write a list of the tiniest steps of courage you could possibly take in the next
day, week, and month. Consider taking one or two this week. Visualize and feel
5 percent more courage in your body during moments of daydreaming. Repeated
completions: "I feel courage when . . . "

Small Question for A.I.M. Potion

What one small courageous thing can I do today?

October 12

Daily Soul Vitamin

Frustration is commonly the difference between what you would like to be and what you are willing to sacrifice to become what you would like to be. ~Unknown

Toast of the Day

Here's to that moment when something frustrating has been resolved.

Awe-Servances

Today is: Columbus Day, World Egg Day, and International Moment of Frustration Scream Day.

Aha-phrodisiacs

Free associate about the word "discovery." Repeated Completions: "I discover . . . "

Free associate about eggs or egg concepts. Write about discovering an egg.

Make a collage of an egg breaking open and have surrealistic things emerging from it.

Go outdoors at 12 Greenwich Time and scream for 30 seconds then write about a remedy or potion for frustration.

Journal Juju

Write a quick list of discoveries you've made, from the minuscule to the large. Doodle or draw what frustration looks like to you. And then doodle, paint or draw a different picture that triumphs over the frustration.

Dose of Mirth

My recipe for dealing with anger and frustration: set the kitchen timer for 20 minutes, cry, rant, and rave, and at the sound of the bell, simmer down and go about business as usual. ~Phyllis Diller

A.I.M. Message

The struggle is optional. Let it go. Breathe when frustrated, hop at least once when discovering something, and lean toward sweetness.

October 13

Name today _____

Daily Soul Vitamin

My whole artistic life has always been about change, change, change, move on, move on. It's the only thing I find interesting. ~Paul Simon

Toast of the Day

Here's to the towns that have character.

Awe-Servances

Happy Birthday to:

Paul Simon, 1941, singer/songwriter icon.

Lenny Bruce, 1925, controversial stand-up comic, satirical writer of the 50s and 60s.

Still Life After
All These Years

Aha-phrodisiacs

Make a quick list of things you could change about your creative endeavor, relationship, or job.

    Pick at least five viewfinders (in back of the book) to help with a new perspective.

    Take the title *Still Crazy After All These Years* and replace the word Crazy with various adjectives for amusement, writing or art inspiration. (e.g. Still Blond . . . , Still Alive, Still Lopsided . . . , Still Restless . . . , Still Purple . . . , Still Lazy . . .)

Dose of Mirth

I hate small towns because once you've seen the cannon in the park there's nothing else to do. ~Lenny Bruce

Journal Juju

Paul Simon said, "My words trickle down, from a wound that I have no intention to heal."

    What wounded part of your soul inspires creative thought? Can you let it speak or make art in your journal? Starter fluid: "If a wound were to speak it would say . . . "

A.I.M. Subliminal Message

Think and feel in your body the intention: I accept and release concern over what I cannot control and I focus on where I can make a difference.

Daily Soul Vitamin

Indeed, I think that people want peace so much that one of these days governments had better get out of the way and let them have it.
~Dwight D. Eisenhower

Toast of the Day

Here's to strawberry shortcake and writing in lowercase.

Awe-servances

Happy Birthday to
Dwight D. Eisenhower, 1890, 34th President of the US.
e. e. cummings, 1894, a poet, painter, essayist, and playwright.

Grandmother's Day.

Aha-phrodisiacs

Expose yourself to some e.e. cummings writings, then write a list of random topics. Choose one and write in e.e. cummings style. Pick an e.e. cummings line and make art or a collage from its inspiration, including the line in the art work.

Journal Juju

Write a letter to yourself from your grandmother; set a place at the table for her today if she's no longer on the planet with her favorite food if you know it. My grandmother liked strawberry shortcake.

Today I get to: _____

Daily Soul Vitamin

The youth, intoxicated with his admiration of a hero, fails to see, that it is only a projection of his own soul, which he admires. ~Ralph Waldo Emerson

Toast of the Day

Here's to the heroes of our lives (including ourselves).

Awe-servances

Happy Birthday to:

Friedrich Nietzsche, 1844, German philosopher, critic of religion, morality, contemporary culture, philosophy, and science.

It's National Grouch Day, National Heroes Day in Jamaica, and World Poetry Day. It's also International Day of Older Persons and National Heart Magic Day

Aha-phrodisiacs

In his book, *How One Becomes What One Is*, Nietzsche titled sections: "Why I Am So Clever" and "Why I Am So Wise." He uses half-joking self-adulation as a mockery of Socratic humility. Invent a character or invent yourself as someone who answers one or both of those questions in an overly self-flattering way. Or invent a list of your own sections: eg. "Why People Like Me So Much," "Why I Succeed at Everything," "Why I Don't Have to Clean the Kitchen Counter." Do it in poetry form if you like.

Invent a new hero. Come up with a name, a cover occupation, a quirky trait, a motivation and a conflict. Write an opening paragraph including all these things. Who or what does your hero save?

Journal Juju

Write a list of seven questions, pick at least one and answer it first from a grouchy point of view and then from a hero one.

Today I get to: _____

October 16

Daily Soul Vitamin
Art is the most intense mode of individualism that the world has known. ~Oscar Wilde

Toast of the Day
Here's to dancing alone with wild abandon in the living room.

Awe-servances
Happy Birthday to:
Oscar Wilde, 1854, playwright, novelist, poet, and short story writer.

It's also Dictionary Day, in Honor of Noah Webster, who was born on
    this date in 1758.
National Boss Day.

Aha-phrodisiacs
Make up at least two words; give them definitions, use them in writing, or make art around them.

Oscar Wilde said, "When good Americans die they go to Paris." Write a beginning rough, rough draft of a short story, a monologue or scene about an American who ended up in Paris (or any other place of your choice) upon dying.

 ### Dose of Mirth
Some cause happiness wherever they go; others, whenever they go. ~Oscar Wilde

Journal Juju
Make up a word that describes how you feel today; it can be a conglomeration of real words. Make it your journal title for today.

Let the bossy side of your personality write a rant; stick in a made-up word. Write an accounting of the day from the point of view of your current boss.

Subliminal Message from the A.I.M. Potion
Pick one of these to think to yourself based on which energizes your body the most, "I'm doing better than I thought," or "I can do this" or "My foolish ways are filled with writing potential."

October 17

Daily Soul Vitamin

Don't let anyone rob you of your imagination, your creativity, or your curiosity. It's your place in the world; it's your life. Go on and do all you can with it, and make it the life you want to live. ~Mae Jemison

Toast of the Day

Here's to first times.

Awe—servances

Mae Carol Jemison, 1956, astronaut, first African-American woman to travel in space.

It's also Black Poetry Day, celebrating the birthday of Jupiter Hammon, 1711, the first black man to publish a poem (1760). (Jupiter was a slave all of his life.)

Aha—phrodisiacs

Word pool from Jupiter Hammon poem: wise, sweet supplies, improve the present day, teach, little children, hastening, coming down, rest upon, declare, quick awake, leave dusty, trumpet sound, the native sky, ground, in the twinkling, the angelic train, the power of where angels stand, cast, joys.

Dose of Mirth

There is still no cure for the common birthday. ~John Glenn

Journal Juju

Astronaut James A. Lovell said, "The moon is essentially gray, no color. It looks like plaster of Paris, like dirty beach sand with lots of footprints in it." Land on a mood and describe it as if you were landing on the moon: what color is it, what does it look like, whose footprints are in it, etc.? Let your imagination orbit.

Message Brought to You by Body Temple

Find a sedating herb essence that works for you and dab it on your temples, smelling it with your eyes closed and imagining the colors and movement of it: Try lavender, chamomile, lemon balm, passion flower, cloves, rose scent, or cedar. Dab some on your pillow for fragrant dreaming.

Name today _____

Daily Soul Vitamin
Show me a sane man and I will cure him for you. ~Carl Jung

Toast of the Day
Here's to the bliss that sets in while meditating.

Awe-servances
Happy Birthday to:
Chuck Berry, 1926, guitarist, singer, and songwriter.
Terry McMillan, 1951, author of *Waiting to Exhale,* one of the first novels to
portray affluent African Americans, who don't have to struggle against
racism or poverty.

Aha-phrodisiacs
Chuck Berry Title Wave: Things I Used To Do, Don't lie To Me, No Particular
Place to Go, Lonely All The Time, Deep Feeling, You Never Can Tell, Diploma For
Two, The Little Girl From Central, The Way It Was Before, Come On

Dose of Mirth
Chuck Berry is "a musical scientist who discovered a cure for the blues."
~Anthony Kiedis of the Red Hot Chili Peppers

Journal Juju
Terry McMillan said, "I don't write about victims. They just
bore me to death. I prefer to write about somebody who
can pick themselves back up and get on with their
lives." Today's journal title: *Picking Myself Up,* write
about a time you picked yourself up or use a current
challenge and write about it as if you triumphed.

Subliminal Message from Awe-wakened Moment Potion
Melt into the pleasure of this moment.
Cultivate pleasure radar.

Name today _____

Daily Soul Vitamin
Writing is like walking in a deserted street. Out of the dust in the street you make a mud pie. ~John le Carré

Toast of the Day
Here's to getting lost in a superbly-written spy novel.

Awe-servances
Happy Birthday to:
John LeCarré, 1931, writer of espionage novels.

Evaluate Your Life Day: Created by Thomas & Ruth Roy.

The Return of the Heart on Wheels

Aha-phrodisiacs
Take this le Carré quote and use it as Starter Fluid: "A desk is a dangerous place from which to watch the world."

Dose of Mirth
Having your book turned into a movie is like seeing your oxen turned into bouillon cubes. ~John le Carré

Journal Juju
Evaluate Your Life Day: Just write down everything you're glad you did and everything that worked for you last week. For the rest, trust the process, take small steps in the direction of your dream, watch for spontaneous signs that emerge during those small steps and follow your intuitive wisdom, question your analytic fear.

Write about spying, however you associate to it. Write about one part of yourself spying on another part of yourself.

Subliminal Message from the A.I.M. Potion
Listen to your heart.

Note to Myself: How many times does my intuition have to prove it was right before I start listening to it?

October 20

Name today _____

Daily Soul Vitamin

If you're hung up on nostalgia, pretend today is yesterday and just go out and have one hell of a time. ~Art Buchwald

Toast of the Day

Here's to making one hell of a good time.

Awe-servances

Happy Birthday:
Bela Lugosi, 1882, known for his role as Count Dracula.
Art Buchwald, 1925, political humorist.

Aha-phrodisiacs

Write about meeting Count Dracula through an internet dating site.

Art Buchwald Title Wave: I Think I Don't Remember and Whose Rose Garden Is It Anyway?

Dose of Mirth

I worship the quicksand he walks in. ~Art Buchwald

Journal Juju

Repeated Completion: "I don't remember . . . "

Pretend today is a yesterday about 10 years ago and write about it.

Subliminal Message Brought to You by the FOOOF potion

Write a list of things you liked about yourself as a child. How do those things translate into who you are as an adult? Write a list of things you admire about kids. Hang around kids and listen for their unique way of looking at things or visit the children's section of a bookstore and open a kid's book as if it had a message just for you. Make sense of it as best you can.

October 21

Name today _____

Daily Soul Vitamin

Lots of people want to ride with you in the limo, but what you want is someone who will take the bus with you when the limo breaks down. ~Oprah Winfrey

Toast of the Day

Here's to autumn leaves backlit in sun.

Awe-servances

Happy Birthday to
Dizzy Gillespie, 1917, founder of "bebop."

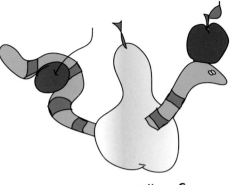

Snake in Still Life

It's National Save Your Back Week, National School Bus Safety Week and Reptile Awareness Day.

Aha-phrodisiacs

Free associate poems, sentences, stories about reptiles and reptile metaphors. Free associate about the word "back," and any of its meanings.

Word pool: oar, headache, nonchalant, express, nuzzle, hub cap, extreme, snake, back, within, taboo, smile, curious, witch, play, odd, assume, opposite, fill, pink, elevate, wise, dizzying, pill, street, bus, bebop, back, snake.

Dose of Mirth

Condoms aren't completely safe. A friend of mine was wearing one and got hit by a bus. ~Bob Rubin

Journal Juju

Any memories or made-up stories about riding in the school bus?
Repeated Completions: "So I'm back . . . "

Write from your snake persona . . . what's in the grass? What are you slithering around?

Message from Inner Awe-lixir Potion

Spend a minute daydreaming about things you want in your life, feeling in your body as if they are already happening.

October 22

Daily Soul Vitamin
You're only as young as the last time you changed your mind. ~Timothy Leary

Toast of the Day
Here's to hitting a string of yellow lights in traffic.

Starter Fluid

BEGIN

Awe-Servances
Happy Birthday to:
Doris Lessing, 1919, writer.
Timothy Leary, 1920, writer, psychologist.

On this day in 1938 the first Xerox copy was made and it's also National Color
    Day, to make people aware of how color affects them.

Aha-phrodisiacs
Doris Lessing Starter Fluid for art or writing: *The Grass is Singing.*

    To honor the Xerox copy, use repetition while doing your writing: repeat a
phrase or word to provide rhythm, or as you edit a piece you have already written,
see where some repetition may provide novelty. Repeating an image in art can also
add interest. Choose one, two or three colors and collage, using those colors with
more attention to the color than the content of the picture.

Journal Juju
Timothy Leary said, "Learning how to operate a soul figures to take time."
Talk about your soul as if it were some kind of equipment that you could
operate. What would generate energy? What mechanism keeps it going? Does
mileage vary? What is its purpose?
    Today's journal title: *Colors.*

Dose of Mirth
*There are three side effects of acid: enhanced long-term memory, decreased short-term
memory, and I forget the third.* ~Timothy Leary

Today I Get to: _____

Daily Soul Vitamin

Life begets life. Energy creates energy. It is by spending oneself that one becomes rich. ~Sarah Bernhardt

Awe—servances

Happy Birthday:

Sarah Bernhardt, 1844, stage actress.

Johnny Carson, 1925, actor, comedian, and writer, best known as the host of The Tonight Show.

Michael Crichton, 1942, bestselling novelist.

It's also the Day of Meditation, when The School of Metaphysics invites people all over the world to meditate as often as possible today.

Aha—phrodisiacs

Crichton Title Wave: Disclosure, Sphere, Timeline, Travel, Runaway, Next.

Make a doodle, scribble, collage, or painting titled *Meditation*. Or write a piece that feels like meditation when it's read. Or just meditate. Meditate on music, on the temperature in the room, on the color aqua, on the sound of the cat purring, on the feel of the autumn air, on the notion of love, on past memories whose essence, encouragement, or healing nature you would like to revisit.

Journal Juju

Do the Astrology Mambo with Scorpio traits even if you're not a Scorpio—Scorpio begins today. Scorpio is intense, determined, powerful, strong-willed, forceful, bold, courageous, enduring, secretive, mysterious, penetrating, psychic, self-reliant, and somewhat introverted or closed.

Dose of Mirth

I was so naive as a kid I used to sneak behind the barn and do nothing. ~Johnny Carson

Message from Kindness and Inner Awe—lixir Potions

Johnny Carson said, "Never continue in a job you don't enjoy. If you're happy in what you're doing, you'll like yourself, you'll have inner peace. And if you have that, along with physical health, you will have had more success than you could possibly have imagined." Meditate on that.

October 24

Name today _____

Daily Soul Vitamin

All the mistakes I ever made were when I wanted to say "no" and said "yes". ~Moss Hart

Toast of the Day

Here's to saying "no" every now and then to protect your sacred solitude.

Awe-servances

Happy Birthday to
Moss Hart, 1904, playwright.
Denise Levertov 1923, prolific poet.
Kevin Kline 1947, actor, Oscar-winning performance in A Fish Called Wanda.

On this day in 1939, women's nylon hosiery went on sale for the first time.

Aha-phrodisiacs

Write a poem or short, short story about a hermit crab named Oscar or an ode about nylon stockings.

    Word Pool: yet, pie, dither, zigzag, abundant, peek, smolder, loud, rose, stare, cloud, beneath, blurry, friction, fish, stockings, mail box, "Of course," nigh, partition, wonder, figure.

Dose of Mirth

I don't go to church. Kneeling bags my nylons. ~Billy Wilder

Journal Juju

Denise Levertov has a poem volume called *Freeing The Dust*. Does that title have any writing juice for you? If so, take a minute and free it.

And Now a Word From Mind Solution

Ask yourself what's been working for you lately. Cock your head with a half smile and appreciate it, then do more.

Question to Myself

Are there times when I should be saying "no" to myself?

October 25

Name today _____

Daily Soul Vitamin

You are never alone or helpless. The force that guides the stars guides you too. ~ Shrii Shrii Anandamurti

Toast of the Day

Here's to the feeling of your shoulders relaxing.

Awe–servances

Happy Birthday to:

Pablo Picasso, 1881, painter and sculptor. One of the most recognized figures in 20th century art, he is best known as the co-founder, along with Georges Braque, of cubism.

Aha–phrodisiacs

Picasso is known for his child-like drawings. Can you translate the spirit of Picasso into poetry? Write with the same abbreviated looseness. Or pick a Picasso painting and write about it.

Dose of Mirth

I was going to have cosmetic surgery until I noticed that the doctor's office was full of portraits by Picasso. ~Rita Rudner

Journal Juju

Pablo Picasso said, "Action is the foundational key to all success." Write about what kind of action figure doll you would be. Picasso also said, "Art is the elimination of the unnecessary." Make of list of things and concepts you can eliminate in the art of your world. Journal Title for today: *Good Riddance 101.*

Awe–vanced Inner Message Public Service Announcement

Action is more pleasant, desirable, and doable when started in small, gentle steps, but every once in awhile a wild energetic unleashed bout of energy accompanied by some favorite music is in order at well. To prepare yourself for action, ask small questions.

Daily Soul Vitamin
Without music, life is a journey through a desert. ~Pat Conroy

Toast of the Day
Here's to leaning against a washing machine during the spin cycle.

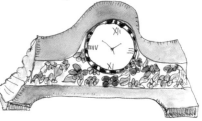

Awe-servances
Happy Birthday to:
Pat Conroy, 1945, author of *The Prince of Tides* and *The Great Santini*, who was influenced by his upbringing and family tragedies.

1858, Hamilton Smith patents rotary washing machine.

Aha-phrodisiacs
Pat Conroy wrote in *Beach Music*: " . . . a sense of smell was better than a yearbook for imprinting the delicate graffiti of time in the memory." Make a list of smells that bring back memories for you and then starting with one of those smells, write in third person about a memory it evokes.

Dose of Mirth
It's better to have loved and lost than to have to do forty pounds of laundry a week.
~Dr. Laurence J. Peter

Journal Juju
Pat Conroy said, "One of the greatest gifts you can get as a writer is to be born into an unhappy family." If you can relate to this quote, expound a bit, with permission to be loose, honest, and free. Write to freeing music. Write about your feelings about laundry.

Brought to You by Inner Awe-lixir Potion
Wayne Dyer said, "I meditate each day to increase my awareness of the divine power within me. Through meditation, I am able to realize the beauty, grace, and love that directs my life and fulfills my deepest desires." Start with five minutes a day.

Today I get to: _____

October 27

Name today _____

Daily Soul Vitamin
Everything in life is writable about if you have the outgoing guts to do it and the imagination to improvise. ~Sylvia Plath

Toast of the Day
Here's to a sweatshirt that's comfortable and fuzzy on the inside.

Awe-servances
Happy Birthday to:
Roy Lichtenstein, 1923, pop artist who used comic strips, etc. in his art.
Sylvia Plath 1932, poet, novelist, short story writer, and essayist. Most famous
as a poet and author of *The Bell Jar*, her novel detailing her struggle
with depression.

Aha-phrodisiacs
Choose a Lichtenstein painting and write a poem, story, song, news report, or caption about it.

Using Sylvia Plath's quote above as inspiration, pick something you thought did not have writing potential, a recent event, an item, a thought, and then let your imagination improvise, embellish, exaggerate, and expound about it.

Dose of Mirth
I don't have big anxieties. I wish I did. I'd be much more interesting. ~Roy Lichtenstein

Journal Juju
Make a list of your anxieties. Pick a few viewfinders from the index in the back and write about these anxieties with a different perspective.

Journal title: *Talk About Anxieties . . .* or *Detailing My Romance with My Creativity.*

Today I get to: _____

October 28

Daily Soul Vitamin
It's fine to celebrate success but it is more important to heed the lessons of failure. ~Bill Gates

Toast of the Day
Here's to a perfectly weighted and beautifully styled fountain pen that glides across the paper.

Awe-Servances
Happy Birthday to:
Bill Gates, 1955, entrepreneur, philanthropist, and chairman of Microsoft.
Julia Roberts, 1967, Oscar award-winning actress.

St. Jude's Day: Patron Saint of hopeless causes.
1886, The Statue of Liberty, sculpted by Frederic Auguste Bartholdi, was dedicated.

Aha-phrodisiacs
Write a journal entry from the Statue of Liberty.

Have a folder of images you cut out of magazines or print from the Internet. Ask a question and pick one or two of your images and write about how they might answer your question.

Get a stack of three books: in the first one copy words from the last line on page 17; in the next book, take a quote from the page that is the same number as your age; the third book, pick a chapter title that intuitively calls to you, then write down three of your favorite words and use all of this as inspiration for writing by combining, subtracting, rearranging, and adding words.

Dose of Mirth
The first time I felt I was famous was when I went to the movies with my mom. I had gone to the loo, and someone in the bathroom said in a very loud voice, "Girl in stall No. 1, were you in Mystic Pizza?" I paused and I said, yeah that was me. ~Julia Roberts

Journal Juju

Write a list of things that bring you hope and rewrite them in a Cure for Hopelessness recipe.

Write what you would do if you were the richest person in the world. Now decide what small part of that you could actually do even if it's in a small, abbreviated form.

October 29

Name today _____

Daily Soul Vitamin
I look forward to being older, when what you look like becomes less and less an issue and what you are is the point. ~ Susan Sarandon

Toast of the Day
Here's to feeling content with what you are.

Awe-servances
National Disgusting Little Pumpkin-Shaped Candies Day.

Aha-phrodisiacs
Write a Halloween or October Haiku.

Write a poem where each line begins with letters in order of the word OCTOBER.

Eat a delicious large-piece of pumpkin pie and experience it with all of your senses—write about the experiences with short phrases in poem form.

Dose of Mirth
I would rather sit on a pumpkin, and have it all to myself, than be crowded on a velvet cushion. ~Henry David Thoreau

Journal Juju
Use a word pool for your journal entry today, attempting to make these words make sense within the events, thoughts, and feelings of your life (or just have fun with them): more or less, peculiar memories, clear and level light of a late afternoon, looking to, voices and laughter, alter, manage, meager, lifted in still air, paralyze, time, kindness, still, easy tears, north wind, waving, welcome mat, disgusting little pumpkin-shaped candies.

October 30

Name today _____

Daily Soul Vitamin
Genius is the capacity to see ten things where the ordinary man sees one. ~Ezra Pound

Toast of the Day
Here's to not taking the refrigerator for granted.

Awe-servances
Happy Birthday to:
Ezra Pound, 1885, poet, musician, and critic.

Halloween Eve's Devil's Night, an occasion for harmless
    pranks by children.
1986 *Discover* magazine reported that almost 43 million
    tons of dust settled on the US each year.
Haunted Refrigerator Night: Who knows what evil lurks
    in the refrigerator?

Aha-phrodisiacs
Write a poem about the fright of the fridge. Make a collage or write a poem
titled, "Halloween Prank." What images do you have of dust? What vision comes
into your mind when you think of that word? Write a list of these images. See
ten things you can do with these prompts instead of one.

Dose of Mirth
Things gone bad in lower tray- can keep you haunted through the day
Smells that send the cats upstairs, all come from scary Frigidaire*.
~The Awe-manac Staff

Journal Juju
Ezra Pound said, "When you cannot make up your mind which of two evenly
balanced courses of action you should take, choose the bolder." Journal title for
today: *The Bolder Decision.*

Note to Myself Get out of your way so you can please you. Let
    your imagination expand your experience.

October 31

Name today _____

Daily Soul Vitamin

I am certain of nothing but the holiness of the heart's affections and the truth of imagination. What the imagination seizes as beauty must be truth, whether it existed before or not. ~John Keats

Toast of the Day

Here's to a people who go all out to make amazingly imaginative Halloween costumes.

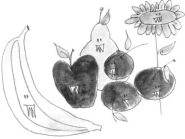

Awe-servances

Happy Birthday to:
John Keats, 1795, poet icon.

On this date in 1941 the Mount Rushmore National Memorial was completed. It's also National Magic Day in honor of magician Harry Houdini who died strangely on this date.

Aha-phrodisiacs

Halloween is a perfect holiday for the imagination. Write about how Mt. Rushmore dresses up for Halloween. If you had an unlimited budget and were not limited by reality, how would you dress for Halloween? As New York City? As a 12-foot man with a neon sign as a hat? As a volcano? As a rabbit pulled out of a hat?

Starter Fluid: "You have what is called . . . ", "Inside the outside of the underside of the day . . ." or "What magic lies under . . ."

Dose of Mirth

Imagination is everything. It is the preview of life's coming attractions. ~Albert Einstein

Journal Juju

Write a list of your personal associations with Halloween then weave it into a tapestry of verse, shorten it for haiku, consolidate it for poetry, embellish it for prose, or abbreviate it for a t-shirt.

Message from the Kindness Potion

Let the magic in the air inspire your imagination. Imagine yourself 5 percent more gentle with yourself today.

THE BODY TEMPLE
Body Blissmas and a Happy New Rear

"There is but one temple in the universe and that is the body of man." ~Novalis

Despite what our rationalizations, sophisticated systems of denial and evolved methods of avoidance would like us to truly believe- exercise, good nutrition, sleep and being-ever-so-kind-to-the-body are immensely important for creativity, compassion, clarity and a firm behind.

Stress, on the other hand, is vital for aging prematurely, discontentment, gradual dulling of wit, emotional vermin, illness, renegade glum, inconvenient lethargy and deposits of seething resentments. Snippiness has also been reported. Stress melts when we exercise regularly and new energy takes its place. Energy is essential fuel for soul-fillment.

Many of us like to pretend we don't need to exercise or we use our creativity to invent robust delusions that support the avoidance of exercise and promote a portrait of ourselves that could be entitled *Still Life and TV*—us being the Still Life. Denial has also reached an impressive level of skill and popularity. Yet when we do exercise regularly and eat well, we experience how vital these activities are to vitality (which is easy to remember). There is no reason why we should surrender to weak or settle for frumpy (neither of which is a seven dwarf). There is good reason why we should embody seductiveness, charm, and allure. (All of which are desirable.)

Assume an alluring pose in this very minute and see how it feels. No really, go ahead, especially if someone is looking but even if you're alone. You have permission to be captivating for the rest of your life. Feeling that we deserve to take care of our body is an issue for many of us. *The Awe-manac* will help you get over problematic feelings of not deserving the best life possible.

POSSIBLE EFFECTS: Feeling a heightened state of well-being and creative exhilaration. Using the energy of the body as guidance for intuition and creativity. Maintaining the use of the temple for a very long time.

Mileage may vary. Not available in any store. Side effects may include peak experiences, break dancing, and a youthful stride. Caution: Eat leafy green things—the un-poisonous ones.

NOVEMBER'S ENTRY WAY

November is from novem, meaning "nine." It was the ninth month of the Roman calendar, which began in March, as we mentioned before. Seems like these months should be renamed or something, since they are no longer accurate in meaning. Let's pause and meditate on what else we might call the months. The word eleven in Latin is undecim, so that would make November, Undecimber and December would be Duodecimber. Hmm. what do you think? With October then renamed December, I think that's way too many December-like words. Let's call November Ned instead. October could be Otto, and December would have a nice holiday quality like, Deeber. I think that's reasonable.

Some Monthly Observances at November's Door

It's International Drum Month, American Indian Heritage Month, Stamp Collecting Month, National Georgia Pecan Month, National Pomegranate Month, National Roasting Month, Peanut Butter Lovers' Month, Christmas Seals Month. The fourth Thursday is Thanksgiving in the US. November begins in Scorpio and ends in Sagittarius

AWe-Manac Invented:

November 30th Comfort day

 ## Suggested Ways to Celebrate

It's a time to think thanks, to think apples and stamps, to honor the American Indian, the Christmas Seal, and the Pomegranate. It's time to appreciate drums, their rhythm and their beat; it's time to drum with drumsticks, fingers, palms, and feet. It's November. Have a fig, a pecan, and a puzzle. Pay some undivided sensory taste bud attention to a piece of pumpkin pie. Taste the spice of late roasted fall, feel the nip of early winter, be grateful for the feeling of slippers.

You have permission to practice a relaxation exercise a few minutes daily in stress-repellent preparation for December. Just one minute of breathing with the intention to relax can work wonders. Think of it as loosening the pressure valve. Practice: breathe-in thinking with both your mind and your body the words "peace be with me," breathe-out thinking and feeling: "I let go of the struggle," breathe-in thinking and feeling "peaceful mind," breathe out thinking: "calm body," breathe in thinking and feeling "I am gentle with my world," breathe-out thinking and feeling "My world is gentle with me," breathe-in thinking and feeling "gratitude" breathe-out thinking and feeling "I am unattached to the way the world needs to look, I let go, (which may be a long exhale depending on how fast you think). Rinse and repeat as often as possible.

weeeeeee

In honor of the number eleven, because November would like to be acknowledged for being the ELEVENTH month, write a poem or a journal entry, or a piece of stream of consciousness prose that has predominately "e" words in it. e.g., Evelyn eventually elevated to the eighth echelon of Exxon corporation's Executive Events Committee in Ellington, England.

Astrological Word-Spells

This month, embody these words with mind, body and spirit 5 percent more than last month. Practice daily.

Aries: grace

Taurus: bold

Gemini: quiet

Cancer: balanced

Leo: calm

Virgo: accepting

Libra: energized

Scorpio: enlightened

Sagittarius: patient

Capricorn: spontaneous

Aquarius: confident

Pisces: strong

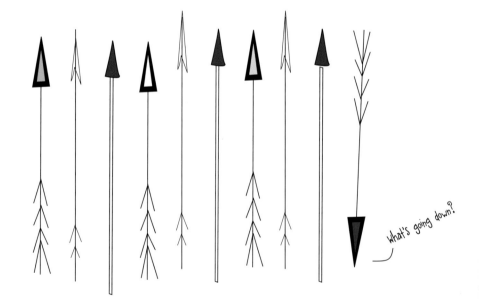
What's going down?

Tides:

Ebbing: What are you letting go of this month (just a little bit)?

Flowing: Where are you expanding this month (just a little bit)?

Vessel of strength: What saying or quote will navigate you and keep you afloat through the month (See Awe-wakened Inner Messages)?

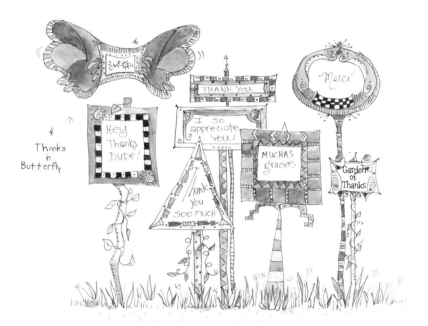

Gardening Information

Flower: Chrysanthemum

Monthly crop: A garden of thanks

Planting Tips: Ponder bless-seeds for 2 weeks, water with gratitudes and pay attention. Place bouquets on the Thanksgiving Day table (or in other countries, on the coffee table in the living room).

November 1

Name today _____

Daily Soul Vitamin
The fear of death follows from the fear of life. A man who lives fully is prepared to die at any time. ~Mark Twain

Toast of the Day
Here's to imagining that a soft breeze blowing across our face is kisses from those we love who have died.

Awe—servances
Happy Birthday to:
Lyle Lovett 1957, singer-songwriter.

Dia de los Muertos (Day of the Dead, Oct 31—Nov 2): A three-day Mexican
   holiday to honor and celebrate loved ones who have died.
National Authors Day.

Aha—phrodisiacs
Lyle Lovett Title Pool for writing or art: In My Own Mind, Nothing But a Good Ride, Working Too Hard, I'm Going to Wait.

   Write a description of you, the author, and a synopsis of your book (real or imaginary) for the book's jacket. Expose yourself to a favorite author; use their influence on you in your writing, begin with your content and their voice.

   Logan Pearsall Smith said, "What I like in a good author isn't what he says, but what he whispers." List what you have whispered in some of the things you have written or made.

Journal Juju
Title an entry: *The lives I Honor and Celebrate, and Why.*
   Starter Fluid: "Who I am whispers. . . " or "Late at night my pillow whispers to me . . . "

Dose Of Mirth
Always go to other people's funerals, otherwise they won't come to yours. ~Yogi Berra

Today I get to: _____

November 2

Name today _____

Daily Soul Vitamin
Spirituality comes from questioning everything but at the same time accepting everything. ~K. D. Lang

Toast of the Day
Here's to the feeling of being accepted.

Awe—servances
Happy Birthday to:

Lois McMaster Bujold, 1949, science fiction and fantasy author. Bujold is best known for her series of novels featuring Miles Vorkosigan, a disabled interstellar spy and mercenary admiral from the planet Barrayar, set approximately 1,000 years in our future.

K. D. Lang, 1961, award-winning singer and songwriter.

Plan Your Epitaph Day: Occurs Nov. 2 to coincide with the last Day of the Dead.

Aha—phrodisiacs
K.D. Lang Title Pool: Use them to write an epitaph, a poem, prose, or to inspire a painting or collage. Black Coffee, Trail of Broken Hearts Crying, Don't Smoke in Bed, The Consequences of Falling, Pullin' Back the Reins Barefoot, Three Cigarettes In An Ashtray.

Journal Juju
Title your journal entry either, *The Consequences of Falling* or *Pullin' Back the Reins* and instinctively write or draw how this might relate to your life, past, present, or future.

Dose Of Mirth
Epitaph: Lawyer Sir John Strange. "Here lies an honest lawyer, and that is Strange."

And now a word from FOOOf
What was your favorite time of the year when you were a child? Walk with child-like energy; if that's difficult, act as if it isn't.

Today I get to:

Daily Soul Vitamin

Love is strange and mysterious. Just like
jelly beans . . . ~Unknown

Toast of the Day

Here's to enjoying the taste of a gourmet
sandwich after a long hike.

Awe-Servances

Happy birthday to:

John Montagu, 4th Earl of Sandwich, 1718, creator of the sandwich.

It's also Bean Day, Housewife's Day, and Cliché Day.

Aha-phrodisiacs

Write an ode to your favorite sandwich. Have a sandwich.

    Write an ode to a housewife. Make a collage of the housewife goddess. Write
about a housewife who talks in clichés and whose specialty is sandwiches.

    Write a piece that is full of clichés. Use a cliché repetitively and reply to it
differently or see where the rhythm takes you. Here are some clichés to play
with: A good time was had by all. A hush falls over the crowd. A penny for your
thoughts. Tag, you're it. Thank you and good night. That's neither here nor there.
That's the way the ball bounces. Funny until somebody loses an eye.

Dose of Mirth

Red beans and ricely yours. ~Louis Armstrong loved red beans and rice so much
he signed his personal letters this way.

Journal Juju

Title a journal entry, *A Hush Fell Over My Soul,* and see what
about your life falls under that theme.

A Message from The Body Temple Potion

The body will serve your creativity if you keep it exercised and fortified with
good nutrition. Find the nutrition that works for you but know that the leafy
greens, the fruits, and the lean proteins can keep your creative engine working
the best.

November 4

Name today _____

Daily Soul Vitamin
The aim of life is to live, and to live means to be aware, joyously, drunkenly, serenely, divinely, aware. ~Henry Miller

Toast
Here's to the flow of conversation that comes from two people with good chemistry.

Awe-Servances
Happy Birthday to:

Will Rogers, 1879, writer, actor and humorist.

It's also Mischief Night, observed in England, Australia, and New Zealand and National Chemistry Week.

Aha-phrodisiac
Write a piece about mischief or use this sentence for Starter Fluid: "My desire for mischief grew when . . . "

Experiment in art like a chemist—steadfast, unwavering, curious, and open to the results. Add different medium together: watercolor with collage, graphic art with acrylics, papier-mache with pen and ink.

Dose of Mirth
I used to be Snow White, but I drifted. ~Mae West

Journal Juju
Make a list of what the word "chemistry" brings up for you and rearrange everything using other words, adding and subtracting to make a word-weaving.

A Note from Arpeggio Spirit
Don't forget how music can transport you. Use it while riding, cleaning, reading, meditating, and finding the slipper that's been at large under the couch for over a week.

Today I get to: _____

November 5

Daily Soul Vitamin
Love yourself and everything falls into line. You really have to love yourself to get anything done in this world. ~Lucille Ball

Toast of the Day
Here's to enjoying the harmony two singers can strike.

Awe-servances
Happy birthday to:
Art Garfunkel, 1941, singer-songwriter and actor,
    half of the famous duo Simon and Garfunkel.
Sam Shepard, 1943, Pulitzer prize winning
    playwright, writer, and actor.

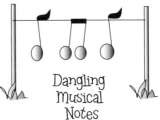

Dangling
Musical
Notes

On this day in 1951, *I Love Lucy* airs for the first time.

Aha-phrodisiacs
Take the Simon and Garfunkel song title, "A Hazy Shade of Winter," and write a poem, paint a picture or write. Begin a stream of consciousness with it.

Use Sam Shepard's play title, *A Lie of Mind* for your own writing or collage inspiration.

As close neighbors, Fred and Ethel would move wherever Lucy and Ricky moved. Invent one or two characters who are that close to you or a character of yours and write a conversation illustrating their personality, occupation, or motivation.

Dose of Mirth
How I Love Lucy was born? We decided that instead of divorce lawyers profiting from our mistakes, we'd profit from them. —Lucille Ball

Journal Juju
Title a journal entry either *A Dangling Conversation* or *Bridge Over Troubled Water* according to which better suits something in your life you would like to write about.

November 6

Daily Soul Vitamin
In the middle of difficulty lies opportunity.
~Albert Einstein

Toast of the Day
Here's to the feeling of sitting between two of your favorite people.

Awe-servances
Happy Birthday to:
Adolphe Sax, 1814, invented the saxophone.
Sally Field, 1946, award winning actress.

Midpoint of autumn.
Colonel Jacob Schick, in 1923, was issued a
　　patent for the Schick dry razor, the world's
　　first practical electric shaver.

Aha-phrodisiacs
In honor of Adolphe Sax's birthday, play saxophone music while writing today (if you don't play the saxophone, play a CD).
　　Since it is the midpoint of autumn, write about being in the middle of something, anything. Begin this repeated completion: "I am in the middle of . . . ."
　　Word Pool: autumn, patent, saxophone, born, surge, trouble, ramble, smear, railroad, party, moody, elephant, laugh, sullen, remarkable, all, flying, shave, trees, resemble.

Dose of Mirth
My agent said, "You aren't good enough for movies." I said, "You're fired." ~Sally Field

Journal Juju
Write a few instances of people who discouraged you in the past in some way and in your journal, tell them they're fired or start with the title: *People I Would Fire If I Could*

November 7

Name today _____

Daily Soul Vitamin

A guilty conscience needs to confess. A work of art is a confession. ~Albert Camus

Toast of the Day

Here's discovering a work of art that you want to stand and stare at for awhile.

Awe-servances

Happy Birthday to:

Joni Mitchell, 1943, musician, songwriter, painter and icon.

Albert Camus, 1913, author and philosopher, often associated with existentialism.

On this day in 1793 the Louvre in Paris was opened for the first time to the public.

It's National Bittersweet Chocolate with Almonds Day.

Aha-phrodisiacs

Use art to express and rid yourself of something with which you feel guilty or disturbed.

Joni Mitchell Word Pool: lamp-shade, free-man, unfettered, groceries, morning, milk truck, blue, clouds, perfume, sleep, wind, calling, crazy, car, hill, conversation, comfort, analyst, told, romantics, fate, meet, cynical, drunk, boring, dark café, mean, clarinet.

Write about getting lost in the Louvre or what paintings do after hours in the Louvre.

Permission to eat bittersweet chocolate and feel compliant.

Dose of Mirth

You might be an artist if: If you've ever drunk the rinse water instead of the coffee. If your cat has chrome oxide green paws-. If you've ever painted an abstract and decided it looked better upside down. ~Jim Lane

Journal Juju

Albert Camus said, "Blessed are the hearts that can bend; they shall never be broken." Doodle a bending heart in your journal. Color it in with color pencils or crayons. Let the repetitive motion and the symbolism relax you.

Name today _____

Daily Soul Vitamin
If you always do what interests you, at least
one person is pleased. ~Katharine Hepburn

Toast of the Day
Here's to losing all sense of time because you are
absorbed in something that interests you.

Dunce
Caps

Awe—servances
Happy Birthday to:
Katharine Hepburn, 1907, a four-time Oscar-winning star.
Bonnie Raitt, 1949, blues singer-songwriter.

Abet and Aid Punsters Day: permission today to be punny.
Dunce Day: the anniversary of the death of Duns Scotus, a medieval scholar who was
responsible for the introduction of the word "dunce" into the English language.

Aha—phrodisiacs
Bonnie Raitt Title Wave: I Got Plenty, Streetlights, What Is Success, Got You On
My Mind. Or write about "What Is Success" using 5 different attitudes from the
Viewfinders Index in the back.
For Dunce day, begin a piece of writing with: "I see dunce people . . . ."

Dose of Mirth
Puns: I wondered why the baseball was getting bigger. Then it hit me.
I couldn't quite remember how to throw a boomerang, but eventually it came
back to me.

Journal Juju
Write about something you have felt dumb about. And then write a note
of forgiveness.

A Message from the Makers of Mental Solution Potion
Keep books filled with facts in the bathroom. Find a lecture to attend. To keep
your brain balanced, shampoo your hair with the opposite hand you usually use,
take a shower backwards, draw with your non-dominant hand.

NoveMber 9

Name today _____

Daily Soul Vitamin

One glance at a book and you hear the voice of another person, perhaps someone dead for 1,000 years. To read is to voyage through time. ~Carl Sagan

The beautiful feeling after writing a poem is on the whole better even than after sex, and that's saying a lot. ~Anne Sexton

Toast of the Day

Here's to the simple joy of taking a walk.

Awe-Servances

Happy Birthday to:
Anne Sexton, 1928, poet and writer.
Carl Sagan, 1934, astronomer and astrobiologist.
Laurie Sparkle Wood, humorist.

Dose of Mirth

Wish on everything. Pink cars are good, especially old ones. And stars of course, first stars and shooting stars. Planes will do if they are the first light in the sky and look like stars. ~Francesca Lia Block

Aha-phrodisiacs

Laurie Wood said, "THE MAGIC CURE: GET OUT OF YOUR OWN WAY!" She said it in caps. Starter Fluid: "In order to get out of my way . . ." or write a list of *10 Ways To Get Out Of Your Way*

Journal Juju

Anne Sexton said, "It doesn't matter who my father was; it matters who I remember he was." Write about any association this quote brings up for you.

November 10

Daily Soul Vitamin
We all dream a lot—some are lucky, some are not. But if you think it, want it, dream it, then it's real. You are what you feel. ~Tim Rice

Toast of the Day
Here's to appreciating everything that feels good about the body in a given moment.

Awe-servances
Happy Birthday to:
Tim Rice, 1944, lyricist, radio presenter, television
    game show panelist, author.

1969, *Sesame Street* premiered.

Aha-phrodisiacs
If you could invent your own kid's show, who would some of the characters be: names, personalities, obsessions, colors, favorite food?
    Starter Fluid: "When you're inside the bubble . . . "
    Use one or more of the following sounds to start poetry or prose, or have the sound/s show up at some point during the piece: shoes squishing with moisture, two people arguing, the doorbell, distant rap music.

Dose of Mirth
The pen is mightier than the sword, and considerably easier to write with.
~Marty Feldman

Journal Juju
Abbe Yeux-verdi said, "Renew your passions daily." Renew your passions by bringing back a passionate memory and imagining your body reliving the feeling of it in the moment, and then writing about it as if it were happening now. Take something you've written, including a journal entry, and revise it for the fun of it by using the Viewfinders page in the back or by making it a specific type of piece: a how-to, a memory, a description, a news report.

Double Dose Daily Soul Vitamin
Neither man or nation can exist without a sublime idea. ~Fyodor Dostoevsky
  The arts are a very human way of making life more bearable. Practicing an art, no matter how well or badly, is a way to make your soul grow. ~Kurt Vonnegut, Jr.

Toast of the Day
Here's to being involved with something rewardingly creative.

Awe-servances
Happy Birthday to:
Fyodor Dostoevsky, 1821, writer who had a profound effect
    on twentieth century literature.
Kurt Vonnegut, Jr., 1922, novelist whose works blend satire,
    black comedy, and science fiction.

Tree Festival in Tunisia.
Mary Gaitskill, 1954, author of essays, short stories, and novels.

Aha-phrodisiacs
How do trees celebrate themselves? Write a poem or a haiku about it.

Journal Juju
Mary Gaitskill said, "My experience of life as essentially unhappy and uncontrol-lable taught me to examine the way people, including myself, create survival sys-tems . . . for themselves in unorthodox and sometimes apparently self-defeating ways. These inner worlds, although often unworkable and unattractive in social terms, can have a unique beauty and courage." Write about your unique beauty and courage. If you do not believe in them yet, write as if you believe you have them.

Note to Myself: Find out where Tunisia is.

Today I get to: _____

Daily Soul Vitamin
Patience is also a form of action. ~Rodin

Toast of the Day
Here's to so many different kinds of art.

Awe-servances
Happy Birthday to:

Auguste Rodin,1840, artist, most famous
as a sculptor.

Edvard Munch, 1863, symbolist painter, printmaker,
forerunner of Expressionistic art.

Shallow Persons Awareness Week; a week to acknowledge and
embrace your shallowness.

Aha-phrodisiacs
Auguste Rodin said, "I invent nothing, I rediscover." Rediscover an idea in
poetry or prose. Start with . . . "Here it is again . . . "

As with many of his works, Munch painted several versions of *The Scream*.
Choose a subject and doodle, collage, draw, or paint several versions of it. Try
using some of the Viewfinders to vary your approach.

Write a poem or essay about any topic (or pick one from the list below) in a
very shallow way: the meaning of life, how to accessorize a Saturday, how to
dust, where the US is on a map.

Dose of Mirth
*Excuse to use when you screw up your art: The wind blew it off my easel; I had to chase
it clear across a field of clover (or ragweed or stinging nettles . . . be creative), and
when I found it a cow had stepped on it. Substitute a goat if cows are rare in your
neighborhood. Don't try this excuse with still lifes.* ~Jim Lane

Journal Juju
Edvard Munch said, "Without fear and illness, I could never have accomplished
all I have." Starter Fluid: "Without . . . "

Daily Soul Vitamin

When you are kind to someone in trouble, you hope they'll remember and be kind to someone else. And it'll become like a wildfire.
~Whoopi Goldberg

Toast of the Day

Here's to a smile of kindness.

Awe-servances

Happy Birthday to:

1850 Robert Louis Stevenson, author of *Treasure Island* and *A Child's Garden of Verses*.
Whoopi Goldberg, 1955, award-winning actress, and comedian.

World Kindness Day.

Aha-phrodisiacs

Robert Louis Stevenson said, "If a man loves the labour of his trade, apart from any question of success or fame, the gods have called him." Whoa . . . what do you think of that?

 Make a collage of the world having kindness bestowed upon it.
 Starter Fluid: "The only way to . . . "

Dose of Mirth

I don't have pet peeves; I have whole kennels of irritation. ~Whoopi Goldberg

Journal Juju

Write about what you love about your job. If you can't think of anything, do this powerful exercise:

 Write about what you love about your job, as if you have a job that you love—make it up. You never know when the wish-portal is open and these messages get through.

Cloud Garden

November 14
Name today _____

Daily Soul Vitamin
*I perhaps owe having become a painter
to flowers.* ~Claude Monet

Toast of the Day
Here's to the inspiration of flowers.

Awe–servances
Happy Birthday to:
Claude Monet, 1840, the French impressionist painter.
Louise Brooks, 1906, dancer, showgirl, and silent film actress.
Yanni, 1954, New Age composer.

National American Teddy Bear Day.

Aha–phrodisiacs
Write a poem or haiku about Monet's famous lily pad painting.
Yanni Title Wave: keys, silence, moments, snowfall, port, swept, steal,
private, love, life acropolis, out, nightbird, take, meet, passion, someday, years,
paths, romantic, reflections, you, on, mystery, away, perfect, optimystique, water,
imagination, nice. For extra credit begin with this sentence: The midnight sky
brought unison . . .

Dose of Mirth
Q: What is a bear's favorite drink? A: Koka-Koala!

Journal Juju
Write about giving things away. Write about keeping things.
Write about giving away intangible things like patience, insight, or courage.
Make a collage called "I think I'll keep it." For extra credit: Give it away.

A Word from Kindness Potion
Louise Brooks said, "I never gave away anything without wishing I had kept it;
nor kept it without wishing I had given it away." Give something away to someone you do not normally give things to. For extra credit: Make it anonymous.
Give a teddy bear to a kid in teddy-bear-need.

November 15

Name today _____

Daily Soul Vitamin

I've been absolutely terrified every moment of my life—and I've never let it keep me from doing a single thing I wanted to do. ~Georgia O'Keeffe

Toast of the Day

Here's to the feeling of a just-cleaned refrigerator.

Awe-servances

Happy Birthday to:

Georgia O'Keeffe, 1887, artist who often transformed her subject matter into powerful abstract images.

America Recycles Day.

National Clean Out Your Refrigerator Day.

Aha-phrodisiacs

Georgia O'Keeffe said, "One can't paint New York as it is, but rather as it is felt." Make a list of things you would like to paint according to how they are felt rather than as they are. Make a list of things you would like to write about by describing an emotion rather than describing details.

Recycle a piece of writing you have—edit out words, changing words to ones you like better, taking a piece of the middle and putting it in the beginning, taking words out so the essence of the piece remains in poetic form. etc. Recycle.

Dose of Mirth

I hate flowers. I only paint them because they're cheaper than models and they don't move. ~Georgia O'Keefe

Recycled Doodle

Journal Juju

Write how it feels to clean your refrigerator even if you do not actually do it.

Fooof and Body Temple Potion Challenge

Prepare something that is both fun and healthy to eat. Optional: share it.

Daily Soul Vitamin

I like to assume that since I drive a car and maintain a respectable credit rating and rarely murder anyone and bury them in the back garden unless they really deserve it, the fact that I hear voices won't unduly disturb anyone. ~Robin McKinley

Queen of Pears

Toast of the Day

Here's to the health and wholesomeness of a home-cooked meal.

Awe-Servances

George Kaufman, 1889, playwright, theatre director and producer, humorist, and drama critic.
Robin McKinley, 1952, fantasy author especially known for *The Hero and the Crown*.

United Nations International Day for Tolerance.
National Fast Food Day.

Aha-phrodisiacs

Write in detail as if you have amazing tolerance with something which you are usually intolerant
    OR Write about your lack of tolerance about something minor.
    Make a fast food restaurant a metaphor for something.
Write about a race between food to see which is the fastest.

Dose of Mirth

Epitaph for a dead waiter, God finally caught his eye.
~George S. Kaufman

Journal Juju

    Write about your early memories of going to a fast-food restaurant.
Write about yourself in the third person or act as the narrator of a documentary of yourself at a fast food restaurant.

Daily Soul Vitamin

A musician must make music, an artist must paint, a poet must write, if he is to be ultimately at peace with himself. What one can be, one must be. ~Abraham Maslow

Two Toasts of the Day

Here's to a feeling of inner peace that lasts more than just a minute. Here's to homemade bread right out of the oven with real butter melted on top.

Awe-Servances

Happy Birthday to:

Martin Scorsese, 1942, prolific director who won an Oscar for
    The Departed.

World Peace Day.

Aha-phrodisiacs

Scorsese trigger: use the word "depart" as a trigger to write, create a collage, or invent a gesture.

Let any associations, stories, or connections to that word lead the way for you. Make a ritual for World Peace Day or light a candle and pause for peace

Journal Juju

What animal, bird, insect, or reptile would you elect to be your symbol? Name it, write a short explanation, and illustrate it with a Googled image, magazine picture, doodle, or painting. Or just name it.

Brought to You by the Body Temple Potion

Do not underestimate the effect your diet has on your body, especially as you grow older. Food will have a different effect on you as you reach midlife. You do not need to change your diet all at once, and everyone is different, so find how food affects you and make tiny adjustments. Believe just 5 percent more that you are worth it. Walk often.

Today I get to: _____

November 18

Name today _____

Daily Soul Vitamin
This above all, to refuse to be a victim. ~Margaret Atwood

Toast of the Day
Here's to amusing one's self with one's writing.

Awe—servances
Happy Birthday to:
Mickey Mouse, 1928. Mickey first appeared in *Steamboat Willie*.
Margaret Atwood, 1939, prolific poet, novelist, literary critic, feminist.

National Adoption Week.
National Game and Puzzle Week.

Aha—phrodisiacs
Write about Mickey Mouse looking for a date on Match.com.

Word Pool: secular night, wander around, alone in your house, it's two-thirty, everyone, this is your story, you remember, out somewhere, suspected, vanilla ice cream, silence between the words, purple, ten years later, reserve a secret vice, you start to hum, that part will come later.

Margaret Atwood said, "Put yourself in a different room, that's what the mind is for." Write what a room that is your mind would look like and include details: what's on the wall, in the closets, what are the windows like?

Dose of Mirth
Arithmetic is being able to count up to twenty without taking off your shoes.
~Mickey Mouse

Journal Juju
What is puzzling in your life? What is the solution?
Repeated Completions: "I'm puzzled . . . ."

And now a message from Inner Awe—lixir Potion
Breathe in peace, breathe out the struggle, breathe in energy, breathe out obstacles, breathe in freedom, breathe out with a blank mind.

November 19

Name today _____

Daily Soul Vitamin

I am more and more convinced that our happiness or unhappiness depends more on the way we meet the events of life than on the nature of those events themselves.
~Alexander von Humboldt

Toast of the Day

Here's to the look and color of bubbles.

Awe-Servances

Happy Birthday to:
Sharon Olds, 1942, award-winning author
    and poet.

1863, Lincoln delivered the Gettysburg Address.
Have a Bad Day Day (created by Tom and Ruth Roy www.wellcat.com). These 24
    hours are set aside for all who shiver with revulsion at being told, yet again,
    to "have a good day."

Aha-phrodisiacs

Take the Sharon Olds title inspiration *The Unswept Room* for your own memoir
entry or prose piece. Or do collage, doodling or a painting..
    Like the Gettysburg address but more fun, write an address yourself. Make a
list first of possible addresses like: The Bad Day Address, The Bullwinkle Address,
The Where-am-I? Address.

Dose of Mirth

Money won't buy happiness, but it will pay the salaries of a large research staff to study the problem. ~Bill Vaughan

Journal Juju

You can have a bad day, but as soon as you set foot on that stage it's joyous. ~Glenn

Tipton, one of the lead guitarists for heavy metal band Judas Priest.
Write about something that shifts you out of a bad mood when
you do it.

November 20

Daily Soul Vitamin

Most success springs from an obstacle or failure.
I became a cartoonist largely because I failed in
my goal of becoming a successful executive.
~Scott Adams

Toast of the Day

Here's to squishy comfy slippers.

Awe—Servances

Happy Birthday to:

Edwin Hubble, 1889, whose discovery and development of the concept of an
expanding universe has been described as the 'most spectacular astronomical
discovery' of the 20th century. As a tribute, the Hubble Space Telescope is
named after him.

It's also Name Your PC Day.

Aha—phrodisiacs

Do you have a name for your PC? What kind of relationship do you have with
your PC?

Starter Fluid: "If it weren't for my PC . . . "

Journal Juju

What are ways you would like to expand your universe? Make a list, keep listing
past the obvious stopping place.

Subliminal Message Brought to You by the FOOOf potion

The sense of humor is crucial to a fulfilling existence as we grow older. To
sharpen up your sense of humor, hang around funny people, read funny books
and articles, watch funny talk show hosts, and pretend that some of the mistakes
you make and quirks you display are caught on camera; see them as entertaining.

Today I get to: _____

November 21

Name today _____

Daily Soul Vitamin

There are men who would quickly love each other if once they were to speak to each other; for when they spoke they would discover that their souls had only been separated by phantoms and delusions. ~Ernest Hello

Toast of the Day

Here's to the moment you realize it is a favorite person saying hello when you answer the phone.

fish from June
saying hello in November

Awe—servances

Happy Birthday to:
Harold Ramis, 1944, director, including *Animal House, Caddy Shack, Ghostbusters, Groundhog Day.*

World Hello Day

Aha—phrodisiacs

Come up with some new ways to say hello

Dose of Mirth

From the home office in Hanksville, Vermont—The top ten new social greetings to replace "Hello," from Eber Lambert:

10) Heimlich! 9) Please hold 8) Sperm Whale! 7) Please wait while I scan you for viruses. 6) TripleShotGrandeNonFatLatte 5) What happened to you? 4) Everybody Mambo! 3) You've got mail! 2) License and registration, please. And 1) Ok, lie to me.

Journal Juju

Harold Ramis said, "My characters aren't losers. They're rebels. They win by their refusal to play by everyone else's rules." Write about a time when you were a rebel. Write about it in third person or from the point of view of someone else. Or write about it as if it were happening right now. Write a time you wish you had been a rebel. List possible times you might be a rebel in the future.

Daily Soul Vitamin

Stand still. The trees ahead and bushes beside you are not lost. Wherever you are is called Here. ~David Wagoner, Poet

Toast of the Day

Here's to sinking into a comfortable chair.

Awe-servances

Happy Birthday to:

Robert Vaughn, 1932, the secret agent man from U.N.C.L.E.

Terry Gilliam, 1940, filmmaker, animator, and member of the Monty Python comedy troupe.

National Stop the Violence Day.

Aha-phrodisiacs

Write about events from your day yesterday but write about how you would have approached them if you were a secret agent. Or use this Starter Fluid: "If I were a secret agent . . . "

Make a collage entitled, "Violence Gone." Visualize peace just for 20 seconds.

Refer to Terry Gilliam's quote below: Make up a story or a poem about one god getting fired and another one getting hired. Include the what, where, who, how, and why of the incident.

Daily Dose of Mirth

Terry Gilliam said, "Actually, I began to think that maybe there is a god, after all. Or maybe it's a different one. The old one got fired."

Journal Juju

Take Wagoner's line, "Wherever you are is called Here . . . " and keep going in your own direction with it.

A Message from Body Temple

Exercise or working out works better 1) when you are doing it with someone else regularly, 2) when it is fun 3) when it is done. Walk, dance, tighten your abdomen while driving, paddle your feet while watching TV—MOVE!

Daily Soul Vitamin
If there were a restaurant for singles it would be a room filled with a bunch of sinks we could eat over. ~Paula Poundstone

Toast of the Day
Here's to eating a juicy apple over the sink looking out into a beautiful day.

Awe-servances
Happy Birthday to:

Billy the Kid, 1859, outlaw.

Rena Tucker, 1962, portrait artist and comedienne. Known for painting portraits of people set in an imaginary, secret life.

Sinkie Day
Sagittarius begins.

Aha-phrodisiacs
Write your name and put "The Kid" after it. Then write about a few of your infamous activities.

During Sinkie Day, people who occasionally dine over the kitchen sink are encouraged to celebrate this casual yet tasteful cuisine. Write about eating over the kitchen sink. Write a recipe or menu for over the sink dining. Cut a sink out of a magazine and make it into something that is not related to a sink.

Doses of Mirth
Everyone should invent bizarre secret lives to have ready for occasions when asked what they do for a living. You should see the PRICELESS expressions on people's faces when they try to act normal after I've just said, with a straightface, that I'm a runway model for Victoria's Secret high-waisted boxer shorts. ~Rena Tucker

Today I get to: _____

NOVeMBeR 24

Name today _____

Daily Soul Vitamin
Do the hard jobs first. The easy jobs will take care of themselves. Do the thing you fear to do and keep on doing it . . . that is the quickest and surest way ever yet discovered to conquer fear. ~Dale Carnegie

Toast of the Day
Here's to watching the flames dance in a fireplace.

Awe-Servances
Happy Birthday to:
Henri de Toulouse-Lautrec, 1864, a French painter,
    printmaker, draftsman, and illustrator.
Dale Carnegie, 1888, writer and the developer of
    famous courses in self-improvement.

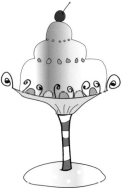

Dose of Mirth
I know that you believe you understand what you think I said, but I'm not sure you realize that what you heard is not what I meant. ~Robert McCloskey

Journal Juju
Dale Carnegie said, "Take a chance! All life is chance. The man or woman who goes farthest is generally the one who is willing to do and dare. The 'sure thing' boat never gets far from shore."

   Write about what boat you are riding through life on. Where is it taking you? What are the sights and sounds? What is it running on? Where is it coming from? Sketch or collage a boat and where you want it to head: metaphorical pictures like this are energizing directors for your subconscious.

A Message from Awe-wakened Moment Potion
What are your favorite parts of this season? When you notice them take a moment to relax your body, mind, and spirit into them as if you were pouring yourself into a Jell-O mold shaping you into favorite seasonal moments.

Question to Self
What flavor gelatin would I be?

Daily Soul Vitamin

It is the mind that makes the body rich. There is no class so pitiably wretched as that which possesses money and nothing else. ~Andrew Carnegie

Toast of the Day

Here's to the essences and sensations of life that are free except for the paying of attention.

Awe-Servances

Happy Birthday to:

Andrew Carnegie, 1835, Scottish industrialist, businessman, major philanthropist, and founder of Pittsburgh's Carnegie Steel Company, which later became U.S. Steel.

Aha-phrodisiacs

Write about a fictional or fantastical version of being paid with the free sensations and essences of life as if you were receiving the most coveted riches in the world.

Word Pool: ransom, wilderness, immediate, top, apprehend, compass, fish, lost, imitate, butterfly, undetected, important, copy, it is all, moon, turning, promise, what kind of, middle, utmost

Dose of Mirth

The only consolation I can find in your immediate presence is your ultimate absence. ~Shelagh Delaney

Journal Juju

Reflect on Carnegie's quote at the top of this page or one or more of his quotes below. Be honest and discuss what these quotes bring up for you both positively and negatively:

"People who are unable to motivate themselves must be content with mediocrity, no matter how impressive their other talents." "No man will make a great leader who wants to do it all himself, or to get all the credit for doing it." "Think of yourself as on the threshold of unparalleled success. A whole, clear, glorious life lies before you. Achieve! Achieve!"

November 26

Name today _____

Daily Soul Vitamin

The way you write science fiction is: you sit down at your writing machine and you open your mind to the first thought that comes through. ~Frederik Pohl

Toast of the Day

Here's to being under a warm down comforter on a chilly night, listening to the wind blowing outside.

Awe-Servances

Happy Birthday to

Frederik George Pohl, Jr., 1919, science fiction writer, editor, and
   fan, with a career spanning over sixty years. From about 1959
   until 1969, Pohl edited *Galaxy* magazine and its sister magazine
   if, which won the Hugo for three years running.
Charles Schulz, 1922, creator of the comic strip *Peanuts*.
Tina Turner, 1938, singer who sang "What You Get Is What You See."

Aha-phrodisiacs

Turner Repeated Completions: "What you get is . . . ." Or "If . . ."
Come up with ten reasons why you shouldn't be writing or doing art. Commit to it and then have your inner critic argue convincingly for why you should.

Dose of Mirth

*Life is like a ten speed bicycle. Most of us have gears
we never use.* ~Charles M. Schulz

What You Get is What You See

Journal Juju

Relating to the Schultz quote above, are there any gears that you don't use that you would like to write about? What gears do you use the most? (Define "gears" however it works for you).

A Word from the Kindness Potion

Are you being kind to yourself? A little dab will do ya.

Daily Soul Vitamin

Changes are not predictable; but to deny them is to be an accomplice to one's own unnecessary vegetation. ~Gail Sheehy

Toast of the Day

Here's to a lone owl's hoot in otherwise absolute quiet.

Awe-Servances

Happy Birthday to:

Gail Sheehy, 1937, writer and lecturer on life and the life cycle.

Jimi Hendrix, 1942, musician and songwriter.

Aha-phrodisiacs

Use The Hendrix song title, "Night Bird Flying" as a title for poetry, prose, nonsensical ramblings, or collage, painting or doodle.

Gail Sheehy in *Pathfinders* defined four phases of the creative process:

1) Preparation, gathering impressions and images.
2) Incubation, letting go of certainties.
3) Immersion & Illumination, creative intervention/risk.
4) Revision, conscious structuring and editing of creative material.

Dose of Mirth

I'm from Canada, so Thanksgiving to me is just Thursday with more food. And I'm thankful for that. ~Howie Mandel

Journal Juju

Write down Sheehy-like stages of any process of yours: Worrying, Vacationing, Response to the Holidays, Relationship Styles, Approaching an All-You-Can-Eat Buffet.

Kindness Potion Reloaded

When going through changes, be patient with yourself. Things usually take longer than we hope or plan, so when that happens just lighten up and trust the process.

November 28

Name today _____

Daily Soul Vitamin
Exuberance is beauty. ~William Blake

Toast of the Day
Here's to Randy Newman's warm and fun movie scores.

Awe-servances
Happy Birthday to:

William Blake,1757, poet, visionary, painter, and printmaker.

Randy Newman, 1943, singer/songwriter and pianist who is notable for often satirical pop songs and for his many film scores.

1922, The first skywriting, "Hello USA," was written over NYC.

Aha-phrodisiacs
Rank where you are today on this scale of Randy Newman titles OR have a Randy Newman Title Wave.

> "I Want You to Hurt Like I Do"
> "Blue Shadows on the Trail"
> "Real Emotional Girl"
> "Good News"
> "Tickle Me"
> "My Life Is Good"
> "Magic in the Moonlight"
> "Laugh and Be Happy"

Journal Juju
If you could write in the sky, what would you say?

> Write about any memories or recent events that involved exuberance.

Dose of Mirth
I like the idea of taking a true classic written by a true genius and destroying it essentially! I like the idea of bringing it down to earth a bit, and even a bit lower than that. ~Randy Newman

NoveMber 29

Name today _____

Daily Soul Vitamin

Far away there in the sunshine are my highest aspirations. I may not reach them, but I can look up and see their beauty, believe in them, and try to follow where they lead. ~Louisa May Alcott

Toast of the Day

Here's to the initial feeling of stepping into a sauna.

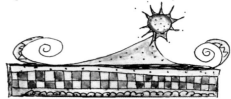

Awe—servances

Happy Birthday to:

Louisa May Alcott, 1832, author of *Little Women*.

Madeleine L'Engle, 1918, writer of children's books, including *A Wrinkle in Time*.

Chuck Mangione, 1940, musician and composer, known for "Feels So Good."

Garry Shandling, 1949, comedian, and actor.

1889, the first jukebox was installed in San Francisco, CA.

Aha—phrodisiacs

Write an alien's description of a jukebox. Use *jukebox* as an adjective. Doodle a jukebox.

Chuck Mangione wrote a song called: "Sun Shower." Use that title for a collage, painting or drawing. Let it be practice. If there were a shower of words, what would they be?

Dose of Mirth

I once made love for an hour and fifteen minutes, but it was the night the clocks are set ahead. ~Garry Shandling

Journal Juju

Madeleine L'Engle said, "Artistic temperament sometimes seems a battleground, a dark angel of destruction and a bright angel of creativity wrestling." Talk about this in your journal in terms of a creative experience you've had.

Today I get to: _____

November 30

Name today _____

Daily Soul Vitamin

I define comfort as self-acceptance. When we finally learn that self-care begins and ends with ourselves, we no longer demand sustenance and happiness from others. ~Jennifer Louden

Toast of the Day

Here's to the awareness that there is something about ourselves which we receive.

Awe-Servances

Happy Birthday to:

Mark Twain, 1835, Twain was quoted as saying, "I came in with Halley's Comet in 1835. It is coming again next year and I expect to go out with it." He did. Twain died at Redding, CT, on April 21, 1910, just one day after Halley's Comet's perihelion.

Jennifer Louden, 1962, author, workshop leader, advocate of comfort, "The Comfort Queen"

Aha-phrodisiacs

Twain Starter Fluid: "When we remember we are all mad, the mysteries of life disappear and life stands explained . . . "

Journal Juju

Write about comfort: Make a list: what furniture makes you feel comfortable? What person, quote, activity, music, exercise, movie, position, texture, clothes, smell makes you feel comfortable?

We Interrupt This Page for a Message from Body Temple and Awe-wakened Moment

What can you do RIGHT NOW to make yourself more comfortable? How can you shift or relax your body? (Or in my case, kill the fly that keeps landing on my knee caps.) What thought can you think that makes you feel more comfortable? Think it a minimum of ten times.

Spots WarraNtiNg ReMovaL:

1. People who don't believe in us, people who are crazy-makers, intolerantly righteous, immoral, untrustworthy, unkind and chronically cranky.
2. Thoughts that torment, ridicule, scare, disillusion, frustrate, distract, disable, undermine, underestimate, limit, belittle, and dement us.
3. Jobs that make us miserable.
4. Relationships where we compromise our values and beliefs WAY too much.
5. Self Sabotage.

BUB BYE!

SPOT REMOVER

HoW to ReMoVe tHe Above Spots, Keyed NuMericaLLy:

1. Create boundaries and in some cases find new people, family, friends.
2. Retrain the mind; come up with comebacks and visualizations. Read *The Awe-manac*, look for Awe-vanced Inner Messages.
3. Plan your escape or balance your job with joy-filled pastimes and people.
4. Form new support systems, pool your resources, and leave.
5. Bring your choice of thoughts, beliefs, and behaviors to your awareness and make a choice based on the desire of your higher self, not your lower patterns.
5. Do Yoga.

POSSibLe EFFectS: Removal or minimization of the cold, dark ruin of the subterranean mental abyss, the lifelong effect of harboring of demons installed by the twisted reasoning of a dysfunctional upbringing, and ring around the collar (due to sweat from pains in the neck).

Side Effects vary according to personality type. Some types should use Stain Removers instead of Spot Removers especially if you are "stayin" in jobs or relationships that are making you miserable for more than four hours, four times a month.

ENTRY WAY TO DECEMBER

December is from *decem*, ten;" tenth month of
the old Roman calendar, which began with March.
December is now the 12th month. Rewrite The Twelve
Days of Christmas with what you would like to get for
the twelve days of Christmas or with what you would
want for the world. Or simply take 12 minutes to lie in
front of a fire (or a candle) and pause between
the flurry of things to be done.
(Caution: Watch for low flying sugar plum
fairies, those wands could poke your eye out).

Some of the December's Observances

It's National Stress-Free Family Holidays Month which we are REALLY emphasizing, as well as Winter Month, Hi Neighbor Month, Read a New Book Month, Safe Toys and Gifts Month, International Calendar Awareness Month, Universal Human Rights Month.

Awe-Manac Invented:
Dec 5 Bathtub Day
Dec 11 Laughter Day
Dec 19 Holiday Pause (paws)

Suggested Ways to Celebrate

The Awe-manac's empirical study of December holidays for the last 40 years (which doesn't count 10 years of childhood) has deemed December a highly probable stress agent. This month *The Awe-manac* expands on National Stress-Free Family Holidays by extending the observance to Stress-Free *Everybody* Month. Focus on breathing, kindness, love, all that is calm, all that is bright.

A guided imagery designed specially for you this month:

Find a place to relax. Arrive fully in the room, in the chair or on the floor, and in your body. Relax your face, soften your jaw. Let the shoulders drop and feel relaxation move down the arms like honey, warming the hands, relaxing the fingers. Relax the belly, the legs and the feet. Feel the breath washing tension away. Let the mind and your breathing become one. Melt like a sugar cube in a warm cup of tea. Feel a warmth of benevolence wash through you, feel your breath slowing and flowing effortlessly like a river of peace through your body, through your extremities, through your spirit. Feel spaciousness replace tightness and feel the limitations of your body merge into the tranquility of space around you. Quiet and slow down your thinking, let your thoughts float quietly above you. Don't struggle to turn off your mind, just let the thoughts be soft and transparent. Open your heart compassionately to your emotions, accepting them and soothing them. Feel the well being of the body; let it expand to all areas. Let the benevolent breeze transport your imagination to a floating reverie. Feel the body traveling high above the noise and tension. See the world as small and the notion of calm grow greater and greater, stronger and stronger with each breath in. With each breath out, release struggle and see it fly away like the release of a flock of doves. Feel the walls of your existence unfold into the brilliance of a beautiful cosmos where entities are in existence solely to soothe your tensions and nurture you with strokes of calming ointments. Get quiet, still and eagerly anticipate that something good is about to happen. Bring a favorite feeling to mind, then to your body and spirit. Listen and watch for a symbol, a word, an essence, a sentence, or a vision in this moment or in the near future, one that brings you strength and confidence balanced with peace and surrender, acceptance and compassion. When one comes to you, write it down. Post it or find an image of it to keep around. Or begin writing with this sentence: "When I am calm I am gifted with . . . "

Astrological Spells For Peace

Aries : Right now, drop your shoulders and breathe in as if you were breathing healing refreshment.

Taurus: Imagine a more peaceful self and write a journal entry from that point of view.

Gemini: Drive around without the radio or CD playing for a few days this month.

Cancer: Add something special to the most peaceful part of your house.

Leo: Hide for 15 minutes at least once this month.

Virgo: Make peace with your perfectionism. Give it a month off and tell it if it plans on coming back it needs a more cooperative attitude.

Libra: Write little sticky notes that say "peace be with you" and deliver anonymously.

398

Scorpio: Imagine a scene of beauty and peace, imagine experiencing all its sensations.
Sagittarius: Create a flower arrangement inspired by the title of "peace."
Capricorn: Do one small thing that brings a little peace with yourself.
Aquarius: Imagine the dawning of the age of peace—breath in a gentle rhythm.
Pisces: When you stand in some store-line imagine a shield of peace lowering over you.

Tides:

Ebbing: What are you letting go of this month (just a little bit)?

_____

Flowing: Where are you expanding this month (just a little bit)?

_____

Vessel of strength:

_____

Gardening Information

Flower: Narcissus
Monthly Awe-manac
Crop: Relaxation
Planting Tips: Lie down on your floor and let a growing sense of relaxation overtake tension and tightness—space yourself at least 6 feet away from anything that brings you stress. Pa rum pum pum pum.

December 1

Name today _____

Daily Soul Vitamin

As the poet said, "Only God can make a tree," probably because it's so hard to figure out how to get the bark on. ~Woody Allen

Toast of the Day

Here's to finding someone with whom you have a bunch in common.

Awe-servances

Happy Birthday to:
Woody Allen, 1935, actor, writer, producer.

1955, Rosa Parks refused to give up her seat on the bus in Montgomery, Alabama on this date. Her arrest triggered a year-long boycott of the city bus system and led to legal actions that ended racial segregation on buses in the South.

Aha-phrodisiacs

Bette Midler said, "I never know how much of what I say is true." Take a recent event and embellish it. Add people, places, powers, poodles, and possibly a parade; keeping an element of truth but commit to whatever fable you are inventing.

Dose of Mirth

It is impossible to experience one's death objectively and still carry a tune.
~Woody Allen

Journal Juju

If you had the will of Rosa Parks, what would you do with it?

Woody Allen said, "Eternal nothingness is fine if you happen to be dressed for it." Write about the proper attire for the following: eternal nothingness, unlimited possibility, and utopia. Or make a list of your own intangible places and their dress codes.

Subliminal message

Take a deep breath and on the exhale, let go . . . .

Today I get to: _____

December 2

Daily Soul Vitamin

Dreams are illustrations from the book your soul is writing about you. ~Marsha Norman

Toast of the Day

Here's to a holiday party that becomes a warm and wonderful time to connect with others.

Awe-servances

Happy Birthday to:

Georges Seurat, 1859, Neo-impressionist Pointillism painter.

1942, Scientists at the University of Chicago achieved the first self-sustaining chain reaction.

Aha-phrodisiacs

Georges Seurat said, *"Some say they see poetry in my paintings; I see only science."*

    Relax by participating in the science of doodle-dotting a picture. Make it an ongoing picture that you can add to over time. Trace or draw a picture with pencil and dot in with thin colored markers. Do it to dot-a-ble music. What would a pointillistic piece of writing sound like? Write a piece that has a pointillistic rhythm of words: short phrases or one and two word sentences. Doodle or collage a picture entitled *Chain Reaction.*

 ## Dose of Mirth

As my guests leave even my most simplest parties, I consistently hear the same thing: "That was the best time I ever had," and it's always me saying it. -Amy Sedaris.

Journal Juju

Write about a real or fictional chain reaction in your life. Something that led to something that led to something else, etc.

Subliminal message

Take a deep breath and on the exhale let go again . . .

Today I get to:

December 3

Name today _____

Daily Soul Vitamin

Creative minds have always been known to survive any kind of bad training.
~Anna Freud

Toast of the Day

Here's to that moment just before the sun disappears over the horizon.

Awe-servances

Happy Birthday to:
Anna Freud, 1895, followed the path of her father in psychoanalysis.
Daryl Hannah, 1961, actress and mermaid.

National Roof-Over-Your-Head Day.

Aha-phrodisiacs

What IS National Roof-Over-Your-Head Day? Make up your own or spontaneous fable you have to having a roof over your head. Word Pool: mermaid, roof, survive, mind, head, associate, notice, embark, scratch, a lot to do with, admired, coast, comfort, squander, so many, names of flowers, off-days, good only for, night.

Dose of Mirth

Bad Training: Pick a fun topic: Jell-O sculptures, tree reading, lampshade hats, something obvious like those—and write a monologue that teaches the topic very poorly. Go off on tangents, talk obsequiously to your students, talk obscurely, be rigid, etc.

Journal Juju

Again related to Anna Freud's quote: Did you have any bad training? Write about how you did or you can survive it. Repeated Completions: "I know I will . . . ?"

Today I get to: _____

Note to self: Relax your shoulders

December 4

Name today _____

Daily Soul Vitamin

God gave us memories that we might have roses in December. ~J. M. Barrie

Toast of the Day

Here's to moments of silence.

Awe—Servances

Happy birthday to:

Wassily Kandinsky, 1866, modern painter, printmaker, and art theorist.

Rainer Maria Rilke, 1875, poet. His haunting images tend to focus on the difficulty of communion with the ineffable in an age of disbelief, solitude, and profound anxiety—themes that tend to position him as a transitional figure between the traditional and the modernist poets.

On this day in 1812 the power lawn mower was patented by Peter Gaillard of Lancaster, PA.

In 1955, mime artist Marcel Marceau appeared on television for the first time.

Aha—phrodisiacs

Have a power lawn mower discuss its relationship with grass, weeds, and sprinkler heads. Write a poem or haiku about a power lawn mower. Drink a wheat grass shooter in celebration of power lawn mower day.

Write about having an interview with Marcel Marceau. Write about your imaginary life as a mime. Mime your imaginary life as a writer.

Journal Juju

Kandinsky said, "There is no must in art because art is free." Doodle, paint or collage what "art is free" means to you. Title a journal entry *There is No Must.*

CHRISTMAS SEAL

Dose of Mirth

It's good to shut up sometimes. ~Marcel Marceau

Today I get to: _____

December 5

Name today _____

Daily Soul Vitamin

Character, the willingness to accept responsibility for one's own life, is the source from which self-respect springs. ~Joan Didion

Toast of the Day

Here's to a lavender bath with grapefruit candles and the Cowboy Junkies.

Awe-Servances

Happy Birthday to:

Walt Disney, 1901, film producer, director, screenwriter, voice actor, animator, entrepreneur, visionary and philanthropist.

Calvin Trillin, 1935, journalist, humorist, and novelist.

It's Take a Soothing Bath Day.

Aha-phrodisiacs

Water can be therapeutic in so many ways. One of them is climbing inside of tub of nurturing warm water. Add a candle and some music. Write while in the tub: See the Calvin Trillin quote below and hypothesize about what happened to the original meal.

Dose of Mirth

The remarkable thing about my mother is that for thirty years she served us nothing but leftovers. The original meal has never been found. ~Calvin Trillin

Journal Juju

Walt Disney said, "The way to get started is to quit talking and begin doing." Quit reading about taking a bath and take one. Write or doodle in your journal in the bathtub. Title an entry: *While Soaking . . .* or use the same two words as Starter Fluid.

A Message from Fooof

Buy a new fun washcloth that has a Disney character on it; they're not just for little kids.

December 6

Name today _____

Daily Soul Vitamin

Deep, unspeakable suffering may well be called a baptism, a regeneration, the initiation into a new state. ~Ira Gershwin

Toast of the Day

Here's to completing a project you have been working on for a long time.

Awe-servances

Happy Birthday to:

Steven Wright, 1955, stand-up comedian, actor, and writer.

Ira Gershwin 1896, Pulitzer prize-winning lyricist.

Aha-phrodisiacs

Have one of your projects write to you what it wants you to do next or what creative angle it would like to give you. Have it talk with other creative projects to get advice or ideas.

Word Pool: pilfer, important, exceed, fetch, ring, click, turnpike, inspector, improve, see, twinkle, dine, under, pertinent, sly, nod, feather, sign, daisy, wiggle, collude, biscuit, never.

Dose of Mirth

I went to a restaurant that serves "breakfast at any time".
So I ordered French Toast during the Renaissance. ~Steven Wright

Journal Juju

Choose an expressive art medium, pastels, paints, collage, doodling. Portray the way a creative block looks and feels to you in the first picture and then do a second picture of a creative block transformed by healing, freeing energy. Let music guide you. Write as if you were the second picture explaining what you are saying in the transformation.

Write or make art about ordering breakfast at a different time in history (See Steven Wright's quote above).

Note to Myself

I should take a moment to agree with a compliment someone has given me in the past.

Daily Soul Vitamin

I started writing down people's conversations as they sat around the bar. When I put them together I found some music hiding in there. ~Tom Waits

Awe—servances

Happy Birthday to:

Tom Waits, 1949, singer-songwriter, composer, and actor. Waits has a distinctive voice, described by one critic as sounding "like it was soaked in a vat of bourbon, left hanging in the smokehouse for a few months and then taken outside and run over with a car."

Willa Cather, 1947, author.

Cowboy Christmas (Dec. 7—8) in Wickenberg, AZ. A gathering of cowboy poets and singers who celebrate ranch life and traditional cowboy life in verse and song.

Aha—phrodisiacs

Write a cowboy/girl verse or song about the ranch at Christmas. Write a poem to yourself giving yourself advice for the holidays in cowboyeze.

In an interview, Waits once mentioned that he likes to overhear things wrong which gives his lyrics an imaginative twist. Eavesdrop (subtly) on someone's conversation and take notes, purposely getting some of the words wrong and seeing if that gives you a poetic edge.

Dose of Mirth

Timing has a lot to do with the outcome of a rain dance. ~Cowboy Proverb

Journal Juju

Make a list of times in your life when you had good timing. Choose one of them to write about in third person point of view.

Write how you associate these two Willa Cather quotes to your life: "I like trees because they seem more resigned to the way they have to live than other things do." "There are some things you learn best in calm, and some in storm."

A Word from Inner Awe—lixir Potion

Breathe.

December 8

Name today _____

HANUKKAH SEAL

Daily Soul Vitamin

Let us not look back in anger, nor forward in fear, but around in awareness. ~James Thurber

Toast of the day

Here's to the moment you are aware your food is placed in front of you.

Awe-servances

Happy Birthday to:

James Thurber, 1894, humorist and cartoonist best known for his contributions to *The New Yorker.*

Bill Bryson, 1951, author of humorous books on travel, the English language, and scientific subjects.

Aha-phrodisiacs

Thurber said, "It is better to have loafed and lost, than never to have loafed at all." Make a list of what other words could be substituted for loafed (which was substituted for love)? Write about the art of loafing well, or about Loaf Potion Number Nine, The Greatest Loaf of All, or Loaf Will Find a Way.

Dose of Mirth

The remarkable position in which we find ourselves is that we don't actually know what we actually know. ~Bill Bryson

Journal Juju

Quickly, without thinking, write list of things you don't know and five subjects, five emotions and five places you know very well. If the Muse stirs, pick one or more and expound. Use the
Thurber title *My World—and Welcome to It* as the beginning of your journal entry today. Or make a repeat completion out of "My world and . . ."

Another Word from The Inner Awe-lixir Potion

Breathe again today . . . a nice deep, long cleansing breath.

Daily Soul Vitamin

No matter how old you get, if you can keep the desire to be creative, you're keeping the man-child alive. ~John Cassavetes

Toast of the Day

Here's to the joy of holding a child's hand.

Awe-Servances

Happy Birthday to:
John Cassavetes, 1929, actor, screenwriter, and director.

Aha-phrodisiacs

Write a list of small things you can do to stay passionate about your creativity. Write seven ways to say "no" to a holiday party and one way to emphatically say "yes" to something creative.

Dose of Mirth

Why is the alphabet in that order? Is it because of that song? –Steven Wright

Journal Juju

Use the alphabet to list 26 ways to stay calm during the holiday season. You can use more than one word for each letter. Example: A: Actually nap; B: Believe in life after the holidays; C: Cleverly avoid certain people; D: Decline too much sugar, E: etc.

A Message to You by the A.I.M. Potion

What little 1-to-5 minute step can you take today toward building a creative commitment or habit? The habit can be to practice feeling and thinking in a way that better serves you, too. What would 15 percent more creative confidence feel like? What would it make you think? What small thing can you do to believe in yourself? Imagine it for 20 seconds, really believing you can surpass your limitations.

December 10

Name today _____

Daily Soul Vitamin
Faith is taking the first step even when you don't see the whole staircase. ~Martin
    Luther King Jr.

Toast of the Day
Here's to palm trees wrapped in tiny white lights.

Bring me the sunset in a cup

Awe-servances
Happy Birthday to:
Emily Dickinson, 1830, poet, recluse; only seven of
    her poems were published during her lifetime.
    After her death her sister discovered over 2,000
    poems which were published gradually over 50 years.

Aha-phrodisiacs
Create a poem beginning with Emily Dickinson's "Bring me the sunset in a cup . . ."
    Like Martin Luther King, Jr. did in today's Soul Vitamin, make faith into a
thing by finishing the sentences "Faith is . . .", and adding an image and an
action. Pick some other intangible feelings and in art or writing present them as
tangible images that create an action: Love, curiosity, cunning, alone, envy,
delight, etc. Don't try to be perfect.

Dose of Mirth
*I have never been jealous. Not even when my dad finished fifth grade a year
before I did.* ~ Jeff Foxworthy

Journal Juju
Play with a list of the chapter titles you would use to write your life story. Start
it today and revise or change as more inspiration emerges.

Today I get to: _____

Daily Soul Vitamins

At the height of laughter, the universe is flung into a kaleidoscope of new possibilities. ~Jean Houston

Life is too important to be taken seriously. ~Oscar Wilde

Toast of the Day

Here's to laughing, a major fringe benefit of being human.

Ha-ha-phrodisiacs

Ways to Use Humor with Yourself: Give your creative projects or work projects names or titles like Alfred, Mission Imperfection, or Un-ga-wa-heelie. Laugh with willing co-workers for no reason at all. Laugh in your car for one minute on your way to work or on your way home. Wear a weird expression on your face. Narrate your actions as if you were on a reality TV show. Do one randomly silly or absurd thing a day. Write down the absurdities of life. Hang with people who you feel funnier with.

Ways to laugh with a friend or partner: exaggerate a hug with someone (without being inappropriate). Echo someone's laugh, laugh when they do. See who can laugh the hardest or loudest. Leave funny messages on answering machines (use different voices) or through email.

Doses of Mirth

Change your habits: Boycott shampoo! Demand the REAL poo! ~Unknown

Sometimes I wake up grumpy; other times I let her sleep. ~Unknown.

Today I get to: _____

_____

_____

MARCH CROP RELOADED

December 12

Name today _____

Daily Soul Vitamins
To be is to do. ~Socrates
To do is to be. ~Jean-Paul Sartre

Dose of Mirth
Do be do be do. ~Frank Sinatra

Toast of the Day
Here's to old "do be do" jokes that are
still sort of funny.

Awe-servances
Happy Birthday to:
Frank Sinatra, 1915, jazz-oriented singer icon and award-winning actor.
Dionne Warwick, 1941, singer.

Poinsettia Day: The poinsettia was introduced to the US by American diplomat
    Joel Roberts Poinsett, who died on this day in 1851.

Aha-phrodisiacs
Come up with 6 images for the winter holidays, then come up with 6 less obvious ones, then come up with 5 sensations, 3 difficult emotions and 3 easy emotions, 5 nouns having to do with the holidays, 5 nouns have nothing to do with
the holidays and one adjective. Let the one adjective repeat throughout, combining all of these together except the first 6 obvious images which are optional.
    Take something that has a bad rap (i.e. finding a parking place, holiday
grumpiness) and give it a new positive reason for its existence.

Journal Juju
Dionne Warwick Repeated Completion: "Here I Am . . . "

Inner Awe-lixir Potion Time Out
Close your eyes and transport yourself to a place of simplicity, comfort, beauty
and calm. Experience it with all of your senses and as you breathe make it more
and more a part of yourself.

December 13

Name today _____

Moonlight is sculpture. ~Nathaniel Hawthorne

Daily Soul Vitamin
When words leave off, music begins. ~Heinrich Heine

Toast of the Day
Here's to the first light of the morning.

Awe-servances
Happy Birthday to:
Heinrich Heine, 1797, journalist, essayist, and poet.

Festival of Lights: St. Lucia was a fourth-century Italian martyr. Her name is
    derived from the Latin *lux*, meaning "light," so she has become associated
    with festivals and celebrations of light.
Ice Cream and Violins Day: Light, piquant, refreshing: just the thing to cleanse
    the palate and eardrums between those rich holiday courses.

Aha-phrodisiacs
Make an artistic definition of "light" using collage, add a quote from today.
Make a list of sentences that use the word "light" in different ways. If one
sentence has more juice than the others, keep going with it freely for awhile,
but keep it light.

Heinrich Heine was quoted as saying "Ordinarily he was insane, but he had
lucid moments when he was merely stupid." Play with this sentence structure,
substituting other words. e.g. "Ordinarily I am. . . . , but I have moments when . . ."

Doses of Mirth
*I just installed a skylight in my apartment. The people
who live above me are furious!* ~Steven Wright

Journal Juju
Write down a quick list of ice cream memories,
thoughts, or feelings, then choose one and write
about it in detail.

Name today _____

Daily Soul Vitamin
I delight in what I fear. ~Shirley Jackson

Awe—servances
Happy Birthday to:
Nostradamus, 1503, physician best remembered for his
    astrological predictions.
Patty Duke, 1946, actress.
Shirley Jackson, 1916, author.

Halcyon Days (Dec. 14-28), The seven days before and the seven days after the
    Winter Solstice. To the ancients a time when the halcyon, a fabled bird,
    calmed the wind and waves.

Aha—phrodisiacs
Nostradamus Word Pool: prophet, muddled, a magical quality, clue, sealed, vague,
rockets, cage, approach, events, claim, swim.
    Write a poem or haiku about the halcyon bird. Halcyon is a synonym for
quiet, peaceful, untroubled.
    Shirley Jackson Starter Fluid: *We Have Always Lived in the Castle.* ..

Journal Juju..
Patty Duke said, "I'm not sure I want all my neuroses cleared up." List what you
believe to be some of your quirks or neuroses then discover or consider some of
their gifts and write about them.

fooof service announcement
Look for faces of children around the holidays. Go to the
mall and watch children sit on Santa's lap. Listen to kids logic.

Today I get to:
_____
_____

December 15

Name today _____

Daily Soul Vitamin

Writers really live in the mind and in hotels of the soul. ~Edna O'Brien

Awe-servances

Happy Birthday to:

Alexandre Gustave Eiffel, 1832, architect who designed
   the Eiffel Tower.
Edna O'Brien, 1930, novelist and short story writer whose works
   often revolve around the inner feelings of women and their
   problems in relating to men.

On this day in 1939 *Gone with the Wind* premiered at Loew's Grand Theater in
   Atlanta, GA.

Aha-phrodisiacs

Take your last name and put "Tower" after it. What would that tower look like if
you had no limitations in designing it? Where would it stand? Would it have any
function or represent anything in particular? Be imaginative and have fun.

   Repeated Completions: "Gone with the . . . ." For example: Gone With the
Poodles, Gone With the Eggnog, Gone with the Lightening Bugs .
. . Then, if any of the titles energize possibilities
for poems, captions or stories, go with it.

Space Left iNTENTioNaLLy SimPLe

Dose of Mirth

*The easiest way to teach children the value of money is
to borrow some from them.* ~Anonymous

Journal Juju

Edna O'Brien said, "In a way winter is the real spring, the
time when the inner things happen, the resurge of nature." Title
a journal entry *A Resurge of Inspiration.*

   Write or collage with this title: *The Hotel of My Soul.*

Note to myself: Today there's more space on the page to
          emphasize simplicity.

Name today _____

Daily Soul Vitamin

To be interested in the changing seasons is a happier state of mind than to be hopelessly in love with spring. ~George Santayana

Toast of the Day

Here's to the variety provided by the change of seasons.

Awe-servances

Happy Birthday to:

Jane Austen, 1775, novelist who wrote *Sense and Sensibility*, among others.
George Santayana, 1863 philosopher and author.
Sir Noel Coward, 1899, actor, playwright, and composer of popular music.

Tell Someone They're Doing a Good Job Week.

Aha-phrodisiacs

Santayana wrote a philosophical work called *Realms of Being.* Make a list of realms of being or seasons of mind in which you alternately reside, write short descriptions of each.

Dose of Mirth

I like long walks, especially when they are taken by people who annoy me. ~Noel Coward

Journal Juju

Charles Fillmore said, "We increase whatever we praise." Write a credit report for things you are glad you did this week.

Jane Austen said "We have all a better guide in ourselves, if we would attend to it, than any other person can be." Let your guide write to you non-stop for about five minutes, try to replace thought with intuitive spontaneity.

Body Temple Reinforcer

You have permission to say no to some of the food served around the holidays.

Today I get to:

DeceMber 17
Name today _____

Daily Soul Vitamin
What I am actually saying is that we need to be willing to let our intuition guide us, and then be willing to follow that guidance directly and fearlessly. ~Shakti Gawain

Toast of the Day
Here's to catching a show of birds in a formation flight.

Awe-servances
Happy Birthday to:
William Safire, 1929, author, columnist, and presidential speechwriter.

1791, The birth of the one-way street.
1903, Wilbur and Orville Wright, were the first people to achieve powered flight.

Aha-phrodisiacs
Write a list or a mind-map of associations to the word "flight." Now write associations to "one-way street." Now see if you can combine some associations from both lists for some interesting poetry or art idea.
    Starter Fluid: "From 17F I can see . . ." Write prose or poetry about a real or fictional experience in an airplane.

Dose of Mirth
Some of William Safire's Rules for Writers: "A writer must not shift your point of view. Proofread carefully to see if you words out. Take the bull by the hand and avoid mixing metaphors. Last but not least, avoid clichés like the plague; seek viable alternatives."

Journal Juju
Journal title for today: *Flying off the Handle*: Write whatever associations come up for you.
    Life is sort of a one-way street because you can not grow chronologically younger. However, you can make a list of: things that worked in the past, journal entries that remind you of who you are, memories or things friends have said that felt good, funny moments, and topics for poems or memoirs.

Administer frequently

December 18

Name today _____

Daily Soul Vitamin

*Once a month the sky falls on my head, I come to, and
I see another movie I want to make.* ~Steven Spielberg

Toast of the Day

Here's to the feel of a café with a ceiling fan.

Still Life and the Sky is Falling

Awe-Servances

Happy Birthday to:

Antonia Stradivari, 1737, the celebrated *Italian violin maker*.

Ray Liotta, 1955, actor in *Something Wild* and many other movies.

Brad Pitt, 1964, actor in *Twelve Monkeys* and many other movies.

Keith Richards, 1943 member of The Rolling Stones.

Steven Spielberg, 1947, Director of *Catch Me If You Can* and many other movies

Aha-phrodisiacs

Doodle a violin and have some pasta to celebrate Antonia's birthday. (Gelato
is optional.)

Each actor, director, or Rolling Stone listed above has a title with which they
are associated beside their name. Use the titles in a Title Wave. They are also
wonderful titles for a painting, a doodle, or a collage.

Dose of Mirth

Why pay a dollar for a bookmark? Why not use the dollar for a bookmark?
~Steven Spielberg

Journal Juju

If the sky were to fall on your head, what idea or reality would it
bring to you? Starter Fluid or Repeated Completions seven times:
"When the sky falls on my head . . . "

Brought to You by Body Temple Potion

Walk a little every day. Purposely find a parking place a little farther away and
notice 1) less stress and 2) you get to walk a little more. Permission to feel a little
smug. If it's cold outside put the *Nutcracker Suite* on and walk around the house.

Daily Soul Vitamin

*Some of the secret joys of living are not found by rushing from point A
to point B, but by inventing some imaginary letters along the way.*
~Douglas Pagels

Aha-phrodisiacs

Pause for holiday stress escape: five cleansing breaths, let shoulders drop, and
forehead release, soften jaw, loosen stomach, and feel stress melt like a sugar
cube in a warm cup of tea.

Journal Juju

Make a list of any holiday stresses, and then at the end write a calming affirmation,
like "I gently release the rush and surrender to the calm." And breathe.

Dose of Mirth

Try to relax and enjoy the crisis. ~Ashleigh Brilliant

Today I get to: _____

Relax

your
•stress is
melting

December 20

Name today _____

Daily Soul Vitamin

Do what you love. When you love your work, you become the best worker in the world. ~Uri Geller

Toast of the Day

Here's to something so simple yet so exotic like a lightening bug.

Awe-servances

Happy Birthday to:
Uri Geller, 1946, performer and celebrity who has drawn both fame and criticism with his claims to have psychic powers.

Aha-phrodisiacs

Nog-Breath award: Drive around decorated neighborhoods with a friend and decide which house has the best Christmas decorations. Once determined, put a $5 gift certificate and an anonymous "Nog-breath" Award Certificate in the Mail Box. Listen to holiday music and sip un-spiked eggnog during the event.

Dose of Mirth

The difference between the right word and the almost right word is the difference between lightening and the lightening bug. ~Mark Twain

Journal Juju

Use this prompt for your journal entry: *Five things I need to throw away and why.*

And now a Message from Arpeggio

Holiday Intervention: Pause. Listen to a song without multitasking and relax every cell into the music as if the song were playing from the inside of you. Relaxation is an anti-aging strategy.

December 21

Name today _____

Daily Soul Vitamin

If we had no winter, the spring would not be so pleasant:
if we did not sometimes taste of adversity,
prosperity would not be so welcome.
~Anne Bradstreet

Winter is Here

Toast of the Day

Here's to the invincible summer in all of us.

Awe-Servances

Happy Birthday to:
Frank Zappa, 1940, rock musician and composer.

Winter Solstice the shortest day of the year and the beginning of winter.
Humbug Day—A day to allow those preparing for Christmas to vent their frus-
    trations. 12 verbal "humbugs" allowed.

Aha-phrodisiacs

Write an ode to winter to welcome it or write 12 humbugs on a piece of paper,
burn them over the sink with a holiday candle, and then have a nog.
    Use this Frank Zappa title as Starter Fluid for art or writing:
"Excentrifugal Forz."

Journal Juju

Winter is a time to go inside. Today's journal title: *When I'm Inside . . .*

Subliminal Message Brought to You by the FOOOF potion

Close your eyes and see if for 15 to 30 seconds you can conjure up
any feelings of wonder you had as a child around the holiday
season, even if it's letting only 20 percent of the feeling in.

Today I get to: _____

420

Name today _____

Daily Soul Vitamin

Whatever you want in life, other people are going to want it too. Believe in yourself enough to accept the idea that you have an equal right to it. ~Diane Sawyer

Toast of the Day

Here's to the look and quiet majesty of new fallen snow.

Awe-servances

Happy Birthday to:
Kenneth Rexroth, 1905, bohemian poet.
Dianne Sawyer, 1945, journalist.

Capricorn begins.

Aha-phrodisiacs

Kenneth Rexroth Title Wave for writing, art, or collage: In What Hour? With Eye and Ear, Beyond the Mountains, World Outside the Window.
Tip for Writing from Rexroth: "The basic line in any good verse is cadenced . . . building it around the natural breath structures of speech."

Dose of Mirth

To shorten winter, borrow some money due in spring. ~W. J. Vogel

Journal Juju

Capricorn is ambitious, organizational, self-disciplined, thrifty, prudent, security conscious, conservative, responsible, practical, persistent, political. Pick three or four or more of these qualities and update yourself on where you are with them even if you are not a Capricorn. Write: "I am _____ (trait) when . . ."

Name today _____

Daily Soul Vitamin
I know a lot of men who are healthier at age fifty than they have ever been before, because a lot of their fear is gone. ~Robert Bly

Toast of the Day
Here's to hearing a song on the radio that makes driving interesting.

Awe-Servances
Happy Birthday to:
Robert Bly, 1926, poet, author, and leader of the mythopoetic Men's Movement.

Feast of the Radishes (Oaxaca, Mexico) Figurines of people and animals are
    carved out of radishes and sold.

HEY.

Still Life and
Radish at a
Christmas Party with Mistletoe

Dose of Mirth
All of us are born with a set of instinctive fears, of falling, of the dark, of lobsters, of falling on lobsters in the dark, or speaking before a Rotary Club, and of the words "Some Assembly Required." ~Dave Barry

Journal Juju
Journal title for today: Me with No Fear. Write about what you would be like without fears. Make fearless art in your journal. Take a step that has 5 percent less fear in it.

Subliminal Message Brought to You by the Kindness and Sharing Potions
Practice in this moment feeling deserving of wonderful things in your life even if it's just 5 percent more today? If that's difficult, imagine what that would feel like.

Today I get to: _____

Daily Soul Vitamin
Doing nothing feels like floating on warm water to me. Delightful, perfect. ~Ava Gardner

Toast of the Day
Here's to the sacred feeling in a silent night.

Awe-servances
Happy Birthday to:
Ava Gardner, 1922, film and television actress.
Mary Higgins Clark, 1927, author of suspense novels.

Aha-phrodisiacs
Ava Gardner Title Wave for writing or art. Fancy Answers, We Do It Because, This Time for Keeps, Lost Angel, Whistle Stop, One Touch of Venus, The Sun Also Rises, The Angel Wore Red, Earthquake, The Blue Bird.
   Mary Higgins Clark title for Starter Fluid: "I Heard That Song Before . . ."

Dose of Mirth
How did it get so late so soon? It's night before its afternoon. December is here before it's June. My goodness how the time has flewn. How did it get so late so soon? ~Dr. Seuss

Journal Juju
Write a list of "soft reflections" and interpret what they mean according to your intuitive urges.
   Starter Fluid: "This day seems to speak of . . ."

A Word from Kindness Potion
Gentle.

Today I get to: _____

Daily Soul Vitamin

Christmas waves a magic wand over this world, and behold, everything is softer and more beautiful. ~Norman Vincent Peale

Toast of the Day

Here's to the sudden end to the seasonal frenzy and the contrast of stillness that sets in.

Awe-servances

Christmas Day, the Christian festival commemorating the birth of Jesus of Nazareth.

A'phabet Day, also known as No-L Day, is a celebration for people who do not want to send Christmas cards but who want to greet their friends. They send out cards listing the letters of the alphabet in order, but with a gap where the L would be.

Aha-phrodisiacs

Lie down on the floor and let the tension of the season melt into the floor. See if you can be awake and present, a state needed for creative thought. Listen and watch for inspiration but have a low-pressure day. Have joy radar and focus the mind on that which brings it to you.

Take the L people left out and write a list of L words for a word pool with alliteration.

To relax yourself, get out a box of crayons and color to music or color in the Mandala provided at the end of the book.

Filling in a Mandala with Color will Center and Relax You

Dose of Mirth

Did you ever notice that life seems to follow certain patterns? Like I noticed that every year around this time, I hear Christmas music. ~Tom Sims

Journal Juju

Use each letter of the word Christmas to begin each new line in your journal today.

December 26

Daily Soul Vitamins

The thing is to become a master and in your old age to acquire the courage to do what children did when they knew nothing. ~Henry Miller

Toast of the Day

Here's to the smell of cloves.

Awe-Servances

Happy Birthday to:
Henry Miller, 1891, writer and painter.
David Sedaris, 1956, humorist, author and radio contributor.

National Whiner's Day, dedicated to whiners, especially
   who return Christmas gifts.
Kwanzaa Begins: a week-long secular holiday honoring
   African American heritage, observed until January 1
   each year.

KWANZA SEAL

Aha-phrodisiacs

Use this Henry Miller quote as Starter Fluid: "What does it matter how one comes by the truth so long as one pounces upon it and lives by it?" Or be a Truth Expert and talk about the art of truth pouncing. Does truth scamper, flutter, or call to us from a distant tree limb? Personify truth.

Dose of Mirth

I haven't got the slightest idea how to change people, but still I keep a long list of prospective candidates just in case I should ever figure it out. ~David Sedaris

Journal Juju

Miller ALSO said, "Develop an interest in life as you see it; the people, things, literature, music, the world is so rich, simply throbbing with rich treasures, beautiful souls and interesting people. Forget yourself." Make a list of treasures, souls and interesting people to get to know better in the coming year.

   Whining on the page can be wonderfully liberating as long as you finish it with: "Now I release this whiny energy and awake to the throbbing treasures of my life." Whine, shift, and complete.

Daily Soul Vitamin

. . . but those to whom we can cling to; those are the brilliant gems of life which provide the nourishment we need so often to reach our destinations. ~Holly Wheeler

Toast of the Day

Here's to a sky so clear that at night you can see more stars than sky.

Awe-servances

Happy Birthday to

Johannes Kepler, 1571, the father of modern astronomy.

Marlene Dietrich, 1901 actress, singer, and entertainer.

Oscar Levant, 1906, pianist, composer, author, comedian, and actor.

Holly Wheeler, 1973, business coach, author.

On this day in 1871, the world's first Cat Show was held at the Crystal Palace in London.

Aha-phrodisiac

Rosanne Amberson said, "In the middle of a world that had always been a bit mad, the cat walks with confidence." Write from the point of view of a confident cat walking through a mad world. Keep going for 5 minutes without stopping to think.

Dose of Mirth

Underneath this flabby exterior is an enormous lack of character. ~Oscar Levant

Journal Juju

Keep going with this Marlene Dietrich quote: "Without tenderness, a man is uninteresting."

List people whom act as North Stars in your life.

Awe-wakened Inner Message

I am patient and satisfied with one small step, and I trust the process.

December 28

Name today _____

Daily Soul Vitamin

My mother never gave up one me. I messed up in school so much they were sending me home, but my mother sent me right back. ~Denzel Washington

Toast of the Day

Here's to a comfortable chair, a good book, and a view.

Awe-Servances

Happy Birthday to:

Edgar Winter, 1946, singer

Denzel Washington, 1954, actor

1849: M. Jolly-Bellin accidentally discovered dry cleaning when he upset a lamp containing turpentine and oil on his clothing and noticed the effect.

Aha-phrodisiacs

Use this Edgar Winter title as Starter Fluid: "Free Ride."

Creativity is filled with accidents. Close your eyes and draw and see if anything happens by accident. Give it a title. Use the title as inspiration for a poem. Write about an accident in your or a character's life.

Dose of Mirth

Accident is the name of the greatest of all inventors. ~Mark Twain

Journal Juju

Make a collage upside down by cutting out a bunch of images, unpeeling a piece of clear contact paper, placing the sticky side face up, and applying the images facing toward the sticky side. Turn it over and see what kind of happy accident is invented. Write about it.

Mental Solution Musing

A quote to ponder: A good style should show no signs of effort. What is written should seem a happy accident. ~W. Somerset Maugham

Daily Soul Vitamin
Having a dream is what keeps you alive . . . Overcoming the challenges make life worth living. ~Mary Tyler Moore

Toast of the Day
Here's to Thomas Edison; if it wasn't for him, we'd be watching television by candlelight.

Awe-servances
Happy Birthday to:
Mary Tyler Moore, 1936, actress.
Paula Poundstone 1959, stand-up comic and author.

In 1891, Edison patented the "transmission of signals electronically."

Aha-phrodisiacs
Write about what really happens when some single woman throws her hat in the air in the middle of a busy city.

Paula Poundstone said, "Adults are always asking little kids what they want to be when they grow up because they're looking for ideas." Thinking like a kid can be a conduit for creative thought; write a list of other questions you could ask one.

Journal Juju
Write a review of a book, movie, or TV show in your journal.

Reminder: Make sure you write in your journal when you are in a good mood so you can refer to it when you're not.

Repeated Completions: "The problem with . . . "

Dose of Mirth
The problem with cats is that they get the same exact look whether they see a moth or an ax-murderer. ~Paula Poundstone

Awe-wakened Moment
Take a moment to reflect on leaving the year behind. What little things felt good about the year?

December 30

Daily Soul Vitamin
Take everything you like seriously, except yourselves.
~Rudyard Kipling

Toast of the Day
Here's to the smell of coffee.

Awe-servances
Happy Birthday to
Rudyard Kipling, 1865, poet, author of *The Jungle Book*.
Tracey Ullman, 1959, comedian, actress, singer, dancer, screenwriter, and author.

On this date in 1817 the first coffee was planted in Hawaii.

Aha-phrodisiacs
Tracey Ullman said, "I used to sit and talk to myself in the mirror and pretend that I was a woman whose husband was in prison and who had three kids and no money." Your turn, but do it on the page. Or write poetry, prose, or make art about being raised by animals in a jungle.

Dose of Mirth
A morning without coffee is like sleep. ~Author Unknown

Journal Juju
Write about your relationship to coffee, hot drinks or waking up in the morning. Journal Title suggestion: *The Caffeinated Me, Waking Up.* Repeated Completions: "Being awake means . . . " Do two entries using the repeated completions, but make one serious and the other taking yourself less seriously.

Awe-wakened Moment
Question: What little things other than coffee truly awaken my spirit?

Cup of Kona

December 31

Name today _____

Daily Soul Vitamin

Somewhere in your career, your work changes. It becomes less anal, less careful and more spontaneous, more to do with the information that your soul carries. ~Ben Kingsley
Comment from the people at FOOOF laboratories (oh galloo gallay, hooray!!)

Toast of the Day

Here's to not taking for granted still being
on the planet another year.

Awe—servances

New Years Eve
Happy Birthday to:
Ben Kingsley, 1943, Actor
Patti Smith, 1946, Singer
Donna Summer, 1948, Singer

awwwhh, that feels good!

The Awe-manac can also be used to press
purple periwinkles flat. They like it.
Happy New Year.

Aha—phrodisiacs

Use Patti Smith's title "Wild Leaves" and write what made the leaves wild that night.. (whatever night that was). Use Donna Summer's title: "I am a Rainbow" as Starter Fluid for a poem, humorous piece of writing, or art. Press periwinkles flat.

Dose of Mirth

He who laughs last didn't get it. ~Helen Giangregorio

Journal Juju

Create your own annual personal awards ceremony: *The Awe-manac* Staff does this every year. Come up with your own criteria and in your journal give end of the year awards to your man, woman, book, learning moment, moment of beauty, movie, vacation, moment of triumph, mistake, eating out experience, new friend, possibility of the year. Do it annually –revisiting these pages reminds you of the high points of your years.

INdeX of A FeW More THiNgS

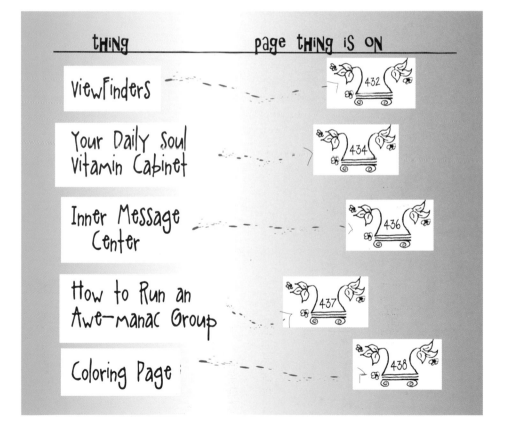

VIEWFINDERS

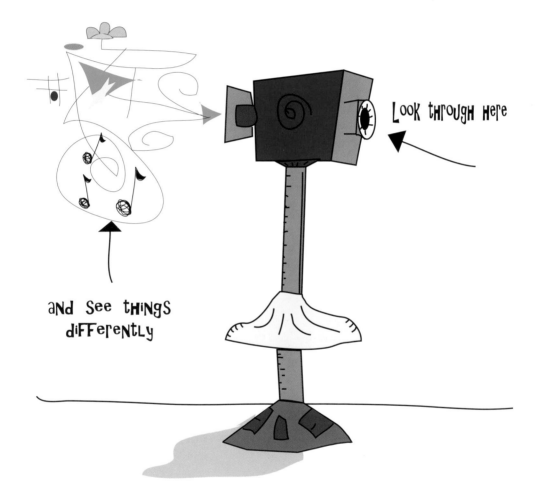

Look through here

and see things differently

VieWFinder's P.A.G.E.

(Personas. Attitudes. Genres. Emotions.)

Choose a persona, attitude, genre, or emotion to view your writing, art, music or life differently. Give it a try.

Attitudes:

absentminded
accident-prone
agitated
aimless
aloof
angry
argumentative
articulate
at wit's end
baffled
belligerent
bitchy
boastful
bossy
brave
bumbling
childlike
clumsy
co-dependent
compassionate
compulsive
cool
cosmopolitan
courageous
cowardly
cranky
crazy
creative
cunning
curious
cynical
deceitful
demanding
devoted
dieting
disgusted
disobedient
distracted
domineering
driven

eager
easygoing
edgy
elated
elegant
embarrassed
empowered
erotic
error-prone
fascinated
fault-finding
feisty
finicky
free-spirited
glib
haunting
helpful
hip
humble
idealistic
imaginative
impulsive
innocent
insensitive
inspired
insulted
intimidating
misunderstood
morose
nosy
over-polite
overprotective
overzealous
paranoid
peculiar
perplexed
pessimistic
playful
reckless
stubborn
superficial

superstitious
talkative
touchy
under a trance
under a truck
under the
 influence of
 love
unsure
uptight

Be A:

bad-ass
big shot
bimbo
braggart
child prodigy
compulsive liar
control freak
copycat
drug addict
fuddy-duddy
hillbilly
hoodlum
know-it-all
name-dropper
nature lover
simpleton
smart aleck
sourpuss
sports
 announcer
taskmaster
thrill seeker
tightwad
wallflower
hypochondriac

Personas:

mischievous
 kid

nun
UFO
meteorologist
bellhop
toll booth
 operator
supermodel
construction
 worker
switchboard
 operator
gardener
handyman
talk-show host
infomercial host
news anchorman
sport reporter
brain surgeon
press secretary
sensationalist
 journalist
movie star
convenience
 store clerk
 tele-evangelist
an animal of any
 kind
bird
an ant

Genres:

musical
slapstick
western
film noir
melodrama
Woody Allen
poetic angst
science fiction
e. e. cummings
Dr Seuss

Your Daily Soul Vitamin Cabinet

a place to copy the quotes that especially
fortify <u>your</u> soul and motivate your mind
almost every time you read them.
Reread these quotes for a dose of thinking that
does your soul some good.

Things to Say Over and Over to Yourself:

It's Close Enough.

Confidence grows with practice and practice and forging on despite imperfection.

Damn the torpedoes, full speed ahead.

I am focused on the intentions of my higher self.

I am gentle with myself.

I am patient and satisfied with one small step and I trust the process.

I breathe calmly into the beauty of this moment.

I can do this.

I can't wait to see what I say and do today.

I choose to focus on my higher self.

I don't care what they think, I LIKE what I'm doing.

I give myself permission to succeed in strength and joy.

I have my own way of doing things that is distinctive and clever.

I love me just the way I is.

I make the choices that serve my higher self.

I proceed imperfectly, but get things done. I don't give up.

I get better with practice as I stay in the process

I release it to a greater power and let it be.

I'll take one small step and the way will be made clear.

I'm going to make this work.

I'm rising to the top because I'm among the 15 percent that won't give up.

If everyone likes what I'm doing, I haven't gone far enough.

If not now, when?

Let it be.

Life is unfolding exactly the way it is supposed to.

My creative path is unfolding effortlessly.

Nothing can stop me from _____. (living my dream, writing my book, relaxing in the moment, etc.)

One gentle moment at a time.

Positive thinking brings me the advantages I desire.

iNNeR MeSSaGe CeNTeR

So what, I'll do it anyway.

Thanks for sharing now get the hell out of here.

The HELL I won't.

This could be fun.

This moment is alive with contentment.

This too shall pass.

What doesn't kill me makes me stronger

What other people think of me is none of my business.

With each step I am more clear and more courageous.

I am NOT an animal. (okay, maybe not that one).

Any positively framed small question:
  What works for me?
  What one small step can I take toward my dream today?
  What's one gentle, nurturing thing I can do for myself?
  How will I be inspired today?
  How will the creative universe amuse me today?
  What's one small way I can make this fun?
  What's one small step I can take with something?

How to Run an Awe-Manac Group

1. Gather a group of friends, family, and tribe members or suggest an *Awe-Manac* Group as a program for an already existing group of people craving a connection and easy creative fulfillment. Have them share creative dreams and what gets in the way.

2. Come up with a regular weekly time to meet in person or on a tele-conference call.

3. Open the group by taking turns reading Soul Vitamins from the week. The group leader picks the sequence of people reading. Have them each pick their favorite soul vitamin and write for five minutes about how they can apply it, what they like about it, what it makes them think of or what small step it motivates them to do. Share.

4. Stand up and stretch (Optional: bend and move to a song with a good beat.) Have some tea and a cupcake. Sit back down.

5. Group leader chooses an Aha-phrodisiac from the week and leads the group in doing it and sharing it. No judgment allowed. After each person shares, say as a group "Way Cool." Invite the group to pick things they liked about each person's sharing.

6. If anyone completed an Aphrodisiac outside of the group, invite them to share. There's no pressure to do any of it.

7. Group leader leads the group in choosing a small step according to their creative or fulfillment dream. There's no pressure to do the step—just an intention. Lead a group meditation with everyone keeping in mind their small step, then imagining the emotion, and feeling in the body positive thoughts arising as if they were engaged in the process at that very moment.

8. End with choosing a member to share their favorite dose of mirth, and remind everyone about the time and date for the next meeting.

Mandala

Color with pencils or crayons. Optional: color while listening to color-inspiring music. For an exercise in focus, color inside the lines. For an exercise in breaking the rules, don't color inside the lines. For an exercise in unconventional thinking, tear the page out and fold into an origami swan or laminate and use for a place mat.

"The speed with which any dream may be realized is always a function of how small the miracles have to be in order not to freak out the dreamer."

—Mike Dooley

thank you for reading

THe AWe-Manac

Be actively engaged with the Awe-Manac community of likeminded individuals at www.themuseisin.com